Joe Foster was born in Bolton, United Kingdom in 1935 and with his brother he founded the sports shoe manufacturer Reebok in the late 1950s, which went on to become one of the biggest sports brands in the world by the late 1980s. Joe remains a global ambassador for the company.

Shoemaker

THE UNTOLD STORY OF THE BRITISH FAMILY FIRM THAT BECAME A GLOBAL BRAND

Joe Foster

**SIMON &
SCHUSTER**

London · New York · Sydney · Toronto · New Delhi

First published in Great Britain by Simon & Schuster UK Ltd, 2020
This edition published in Great Britain by Simon & Schuster UK Ltd, 2021

1 3 5 7 9 10 8 6 4 2

Simon & Schuster UK Ltd
1st Floor
222 Gray's Inn Road
London WC1X 8HB

www.simonandschuster.co.uk
www.simonandschuster.com.au
www.simonandschuster.co.in

Simon & Schuster Australia, Sydney
Simon & Schuster India, New Delhi

A CIP catalogue record for this book is available from the British Library

Paperback ISBN: 978-1-4711-9404-7
eBook ISBN: 978-1-4711-9403-0

Typeset in Bembo by M Rules

Printed in the UK by CPI Group (UK) Ltd, Croydon, CR0 4YY

This memoir is dedicated to the memory of my daughter, Kay,
who was taken from us far too soon

CONTENTS

1	Some People Run to Win	1
2	First World Records	11
3	Lessons in Survival	21
4	Taking My Place	31
5	The Beginning of the End	41
6	The Showdown	50
7	Mercury Rises	54
8	It's All About the People	66
9	Changing Names	73
10	A Challenge	80
11	A Spell on the Road	86
12	Time to Move	95
13	America on My Mind	105
14	An Opening to the World	114
15	A Near-death Experience	121
16	New Openings	127
17	A Key to America?	132
18	Dad, Death and a New Distributor	140
19	Back to Square One	148
20	Fated	155

21	Finding Fireman	160
22	The Waiting Game	169
23	Hong Kong and Beyond	180
24	Back to Boston	191
25	My Brother Jeff	198
26	A Major Fault	204
27	Our Angel	214
28	Keeping Up	221
29	Changes Afoot	229
30	Dealing with the Rest	239
31	Reebok Goes Celebrity	245
32	A Clash of Cultures	251
33	A Rollercoaster Ride	261
34	Death, and a Rebirth	267
35	A Founder's Role	273
	Afterword: Who and what made a difference	283
	Acknowledgements	295
	Index	297

CHAPTER 1

Some People Run to Win

I have a confession. Two confessions, in fact. The first is, I don't like running. The second is that I'm a lousy shoemaker. By that, I mean it's not where my particular set of skills lies. There, it's out there. I feel better now.

Though for a book about the founder of Reebok, a book titled *Shoemaker*, you might be confused. Hopefully, you're also a little intrigued. You should be. My story, the Reebok story, is not a standard business tale about how I worked hard, hunched over a shoe last for thirty-five years. Nor is it a linear journey along a well-thought-out path, or a tale of how I risked millions and came out smelling of shiny leather. It *is* a book about motivation and the importance of gripping onto an opportunity when Lady Luck presents it.

But there's more to it than that. A *lot* more. Like every success story, there's been a sacrifice, a muddy pay-off for the glitter and gold that comes with industrial celebrity. There's only room for one love when your heart is fully invested in your passion.

Somebody once said, 'You can't get to the top without standing on a few heads,' or something like that. But that wasn't my way, at least I like to think it wasn't. There were no people harmed in the making of this business, and subsequently this book, although I could be wrong, of course.

I was brought up in a world of the remarkably average, where aspiring to be better was frowned upon. It was an era of 'know your place', 'don't rock the boat', and other edicts injected into the masses to keep society in order. And it was also a time when old-fashioned values were in place, when people were generally kind to their neighbours, their elders and even to their peers.

Decency was paramount, my mum had always instilled that in me, alongside respect for others. But in my mind, contrary to societal expectations, so was growth and improvement through challenging myself, and it was on these foundations that my (eventual) success in industry was founded.

The path to that success wasn't straight, nor was it defined. A lot of it was based on decisions that were made on the hoof. Many of those decisions were reactive rather than proactive, but always with the same aim in mind: to sell more shoes than the day before.

It seems to have worked, though it took thirty-one years to grow from a start-up to the world's number one sports brand. Perhaps if I had made different decisions it would have arrived sooner, but I know for sure that, without the long and meandering journey, I wouldn't have been prepared for the destination.

At the end of the day, many things needed to fall into place as I steered the Reebok ship along a path to success. Some of it was my doing, some of it was that of others. Some of it I'd like to call business acumen, but most of it was not. It was more a matter of good fortune, a dogged determination (some would say obsessive), and an ability to think creatively to turn misfortune into opportunity.

It was also about the importance of timing. Any brand that goes from zero to hero relies on good timing. And where better to start talking about timing than when the starter gun went off.

Some people run to beat others. I ran to beat myself.

Bang!

I closed my eyes but saw no darkness, only a clear path laid out. A narrow track devoured with every step.

I heard my dad shout, 'Come on, Joe, push-push-push,' the nicotine-grated encouragement fading with every stretch of sinew. I pushed, dug deep, but not for him. Even at that age, I knew his encouragement was more to do with the bets he had placed on me than any pride in his seven-year-old son.

I wasn't particularly bothered about winning . . . though I greatly preferred it to losing. The prizes for coming first in my category hardly acted as an incentive. Not many seven- to ten-year-olds will put an extra spring in their step for a piece of cutlery or an ugly ceramic farm animal.

The act of running was hard work, tiring, uncomfortable. Running to win meant pushing your lungs to the point of explosion, forcing your heart to beat so hard it floods your brain with extra blood until you're desperate for your head to pop to alleviate the excruciating throbbing in your temples. No, running hurts, especially if you want to run faster than the fastest. The physical challenge held no attraction. So why did I do it? I had other motivations.

Coming first meant attention from my dad, a scarce commodity in the Foster household. Conversely, losing meant being ignored. But that was nothing new. It was the default setting in our Victorian terraced home on Hereford Road, north of the town-centre chimneys that choked the Bolton skies.

I wasn't born particularly athletic; in fact, I was more weed than flourishing plant – shy, introverted and gangly. But I always knew that if I wanted something badly enough, I alone had the power to achieve it; others weren't going to just give it to me.

I longed for praise from my dad, devoured any crumbs of pride he occasionally threw to me, the middle one of three sons. I taught myself how to get him to scatter a few, principally by winning him money when I raced. But even that wasn't guaranteed.

I devised other ways to seek pleasure out of the monthly athletics events he thrust me into. And gradually, instead of seeking gratification through Dad's praise, I sought it elsewhere, from the pride of knowing that I had done everything I could to maximise my performance, for myself, whether I won or not.

I would never be considered among the best athletes in the world, or the UK, or even Lancashire, for that matter. For that, you needed a genetic advantage. You had to have been born with the DNA of a runner. I hadn't. But looking back, I *had* been born with the DNA of an 'improver'. I could figure out how to do things better, faster, the best way that you could, always looking for slight improvements, things that would give you a minuscule advantage, even at the age of seven.

So, while I couldn't move my whole body faster than the others, I could focus on the poise of my head, the swing of my arms, the gait of my legs, the angle of my soles as they hit the ground, my breathing. The sum of each tweak was enough to gain a few yards on my competitors. But the rest of my physiology, I couldn't change. Which only left the tools of the trade. And there I had another advantage.

I was from a family of shoemakers. Not an advantage in itself, admittedly, but this was no ordinary shoemaking family. This was J. W. Foster & Sons, makers of hand-sewn sports shoes. And when red-faced rivals watched me accepting my winner's trophy – a shiny spoon, a pot pig, or a dull-as-ditchwater reference book – and wondered how this scrawny mite had beaten the best runners in their athletics club, I would brace myself for the inevitable claims of 'cheat, cheat' as their gaze fell to my feet.

While the other boys ran in regular, flat-soled plimsolls, I wore spiked running shoes specifically designed and constructed for the precise conditions of that particular race meeting. I was perhaps the youngest 'athlete' in the country to wear customised running footwear. But before you start jumping to conclusions and thinking I was from a privileged background, my parents affording every advantage they could lay their hands on, let me explain.

Race shoes apart, I was like every other boy from a typical working-class family in the 1940s, appreciative of the small clutch of toys and games in our possession. But when it came to athletics, I had one distinct ancestral advantage – my grandad had invented the spiked running shoe. So I guess before the Reebok story *really* starts, a little historical catch-up is necessary.

Like many towns in the northwest of England, Bolton thrived in the boom of the cotton industry in the eighteenth and early nineteenth centuries. It became a standout example of innovation and rapid growth when, in 1779, Bolton industrialist Samuel Crompton invented the 'spinning mule', a machine used to spin cotton faster and more efficiently than handheld tools, thus reducing the number of mill workers needed and weaving more profit for the mill owners.

Towards the end of the nineteenth century my grandad, also called Joe Foster, became a purveyor of invention almost by accident. As a fifteen-year-old, he had two main interests in his life: running in his local athletics club, the Bolton Primrose Harriers, and repairing shoes and boots in his bedroom above his dad's confectionery shop. The latter pursuit he was good at; the running, like me, not so much.

What Grandad Joe did have, though, was an inventive mind. Fed up with being a backmarker in every race, he figured he would combine his two skill sets to see if he could get to the finishing line quicker.

Grandad Joe likely learned his cobbling skills through visiting his grandfather Sam's shoe workshop in Nottingham. Sam reputedly repaired the soles for lots of local sportsmen, and Joe had maybe seen the spiked cricket boots that his grandad had made to give them more grip. Perhaps a seed had been planted then, that this means of extra grip could be applied in other sports.

As it was, in his bedroom at 90 Dean Road, my grandad Joe set about designing a pair of spiked running shoes for himself.

In 1895, to test their effectiveness, he decided to try them out at his local athletics club, in a middle-distance track event.

The night before his first race, the shoes were still not finished. He had hand-sewn only one of the clumps – the added outer sole on the front of the shoe from which the spikes protrude. Working by candlelight late into the night, he had neither the visibility nor the patience to sew the clump onto the other shoe. Racked with frustration, he simply hammered it on with nails.

His fellow racers were both intrigued and amused. What right did this quiet, unassuming runner have to think he could be different from them? Did he really need to cheat to win? And how on earth would these ugly, and mismatched, shoes give him an advantage over standard plimsolls? Some laughed, some sneered, but as Joe readied himself at the starting line, he believed those to his left and right would soon be in awe when he left them in his wake.

As the starting gun went off, Joe's spikes dug into the cinder track, giving him a perfect kick-off into his stride, his feet lifting light in shoes that felt barely there. By the first bend, he was already several yards in front. As his body leaned into the bend, where the others' plimsolls would lose microseconds with tiny movements sidewards, Joe's spikes forced all motion forwards.

With virtually no cushioning, Joe could feel his feet locking onto the track as soon as his toes touched the surface, propelling him forwards fractions of a second quicker than the rubber-soled feet of his competitors. The gain in traction was minute with each step, but the sum total was enough to continue widening the distance between him and the chasing crowd.

Carrying less weight on his feet and experiencing more straight-line efficiency, Joe could feel the physical advantage. It was slight, but it was there, and as he reached the halfway point he recognised he still had reserves of energy. His lungs weren't trying to suck in air as desperately as in previous races; his legs were not as leaden as usual. *Maybe it was psychological*, he thought as he began his last lap. Perhaps it was just a placebo.

He just had time to decide it was probably a combination when he felt a strange sensation in his right foot. The ground didn't feel as even. It felt like he was running over pebbles. Then it felt like he was running over glass, every step sending agonising needles of pain through the ball of his foot and up his leg, telling his brain to ease the pressure. Finally, he felt something give way. He stumbled over an invisible rock, his bare toes grazing against the coarse cinders.

As he tried to resume the pace, he looked behind to see the second- and third-place runners catching him up. But, even more worrying, in between him and the challengers he spotted the dusty, spiked clump from his right pump lying on the track like a dead rat. With his balance thrown and every step a burning agony, he slowed to a limp, dejected as the chasing pack caught up, each one giving him a desultory smack on the back of his head as they passed.

Joe finished second to last. He snatched off what was left of his running pumps and hobbled home, where he tossed the pumps into a cupboard under the stairs and slammed the door on them. The humiliation he felt at that moment suffocated any desire to seek improvement on the race track again. But Joe was made of sterner stuff.

This gut-wrenching experience was just a reminder that there are no short cuts. His next pair wouldn't let him down and, for the next few months, he worked again on the design, making the shoes lighter and softer until he had what he considered the finished product – the perfect, lightweight running pumps. This time he would give them an outing on solo test runs to make sure there would be no repeat of his initial embarrassment.

When he tried them in a race, he didn't win but came a very unlikely second. Now his clubmates weren't laughing. Now they all wanted a pair of these new wonder shoes, and Joe had no choice but to oblige.

Several months later, after Joe had delivered his final pair, rival athletics clubs didn't take long to notice that Joe's club, Bolton Primrose Harriers, were becoming the team to beat. It took even less time for them to work out why, and then, unsurprisingly, more orders for Joe Foster's running shoes were placed.

Before long, at every race meeting, Joe was surrounded by other runners hounding him to make them a pair. As word spread further, Joe began to spend less time on the race track and more time in his bedroom hand-sewing shoes to satisfy the queues that had started to form outside his door.

In 1900, four years after the first-ever modern Olympic Games had been held in Athens, demand for Joe's shoes forced him to expand. He created J. W. Foster (Athletic Shoes) and moved into new premises at what was soon to become known as the 'Olympic Works' at 57 Deane Road in Bolton, next to the Horse and Vulcan pub.

The latest requests were for one-off designs, custom shoes based on the running style of a particular athlete, or shoes tailor-made for a particular track, even shoes optimised for just one specific race. In no time at all, J. W. Foster had become *the* shoemaker for hand-sewn specialist running pumps. If you wanted the best, no matter where you were based in the UK, Joe was your man.

Never in his wildest dreams could this Bolton cobbler have imagined that just four years later, in 1904, his running pumps would be instrumental in breaking three world records in one race.

CHAPTER 2

First World Records

On a grey November day in 1904, the rain slewed across the crowds huddled on the terraces of Glasgow's Ibrox Park stadium. The fat, grey clouds had sucked any colour and excitement from the athletics meeting. Legions of dedicated friends and family members looked on, collars upturned, quietly cursing the Scottish weather.

When a short, stocky figure stepped onto the race track the murmurs grew louder, the rainstorm forgotten. All eyes were on one man – amateur middle- and long-distance runner, Alfred Shrubb.

Alfred took his place at the starting line, smoothed down his glorious handlebar moustache and glanced at the crowd. He didn't look like a world-beater poised next to the field of taller, more athletic-looking runners. If he felt the pressure, he didn't show it, but he knew what was expected of him.

Stories of his superhuman speed had bolstered his reputation to that of quasi-legend. Tales of his running feats were repeated at race meets over and over; of Alfred having to compete against horses, or run solo against relay teams, as there was no single human on the planet capable of keeping up with him.

Alfred didn't disappoint. He never did. Like all other race days, he quickly tore away from the pack, leaving them trailing far behind. On that day he broke the 6-mile record, the 10-mile record, and then set another world best by covering 11 miles and 1,137 yards in one hour. And he did it all in Foster's shoes.

Grandad regularly attended events to give out his shoes not just to athletes, but to reporters too. Inevitably, they would go on to write articles about Grandad's company, while athletes would immediately notice the advantages gained by wearing his 'gifts' and spread the word even further. He recognised the power of influencers back then, just like brands do today.

All across the country, the running world went wild about Alfred. Competitors wanted to know everything about him – his training regime, his breathing technique . . . his footwear. While most of the other runners were still competing in heavy boots, Alfred wore black, hand-sewn pumps featuring running spikes. Were these the secret to his success?

It seemed that many people thought so. Business at J. W. Foster increased dramatically as more and more running associations placed their orders for the remarkable shoes that Alfred Shrubb had brought to their attention. But he was just one catalyst that propelled the prosperity of Grandad Joe.

There's no denying that Grandad was an innovator in the field of shoemaking, but he was also ahead of his time when it came to marketing too, and, in my eyes, with that combination, he was a genius.

Genius doesn't just rely on creativity, invention and

production. It also needs recognition. Without being recognised, you can't be perceived as a genius. With his spiked running shoe, Grandad Joe had created a brand-new product, and he employed many ways to let people know about it.

His shop front on Deane Road was the early twentieth-century equivalent of a Piccadilly Circus billboard. Every inch of the frontage was used to advertise Foster products and services. While the shop window displayed dozens of athletics trophies and shoes, the redbrick fascia featured hand-painted adverts for anything from gents' sole and heel repairs at two shillings and sixpence, to wholesale running pumps and the manufacturing of football boots.

His marketing efforts didn't stop there, though. Grandad's tactics involved long-term thinking, too. As both local athletics clubs were struggling with membership, he suggested uniting Bolton Primrose Harriers and Bolton Harriers to form Bolton United Harriers. Club presidents saw it as an opportunity to further their stranglehold on the northern running scene, but for Joe, with both clubs winning trophies in Foster pumps, it was a chance to create an even bigger platform from which to promote the near-unbeatable performance of his shoes.

It took until 1908 before Joe was able to found the new Bolton United Harriers out of the wreck of the two clubs, eventually growing the membership to seventy. The new club entered teams in events throughout the local area and beyond. Invariably it won many races. On one occasion it won them all. Plenty of eyebrows were raised, and tongues started wagging.

By 1912 the club had become relatively wealthy and built a clubhouse for the lofty sum of £800. Spurred on by their fine financial standing at the time, they organised an ambitious race meeting on the Old Horse Show field.

A lot of the club's money had been spent on promoting the event, creating plenty of interest both from runners and spectators, particularly as the club had invited Olympic gold medal winner Willie Applegarth to compete. As it was, the event was a washout, literally. Lancashire's damp climate conspired to produce a day that was conducive to nothing but staying indoors and watching raindrops race down windowpanes.

Having taken a great financial hit, the club decided to recoup their losses with a Grand Gala. Again they invited Willie, along with a host of American athletes, and again the sullen Lancashire skies emptied their clouds and ruined the occasion. It was only the combination of less ambitious events and more co-operative weather that managed to put the club back on its feet.

Undeterred by the problems at his beloved athletics club, Grandad continued to market his business countrywide. He placed audacious ads in sporting papers and continued travelling to national race events to gift his shoes to the country's leading runners. He also began paying the elite to wear his running pumps, predating Adi Dassler's similar supply of free shoes to Jesse Owens for the 1936 Berlin Olympics by some thirty years. It was possibly the very first form of sportswear sponsorship in the industry. And it worked.

More and more of the UK's top athletes would refuse to run in anything but Foster's shoes. They wanted the same advantages. And once the fervour took hold, it spread like an epidemic.

At the London Olympics in 1908, Arthur Russell won gold

in the 3,200 metres steeplechase, crossing the finishing line in Foster's shoes.

During these initial 'golden' times for the business, my dad was born in 1906. In line with family traditions, he too was christened with the same initials as my grandad, J. W., only his name was James, or Jim as he became known.

With the family business flourishing, it wasn't long before every hand in the Foster family was conscripted to help with orders, and so, at the age of eight, Jim, along with his brother, Bill (thirteen), became factory workers at the newly renamed J. W. Foster & Sons.

Business was booming so much that Grandad bought the Horse and Vulcan pub next door on Deane Road and converted it into extra workspace. But although production was at full capacity and the Foster family business was flourishing, like everybody else in the UK Joe had an anxious eye on what was unfolding overseas after the assassination of Archduke Franz Ferdinand and his wife on 28 June 1914 in Sarajevo.

The ramifications of those events hundreds of miles away would prove to have massive consequences for everybody from Britain to Germany and beyond as the First World War heaped misery and devastation on humanity *and* the economy.

Although Bolton was not deliberately targeted, in 1916 a stray German Zeppelin airship believed to be aiming for somewhere in the Midlands killed thirteen people when it dropped a bomb on Kirk Street, just behind the Olympic Works. The factory was left relatively undamaged, but that close call struck terror into the work staff as they realised nothing and nobody was safe during the war, wherever they were.

Any yearning from budding athletes to be the fastest

runner on a track was drowned in a sea of survival anxiety. Consequently, the demand for racing footwear all but stopped. For Grandad and his family, the days of fame and glory as an elite athletic shoe supplier had come to an abrupt end. Instead, J. W. Foster & Sons became one of many shoe manufacturers in the north commissioned to repair army boots recovered from the front line.

For the next few years, Grandad and his two sons would be found crouched around tin bathtubs, the water murky red as they scrubbed mud and blood from those boots removed from the young soldiers who lay dead in the Flanders trenches.

At the end of the war, Foster's had to start again from scratch. As the troops came home, Grandad and the family returned to their niche, producing hand-sewn sports footwear. Those runners who had turned from amateur to professional just to earn some money were allowed to revert back to amateur status. Some widened their running repertoire into different branches of the sport and Grandad immediately began to expand the Foster's range to include even more specialist shoes, including hurdling shoes with spiked heels and cross-country pumps that had ankle straps and extra-short spikes.

Quite by accident, he discovered that these new cross-country shoes were ideal for football and rugby training too. He set about marketing them to top clubs up and down the country through newspaper ads and personal contacts. Within months, rugby league teams like Salford, Hull and Saint Helens were wearing Foster training shoes, along with Arsenal, Liverpool, Manchester United and nearly every other club in the top four divisions of English football.

This included Bolton Wanderers, one of the most famous

football teams in the 1920s. They had helped bring the sporting spotlight to the area after the first-ever Wembley FA Cup final in 1923.

Here, an estimated crowd of over 200,000 crushed into the brand-new 126,000-capacity stadium. The image of a single policeman on a white horse controlling the overspilled crowds is iconic in FA Cup history.

Wanderers triumphed in the match, winning 2-0 against West Ham. They lifted the trophy again in 1926, beating Manchester City, and once more in 1929, with a 2-0 win over Portsmouth, making our local team the talk of the decade.

Like Bolton Wanderers, J. W. Foster & Sons was at the top of its game again and, for now, it seemed Grandad could do no wrong. He was the man with the Midas touch for leather.

At the 1920 Antwerp Olympics, Albert Hill finished first in both the 800 and 1,500 metres, and in 1924 Harold Abrahams and Eric Liddell boosted the Foster brand further, both winning gold in Paris. The latter two runners were later immortalised in the film *Chariots of Fire*, along with Lord Burghley, who won the 400-metre hurdles in the 1928 Amsterdam Olympics. And, of course, he did it in shoes hand-made at Grandad's Deane Road factory.

Naturally, as was Grandad's way, he made the most of the great publicity that these wins brought to his company, especially in the local press. His eldest son, Bill, was an excellent athlete himself, and well-known on the local running scene, not just as club champion but also through writing the athletics column in the *Bolton Evening News*.

Grandad made sure Bill never missed an opportunity to promote the family business. In one column, Bill wrote: 'The Harriers are favoured in that they have Joe Foster to attend their shoes, for he will be able to not only advise as to the type of gear that is likely to be most suitable for the Castle Irwell and Crewe courses, and to provide such, and I would advise the lads to get the shoes they require now, and not leave such provision to the last possible minute.' I don't know how he got away with such blatant family business promotion, but he did, and his column ran for many years.

Female runners were also starting to make their mark in the international athletics world, and they too carried the name of Foster's shoes with them. In 1932, Bolton United Harriers runner Ethel Johnson broke the 100-yard world record at the WAAA Championships, and the formidable Nellie Halstead smashed several records in Foster's. She later became known as one of Britain's greatest ever female athletes.

Grandad was one of the first in the industry to recognise and provide for this growing sector. As with many things, he was way ahead of his time. He was not to know, of course, but fifty years later the women's sportswear market would be the source of unprecedented success for this shoemaking family. But before that, in 1933, it was a woman closer to home who became a major force in the evolution of Foster's. After Grandad died suddenly of a heart attack, Grandma Maria, rather reluctantly, took over the running of the business.

At five foot two, what Maria lacked in authoritative height she more than made up for in fieriness. She would suffer no fools and made sure that the factory not only ran like clock-work but was also kept immaculately tidy. Her dedication to cleanliness had been exhibited in a rather unusual way some four years earlier. The body of Grandad Joe's own dad, who'd died at the age of eighty-five, had been laid out in an open coffin in the Olympic Works for several days before his funeral. Every evening Maria took it upon herself to fastidiously dust him down, brushing off the leather dust that had settled on his body during the working day.

When not brushing down corpses or barking orders at J. W. Foster & Sons, Maria was overseeing the birth of first my brother Jeff, and then me, two years later, on 18 May 1935, the same date my grandad was born, and just eighteen months after he had died. Maria believed it was a message from her late husband and insisted, or rather commanded, my mum, Bessie, that my name would also be Joseph William, and, again, Joe for short. Nobody dared argue with her.

In the few hours when she was not naming children or toiling in the factory, Maria could be found easing the stress of business ownership sitting around a crate of Guinness with her friends at the Wheatsheaf pub. As those stresses grew, so did the alcohol consumption. She would often be found asleep outside her house, too drunk to navigate a way through the front door.

When not hungover, one of her most challenging roles at the factory had become keeping a lid on a simmering feud that was building up between her two sons, my dad, Jim, and his elder brother, Bill.

Dad saw the need for change in the factory. He wanted to reduce costs, to offer a range of lower-priced athletic shoes and boots. 'Not everybody can afford a pair of "Foster's hand-sewn",' he would argue. Bill, on the other hand, saw hand-sewn as the heritage, the foundations on which the Foster reputation was built, and he was damned if he was going to throw that away now. They were both right, which made their dispute so unresolvable, and Maria's position as peacekeeper impossible.

Finally, Maria could take the strain no longer. Both sides were adamant about which way they wanted her to take the company and the business began to suffer. The harmony and efficiency that Maria had fought so hard to achieve had disintegrated. The mood in the Olympic Works began to nosedive and, with it, the profits.

Maria wanted out. She decided to relinquish control of Foster's, but only on the proviso that Dad and Bill formed a limited company, each with an equal, 50 per cent ownership.

The result was two disparate companies united in name alone. Dad set up the machinery to produce his 'Flyer' machine-sewn running shoes in 59 Deane Road, while next door, at number 57, my uncle continued the hand-stitching of their 'heritage' range. Neither spoke to the other, except to fling the occasional insult on passing.

Although no longer the owner, Maria still kept herself busy in the factory, sweeping and mopping, anything so she could keep an eye on her sons and jump in when arguments started. Her presence remained the glue that held the two fragments together and, for a few more years at least, it held.

CHAPTER 3

Lessons in Survival

While Maria was just about managing to keep the peace at the Olympic Works, Britain went to war again in 1939. Ironically, it came at a time when the fortunes of J. W. Foster & Sons were on the rise due to more Olympic success.

C. B. Holmes, originally a member of Bolton United Harriers, had competed in the 1936 Berlin Games, an event marked by the brilliance of Jesse Owens on the track, and overshadowed by Adolf Hitler off it. Holmes wore special shoes made by Uncle Bill, which were so tight-fitting they could only be worn once. Jack Lovelock, a New Zealand runner who clocked a new world record in the 1,500 metres wearing Foster's shoes, won Olympic gold in the German capital, which was festooned with Nazi symbols and swastikas.

These successes brought more business for my dad and Bill and eased the tension in the factory for a while. But it was only a temporary respite. The war clouds had gathered, and then, just three years after the Berlin Olympics, all hell broke loose.

As Foster's were once again forced to repurpose in order

to repair army boots, Dad wisely diversified into making sandals. Leather was scarce and this footwear needed very little material, just straps rather than complete uppers. This became a vital source of not only income, but coupons too, and coupons had become essential currency. They played a major part in how the company and our family managed to get through those incredibly difficult and tragic times.

Paradoxically for me, the war brought harmony.

In a blacked-out upstairs bedroom of a terraced house off Chorley New Road, my back warmed by my mum's soft torso, I stood watching distant flames flickering through condensation on the windowpane as, outside, the air-raid sirens wailed. Although fascinated by the smouldering horizon, my eyes were drawn to a hazy reflection in the framed glass – a family huddled together, a cosy portrait of comfort, safety and belonging. In the picture, Mum pulled Jeff and me tightly together, her arms across our chests like safety belts. By her side, Dad enjoyed his moment of accepted patriarchy, quietly explaining why the German Luftwaffe were constantly bombing Manchester's ship canal, docks and industrial estates, and how here in Bolton we were well out of danger. It was the closest I got to him reading bedtime stories, a rare occasion when I felt embraced in family unity.

Like all the homes in Hereford Road and the rest of Bolton, part of our back yard was commandeered to make room for an air-raid shelter. For Jeff and me, it was a cosy den where all the family huddled together when the almost nightly wail of the air-raid sirens began. There we would fall asleep on Mum or Dad's lap, only to be wakened by the sounding of the intermittent all-clear, and, with half-closed eyes, Jeff and I would be carried back upstairs to our beds.

The happy family status quo was disrupted when Jeff and I returned home later than we should have one summer evening after kicking a ball up and down the cobbled lanes, only to be turned around at the door and bundled straight into a neighbour's house. I wondered what we had done. Instead of the expected admonishment, we were fussed over and fed sweets and cakes until we could eat no more. And there we happily stayed for the next month, with Dad popping in now and then to pay money for our upkeep.

I never questioned why, and nobody bothered to explain. Jeff and I just accepted that it was an extended sleepover, and the chance for endless days of playing knock-a-door-run and street football without the usual rules and dictatorship of home life. In reality, the situation was rather more serious. Mum had contracted meningitis, her life teetering on the edge. Thankfully, she survived and our 'holiday at the neighbour's' ended as abruptly as it had begun.

With Mum back from hospital, the wartime family harmony resumed, especially when a bomb flattened Punch Street close to the Olympic Works, shattering the Foster's shop frontage facing onto Deane Road. Dad drove us the 6 miles from our house to the factory so we could look at the damage, our feet crunching on the shattered glass as workmen hammered wooden boards to the splintered window frames. Grandma Maria lived at the back of the factory and, after checking she was okay, Dad handed us a piece of shrapnel that he'd found in the workroom. Jeff and I gazed at it in awe. It was foreign, from a plane with guns, a plane that was now most certainly sitting on an airfield in Germany, about to take off and drop more bombs over Britain. If it hadn't been shot down already by a heroic

Spitfire pilot. The exciting scenarios in my imagination were innumerable.

Jeff and I gave this treasured gift pride of place in our shared bedroom. We stared at it every night as we lay in bed, arming our minds with dreams of adventure. I tried to picture the face of the German airman who'd released the bomb above our town, wondering if, as he'd looked through the rushing clouds from the plane's underbelly, he had spied Dad's factory and deliberately targeted it. I wondered if it was personal, if he somehow knew Mum, Dad, Grandma, Jeff and me – if he was specifically trying to kill *us*. Why would he do that? What had we done? What had *I* done? Maybe a spy on Deane Road had told him about our family? The questions ran and ran in my mind.

The only time I was actually close to danger was when a local RAF pilot decided to show off to his wife by buzzing the family home at low altitude. I was playing army with my best pal, Jack, using sticks to sniper-shoot neighbours and passers-by from around the corner of the local sweet shop. My stick was aimed at the head of the local priest as he stepped off the kerb, whistling tunefully as he came towards me. I curled my finger around the imaginary trigger, ignoring the buzzing sound that was growing in my head. The priest was nearly in range. The buzzing grew to a roar. I tightened my grip, pulled the trigger. The priest suddenly looked up, his face portraying sheer horror. For a moment I thought that by pure will and imagination I'd turned this thin piece of birch into a real rifle and actually shot him, that I had the power to do that.

'Duck!' screamed Jack over my shoulder. The priest threw himself to the floor as a black shadow engulfed the road, followed by the dragon-grey underbelly of a Tomahawk fighter so close it felt like my hair had been ruffled. The priest remained crouched, hands protecting his head, as we watched the plane skim across the top of the houses in the immediate vicinity, then plough into a roof two streets away. Tragically the pilot died, having first destroyed two houses and injured three terrified locals.

More awed than shocked, the reality of lives suddenly ending became more and more commonplace in my world, and not just during wartime.

After the war, football became an outlet for people to let off some steam, but the town of Bolton suffered a major tragedy in March 1946 when a human crush of spectators at Bolton Wanderers' Burnden Park stadium resulted in the deaths of thirty-three fans and injuries to hundreds. At the time it was the biggest stadium-related disaster in Britain. Both of my parents were at that FA Cup tie, and luckily both escaped shocked but unscathed.

Subconsciously, a seed had been planted that the spectre of death was never far away, and if you wanted to do something there was no point in hanging around, you'd better just get on and do it.

Having said that, my childhood was very much like any other in the redbrick suburbia of Bolton. It was a time when front doors were left open and any stretch of tarmac was a football pitch. We had the freedom to play whatever, wherever and whenever ... at least until our names were bellowed in the dark. Back then, playful creativity wasn't stifled by the warnings of parents petrified by the social ills of today. Our imaginations held no bounds and, in our heads, anything was possible.

In the Scouts, too, often another bastion of communal conformity these days, we were allowed to flourish, to explore our capabilities beyond what would be considered convention, both physically and geographically.

Being in the Scouts was a fantastic source of enjoyment and comradeship for both me and Jeff while we were growing up. We now had a baby brother, John, born in 1948, but, being thirteen years younger than me, he was still an infant and not part of our play, social or activity group.

I remember one frosty week at the end of December spent hostelling in the Lake District with the St Margaret's Church Scout troop. We were on a day-long mission to hike from Ambleside to Patterdale, via the Langdales, a series of five peaks cupping a U-shaped valley.

On a pleasant summer or spring day, it would be a moderately strenuous 10-mile trek. On a cold winter morning, with the wind bullying the falling snow into 4-foot drifts, it turned out to be a monstrous challenge.

After a late breakfast, our youthful Scout master, Skip, ushered me and four other bleary-eyed, junior adventurers from the cosy confines of Ambleside Youth Hostel, through the front door and into what was promising to become a blizzard.

The light of day could find no way through the slate sky. A single spotlight mounted high on the stone building cast a yellow pallor over the white-encrusted garden.

Waiting for our great leader to finish studying the map in the shelter of the hostel's porch, our cherubic regiment of red-cheeked Scouts huddled together on the lawn, watching spirals of snowflakes dance in sporadic gusts before collapsing in showers of white sparks. Light-brown Scout jumpers, corduroy shorts and long socks pulled over our knees were our only physical defence against the wild elements. Mentally, we were already on the verge of submission before we had begun.

Suddenly Skip charged past like a cavalryman, arm extended towards the distant hills as if holding a sword. 'This way!' he bellowed above the howling wind. We followed dutifully, snaking a path behind him in the shin-deep snow. Within minutes our legs had numbed beyond the point of caring.

The path up the first hill had been completely obscured by the fresh fall, but, undeterred, Skip strode on, the map still flapping in his hand. We kept a tight line at first as we slowly ascended the frosted slopes, but as the wind thrashed our bare thighs with splinters of ice, the pace slowed even more and the gaps grew wider.

From up ahead, we heard a shout. Skip had suddenly sunk up to his shoulders in a concealed drift. We helped him out, then, rather belatedly I thought, were shown how to use the chin-high Scout poles we carried – standard kit for any intrepid Scout pioneer. We continued, poking at the ground in front as we walked, testing the depth of the snow to avoid the same fate and being swallowed whole into the jaws of winter.

Having reached the peak, a lot slower than anticipated, descending the other side was even more treacherous. What little daylight that had bothered to show up had already begun to dissipate by two in the afternoon as we edged down sheets of ice. Skip beckoned us to pick up the pace. This was not an environment we wanted to be in when night fell, he warned.

I focused all my efforts on each step down, angling my foot in different ways to find the most secure footing. After twenty minutes, my thighs and calves were burning with the effort. I stopped and glanced behind me to check on Brian, the youngest of our group. In the dim light, I could make out the silhouettes of bushes cloaked in smooth curves of white, and the black edges of stony crags that pierced the snow. But there was no sign of Brian.

I shouted ahead and we all retraced our steps back up the hill. A few minutes later a small voice from below cried out in the half-light. Brian had stood on a frozen stream and slid off-track into some rocks below. He was bruised and cut but, fortunately, nothing was broken.

Instead of heading straight to the hostel, we helped Brian hobble towards the lights of a farmhouse in the foothills. Inside, sipping from a mug of hot chocolate in front of a log fire, I stared into the flames as, behind me, the farmer's wife ripped into Skip, admonishing him for risking our lives in such treacherous conditions. I felt sorry for him as he stood silent, berated in front of his troops. Skip was barely out of childhood himself. But I also knew the woman had a point. If I hadn't looked back at that moment, we would have trudged on unaware and Brian's predicament may have been a lot more serious.

With the withering words of the farmer's wife following us out into the cold, we trudged the last 2 miles to our hostel. We'd been expected four hours earlier and mountain rescue had been put on standby. Again, Skip got it in the neck from both the hostel manager and a member of the rescue team, who had popped in to 'offer a little advice'.

Until then, I'd had complete faith in our leader, trusting his age and 'experience' without question. Skip didn't try to defend himself. I felt pity, but also began to question my blind faith in others' ability. Skip had decided to proceed with the hike and lead us into a dangerous situation even though the sensible course of action would have been to stay inside. And, as expected within the Scouts, the army and all regimented institutions, we, the troops, were expected to follow orders without question, even if that entailed risk to our lives.

I didn't know it at the time, but it was a moment of change, when something shifted in my mind. My fate, my life, was my own. I was in charge of my destiny, and I was the only one I should trust to make decisions that were right for me.

In later years, as my glands delivered a heady dose of testosterone and my body veered towards manhood, decisions were governed by hormones, not logic. My time was torn between a primal urge to chase girls and my love of sport. No, not running. I had long since decided that pushing your legs beyond their limits, to the point where you involuntarily threw up, held little appeal.

Unless you had a genetic predisposition to fleetness, there came a point where you would hit that wall, and there was nothing you could do. Yes, you could have the advantage of running in the greatest shoes on earth, and that would buy you time – literally. But on a level playing field, with such vantages neutralised, running was a sport where DNA would ultimately be the deciding factor, and if you didn't possess the right genes, there was nothing you could do about it. Past experience told me that nobody was interested in a loser, so why continue with a pastime that led to such self-labelling?

My sport of choice had become badminton, a game more suited to my genetic makeup. It requires short bursts of energy, extreme agility, fast reflexes (both physical and mental) and, just like in business, an ability to quickly analyse and formulate a tactical game plan while simultaneously coping with pressure. It was a game I could win, and often did.

Conveniently, my parish church provided all I needed to satisfy both elements of my adolescence. It was the epicentre of evening and weekend activities, first at Scouts or on St Margaret's badminton courts, and later in the parish hall, where the telescopic eyes of Canon Kiddell and his collared wingmen guarded over our souls while we eyed girls on the dance floor.

After my friends and I had been rebuffed by all the romantic possibilities in our own parish, we moved further afield, weighing up our chances at the town hall and the local Palais dance hall. It was here I met Jean. Her smile was the first thing that caught my eye from across the dance floor. It radiated genuine warmth, not like all the other wallflowers with grins manufactured simply to lure the most dance invitations that night. Naturally, her Elizabeth Taylor movie-star curves helped too. I was also gladdened by her chattiness. I was shy, an introvert, so her propensity to talk perfectly matched my preference to listen.

I was seventeen, Jean sixteen, and our romance blossomed the way of many new amours of that age. We spent as much time together as possible, both in our social group and alone, showering each other with so much love and support that eventually we melded into one. She was my other half, and I hers, and at the time there was no way we could foresee it ending.

CHAPTER 4

Taking My Place

Around the same time as I fell in love with Jean, I dutifully took my place in the Foster family business. I was to be paid ten pounds, five shillings and sixpence for a forty-hour week, a standard wage for production-line labour.

On the first day in Deane Road, my dad handed me a clicking knife, a curved blade used to cut out patterns of shoe uppers. I was positioned in front of a stack of 8-square-foot, wafer-thin calfskins, given a very brief lesson by Jeff, and told to get on with it. I'd watched Dad and Bill carry out the same task for many years, so it was nothing new or challenging, but I made it more interesting by seeing how many uppers I could produce in one hour.

For the lightest premium running shoes, we would use kangaroo instead of calfskin. It wasn't the cheapest option but it was by far the strongest and most popular leather available, weight for weight. Other skins would be priced down if they had blemishes like tick marks, barbed-wire scratches or other wound scars, but these discounts didn't apply to kangaroo skin, which was usually so badly scarred it was just considered a feature of the leather.

There was little heating in the factory. My dad, Jeff and the other workers were constantly trying to warm their hands by blowing on them, tucking them in their armpits or holding them outstretched over an open fire glowing in the middle of the work floor. I was the only one spoilt by Grandma Maria. I was the chosen one, a living connection to her late husband. Maybe she saw me as a reincarnation of my grandad. Whatever the reason, I wasn't complaining. Several times a day she would stoke the fireplace in my workroom with coals and bring me pint mugs of steaming-hot milk. Cupping my hands round the chipped ceramic helped counter the numbness brought on by the cold wind that blew in from where the window frame was coming away from the brickwork.

Grandmother's fussing apart, I worked in isolation and relative silence. The only soundtrack was from the click of cold steel on leather as I turned the stubby knife blade at the end of each cut, accompanied by the occasional hum of sewing machines operated by two ladies in the room across the staircase, or the cheery whistling from my brother in the production area below.

Jeff had already been in the business for four years. After mastering the art of sewing the uppers, he had been 'promoted' to working the machines in the shoe-assembly process. He knew how to operate all of the machinery, except the Blake sole-sewing machine. This was held in almost sacred reverence by Dad, and for years nobody else was allowed to go near it. 'It's a temperamental beast and a bugger to fix,' he would warn, which made me want to use it all the more.

When Dad wasn't in the factory, I would practise using the Blake. I held the upturned shoe steady on a 'horn' as a needle punched down from above, stitching a path around a sole that had been temporarily glued to the upper. The speed of the needle was controlled by pedals. The skill was in the ability to accurately steer the needle at a fast speed, but only my dad could operate it at maximum velocity without punching errant holes throughout the sole. Running shoes have a very narrow sole around the heel, so for the uninitiated like me, 'crashing off the track' was a regular occurrence. Having peppered my first few attempts with unwanted holes, I plugged the perforations with a wax filler and hoped my dad never noticed.

It's been on my mind for quite some time now, so I'd like to take this opportunity to apologise to the dozens of customers in the early 1950s who were left scratching their heads at all those mysterious holes that appeared in their Foster's running pumps when the filler wore off. If it's any consolation, and you still have them, those shoes are probably worth a fortune on eBay now – *faulty Foster's badly sewn by the future founder of Reebok!*

I did get better on the Blake eventually, but just as I was becoming accustomed to all the various aspects of life in a shoe factory, my apprenticeship was cut short. I was snatched away from everything I had known for eighteen years and thrust into the cold world of square-bashing discipline thanks to national service conscription.

Along with losing the comfort of family and friends, my one-year relationship with Jean was also severed. We, or rather I, decided that it would be mission impossible to maintain a long-distance relationship. I neglected to mention that another conscript friend had warned me that while on national service I'd be surrounded by WRAFs, members of the Women's Royal Air Force.

On 3 September 1953, four months after I'd turned eighteen, I caught the train to Bedford, where, along with ten other conscripts, I was transported in the back of a 'gharry' (a lorry with a canvas cover on the back) to the RAF Cardington Reception Unit for initial kitting out, medical checks and jabs.

I opted to train as a radar operator and was posted to RAF Bawdsey in Suffolk. But first, like all conscripts, eight weeks of initial training were obligatory to 'knock us into shape'. This highly regimented period at Padgate near Warrington involved ludicrously early mornings, lots of pointless marching, and plenty of menial tasks like cleaning floors and polishing boots. In essence, it was all about learning self-discipline, time management and hard work, traits that would hold me in good stead later.

I'd been forearmed for this during my time in the Scouts, when I'd spent weekends away with my troop. So, by the time we were ready to move to our postings, I was in much better shape mentally than many in my group, who were feeling homesick and in shock at having to endure such a disciplined environment.

Parents were invited to the passing-out parade. Mum came, Dad didn't. I hadn't expected him to as it was a working day, but I did note the number of other fathers who attended, having managed to take time off for the occasion.

Following boot camp, my initial radar operator training was at RAF Yatesbury, not far from Swindon, where a few of us would spend Saturday nights cleansing our minds of technical education while engrossed in the sounds of the Joe Loss dance band.

After six weeks I was bestowed with my first 'sparks', a wireless/radar operator arm badge. RAF Bawdsey was still under construction, so I was sent to RAF Felixstowe instead. This had been the base for air and sea rescue during the Second World War, but as I was driven through in the RAF gharry from the train station it was clear the town had seen more recent action.

The lower half of the town was still recovering from massive flooding and a high-water mark could be seen 4 feet up the walls of houses, the shattered residents desperately trying to salvage whatever they could from the sodden rooms within. The clean-up was already well underway and I hoped that we would be deployed to help, but as our convoy drove further out of town I realised this was not going to happen.

Instead, I was introduced to the 'sophisticated' world of technological espionage. I'd dreamed of listening in to coded conversations between foreign generals, of becoming the hero who foiled aerial attacks from the cosy comfort of a futuristic bunker. In reality, our radar station was a cold shed at Trimley Heath, a relic of the war. Shivering within an itchy, standard-issue RAF greatcoat, I watched indecipherable dots on a fuzzy green screen that required constant slapping to keep it from shutting down.

Deeply disappointed, I assumed that that was the extent of the UK's radar operations until RAF Bawdsey was finally ready. There, my eyes were opened to the world I'd hoped for. Within an underseas command centre reached by half-mile corridors, I sat in the warmth of a fighter control cabin at my console studying state-of-the-art equipment that cast a warm, orange glow throughout the station.

I was in one of four fighter control cabins, all overlooking a large map of England's east coast and across the North Sea to continental Europe. WRAF movement plotters were stationed at each side of the map. Their job was to keep tabs on all the aircraft within our sector using information fed from a tracking system. Our fighter cabins were relatively calm until Sabre or Hunter jets from the local RAF bases or American airbase were scrambled. The fighter pilots were the heroes, and not just in the glinting eyes of the WRAFs. These were the cool guys at the business end of the action and I longed to be one of them, to be the one called on to 'take care' of the enemy. It wasn't that I disliked my less heroic role. I was at the forefront of communications technology and my eyes had been opened wide to a world that was advancing rapidly. But hey, who wouldn't want to be revered as a fighter pilot, especially by the WRAFs?

The command centre was manned by two crews. One did the 8 a.m. to 1 p.m. morning shift, then the other took over until 6 p.m. This gave us plenty of time to explore the grounds of Bawdsey Manor, with its woodland, sunken garden and cliff walks that zigzagged down to a private beach. The only disturbance to this charmed life was when fighter pilots practised air interceptions during the hours of darkness. Thankfully, this didn't occur too often, but if you happened to be on the morning shift on a day that night flying was announced, you had to cover a double shift, recommencing at 6 p.m. Although the fighters were equipped with radar, they relied on the controllers in the command centre to guide them into position. The shift continued until our control cabin had sent all fighters under its control back to the base. Our team of up to four radar operators and two WRAF girls on the plotting table were then stood down and allowed to go back to RAF lines, a walk of over half a mile through unlit forested grounds. Having to escort WRAFs through a forest at midnight changed many of my fellow operators' opinions of the night shift.

While I was involved in active service, advances in sports were also being made. People jumped higher, swam longer, ran faster. For one, Roger Bannister had broken the four-minute mile, a feat previously thought impossible. The race, and subsequent publicity, generated a surge of interest in athletics. Unfortunately, Bannister wasn't wearing Foster's. His running spikes were made by Dad's biggest rival, G. T. Law & Son. To the untrained eye, there was no difference in Foster and G. T. Law spikes, but, being based in London, they had much easier access to many of the top, southern-based athletes like Roger Bannister.

In addition to my wonderment at Bawdsey, Roger Bannister's record cemented my ideology that, just because it was widely assumed that something couldn't be done, it didn't mean it wasn't achievable.

Thanks to my prowess in badminton I spent most of my time detached from any one station, and much of my posting was taken up with battling with a shuttlecock. Finally, as my two years in national service were coming to an end, I was asked to step into the room of the personnel officer. He invited me to sit and asked if I would be interested in signing on to a full-time career in the RAF. If so, I would be immediately posted to officer training. Silence. I hadn't expected this. I'd thought it was just going to be a debrief session in preparation for my return to civilian life.

I still hadn't said anything. The officer looked at me, cocked his head to one side. 'Well?' My mind was assessing what was being offered. It was a step towards training as a fighter pilot. I thought of the WRAFs. I was sorely tempted, but something in my mind told me there was another destiny waiting.

And so I returned to Bolton in September 1955. Once again, I took my place in the family business. Many things had changed in those two years away, myself included. I'd finally broken free of the parochial mentality that insulated you from a view of the wider world. I could see beyond the smoking mill towers of Bolton, the redbrick Victoriana and the preordained treadmill of a Lancashire lifespan – birth, labour, death – interspersed with football devotion on the first day of the weekend, religious veneration the next.

I now knew there was a big, wide world out there, that the focus of my yearning for attention, praise and approval had turned 180 degrees from my inner sanctum to the outer world. I wanted to prove myself, be part of the global evolution; I just wasn't sure how yet, even though it was right under my nose.

Bolton Wanderers were now one of the great football teams of the 1950s, bringing international sports media attention to the town. This, along with the surge in athletics interest, meant that orders for Foster's running pumps should have continued flooding in from sports shops countrywide. But while I'd been away that flood had turned into a drip.

Not that my absence was anything to do with the downturn. New sports footwear companies had started to make their mark in the industry. While the likes of Adidas and Puma were rampant in taking new designs to the market,

J. W. Foster & Sons were still operating on the thesis of 'build it and they will come', expecting the market to continue coming to them. If there was one constant still prevalent, it was the non-progressive attitude of my dad and uncle.

Still widely known for their expensive hand-sewn athletic shoes produced by Bill, there had been one advancement made by the company. Through friends of friends, Bill had managed to secure a distribution deal in the USA involving regular monthly shipments of 200 pairs of hand-sewn 'DeLuxe' spikes to Frank Ryan and Bob Geinjack, head coaches at Yale University. It was a foot in the door of the hugely lucrative North American market, though I don't think either of them realised just how big an opportunity this presented.

When I stepped back into the fold after my time doing national service, I was keen to expand on this deal, to see what other lines we could open on the richer side of the Atlantic, but Bill and Dad weren't interested. They were content with this no-fuss deal, and unconcerned that even this arrangement was at risk from the Dassler brothers' Adidas and Puma brands, which were gaining traction both here and abroad. If we didn't fight back, I figured, the Dasslers would muscle Foster's out of the game.

This wasn't my only frustration. Reps on the road were calling into the factory to sell us leather, so why, I reasoned, could we not take our shoes out on the road to sell them? It was logical. It was essential. But again, Dad and Bill were having none of it.

My dad and uncle were trapped in a bubble of complacency, oblivious to the shifting commercial scene. By now, for them, the goal was not to elevate the status of the company with new designs, improved models and more aggressive marketing. Their focus was on sustaining a nice, steady income for each of their families. It was no more than a job, a way to put food on our table, rum in their glasses. Anything that rocked the boat, that involved more thinking, was dismissed immediately. There was no passion, just a lust for comfort, contentment and security.

Expansion was out of the window. It was hard enough maintaining the status quo. They couldn't agree on anything, from where to order leather to what packaging should be used for the shoes. For every decision that had to be made, the other brother had a counterargument, essentially causing delay after delay in whatever action was needed.

I looked on in frustration at a once-thriving company now in decline, hamstrung by the two owners' obstinacy. Grandma Maria was the only thing keeping the company from imploding, stepping in when her two sons came nose-to-nose. 'Don't be so bloody stupid,' she would interject, her slight frame and wooden-handled broom the only things stopping them from coming to blows. 'Do you want me to bang your heads together, you silly fools? Now get on with it!'

By now, Maria wasn't the only one running out of patience with Dad and Bill. Something had to be done.

CHAPTER 5

The Beginning of the End

Bill and Dad's indifference to developing Foster's had begun to quash my ambition and interest in the business. What was the point in a junior officer trying to save a sinking ship if the two captains were blind to the rising waters?

I began to pay more attention to my social life again. I'd also resumed my relationship with Jean. We picked up seamlessly where we left off, but she could see that I wasn't as light-hearted or free-spirited as before. Whereas the conversations were once easy-going and breezy, now they were deeper, more concerned than before I went off to do national service. Often on dates I would offload my frustrations: 'It's just a job,' she would say. 'Do what you need to at work, then forget about it.' And I did, as much as I could. But at the back of my mind, I knew that there would *be* no job if things continued as they were. Not just that, it was wholly unsatisfying to work for a company that had no vision, especially when that company was your family's.

Having deferred his national service, Jeff returned nine

months after me. He could also see straight away that the company was heading for the rocks. It was good to have my brother back, to hear a like-minded voice of reason, but Jeff, like Dad, was very much a follower of the path of least resistance. If the factory had to close, he reasoned, he'd get a new job elsewhere. My brother wasn't as outspoken as me. Where I would voice my concerns, he would keep quiet, allow nature to take its course. I guess Jeff was reactive, whereas I was more proactive. Jeff would take action when there was no other choice. I would take action to avoid the point where there was no choice left.

Perhaps nothing would have altered at Foster & Sons if Jeff hadn't been forced into change. No sooner had he donned his beige factory coat when Dad was rushed to hospital with suspected tuberculosis. This meant that Jeff and I had to take over Dad's side of the business, while Bill continued with the specialist hand-sewn shoes. Life at the factory continued relatively untroubled, free from the daily disputes between the two brothers, and Bill was happy to let us get on with our side of it.

Dad's absence reignited my enthusiasm for the business, as well as Jeff's. Unsupervised, we had the freedom to do what we liked. It was the first time that we had the opportunity to stamp our own mark on a product. We wasted no time in developing two new models of running shoes, the white Trackmaster and the Sprintmaster. If we could instil a sense of innovation from within Foster's, perhaps we could start to steer the company away from disaster, we figured. And then Dad returned.

Most people after a near-death experience would perhaps have a lighter take on life, stop to smell the roses, so to speak.

Not my dad. He couldn't wait to resume the battle with his brother, and, on that first day back, Maria was at her wits' end trying to silence their sniping again. Soon after, all development was stopped, and the company sank to new lows when, as I'd predicted, other brands bit even harder into our market share. With my hands tied, my interest waned again, and my focus switched to life away from the factory.

A year to the day that I returned from national service, Jean and I got married in a small ceremony at the Unitarian Chapel in Ainsworth, the small village where Jean's parents resided. We would live with them for twelve months before taking a mortgage on a bungalow in Harwood, north Bolton.

For a while, we enjoyed our contentment in our bungalow. As per Jean's advice, I'd managed to compartmentalise. Work was work, and home was home. It was comfortable and convenient, but I could also sense a simmering frustration within that I had slipped back into a bubble of provincial cosiness, that my life was going nowhere. It would take a death in the family to burst that cocoon.

Maybe it was aggravated by the stress of keeping Dad and Bill apart, maybe the excessive drink, or maybe it was just her turn, but in 1957 pneumonia took hold of Grandma Maria. She was forced to her bed, agonising as her own lungs drowned her. Thankfully for her, the misery lasted only a few days.

The funeral was solemn, as funerals tend to be. But as I stood in the rain watching damp soil thud on a mahogany coffin, there was a foreboding undercurrent, a sense that Grandma's passing didn't signal the end of family feuding, but the beginning of darker times ahead. It was evident in

Dad's furrowed brow, in Bill's low mutterings, in the distance they kept between them. Jeff and I looked at each other and rolled our eyes.

With Maria gone, there was nobody left to keep Dad and our uncle apart. We had hoped that their mother's sudden death would make them see reason, imbue a sense of sibling solidarity. We had been wrong and wondered what would happen next. We didn't have to wait long.

The following Friday after the funeral, Jeff and I were working on the machines in the Olympic Works when we heard voices being raised in the office along the corridor. We'd grown used to their shouting, but this was different – louder, more aggressive. We rushed towards the melee.

Dad had Bill pinned against a filing cabinet. Bill's face was bright red, spittle spraying from his mouth as he tried to free his arms. Dad's eyes were wide, wild like I'd never seen before. The veins on his arms bulged as he fought to keep Bill's fists from rising. I wrestled Dad away while Jeff grabbed Bill.

'What *are* you doing?' I yelled.

'He's a no-good drunk,' said Dad, jabbing a finger towards his brother. There was no denying Bill stank of rum, even first thing in the morning, and usually even more so after lunchtime. He was operating machinery that could easily amputate a finger of even the soberest of workers. It was a miracle he still had all ten digits.

'You and me, we're finished,' slurred Bill.

'Suits me,' said Dad.

Jeff managed to bundle Bill out of the living room while I tried to calm Dad down, make him see sense, but he was in no mood to listen, especially to his son. I'd long since realised that his children were towards the bottom of the list when it came to people he respected in life. Offspring were just that, like offcuts of leather, irrelevant by-products that were only useful for filling in when needed.

Following that day of fisticuffs, Bill and Dad point-blank refused to speak to each other, which, as you can imagine, was not exactly conducive to running an efficient company. Invoices remained unpaid, the stock became depleted. Their self-imposed silence had a bright side, though. They rarely bothered Jeff and me, so we resumed our work on new designs.

While we were now progressing on the development side, we were still way behind the competition when it came to sales and distribution. I had implored Dad to take on a sales representative to expand our territory, but like all my ideas this had been completely dismissed. He was happy to continue fuelling the business with nothing more than a tepid mixture of reputation and local contacts, along with a sporadic boost of business exaggeration.

The *Bolton Evening News* had recently interviewed Dad about the Foster business, during which he claimed he had twenty employees.

'Twenty employees, Dad?' questioned Jeff as he peered up from the article.

'It *is* twenty if you include the postman, the bin men and all the delivery drivers,' he said, satisfied that it was a legitimate claim. We actually only had eight people working in the company, including Dad, Bill, me and Jeff, but it was refreshing to see him using a bit of marketing prowess for once.

Despite the misinformation, by the mid-1950s the company was stagnating. J. W. Foster & Sons remained boxed in the mindset of the 1930s. Dad's motto was 'don't fix it if it's not broken'. The problem was not that we had anything broken as such — the relationship with his brother apart — it was simply that competitors were improving, moving onwards and upwards rapidly, while Jeff and I could see we were heading in the opposite direction.

Although my oldest brother and I weren't what you would call 'best buddies', we did have a mutual appreciation and respect for each other, both watching the other's back. Socially, we moved in different circles and had different sports as hobbies. Jeff cycled daily, while I still played badminton three or four times a week.

We *did* cross paths at civic dances, and it was here, while I watched Jean swirling her frock with a friend on the crowded dance floor, that I suggested to Jeff that we both approach Dad about setting up a new company with him, away from Bill. Jeff frowned. He didn't think it fair to Uncle Bill. It would seem like a betrayal. I told him that Bill's side of the business would thrive without the ongoing feuds, that maybe he'd even stop drinking as much if he wasn't under so much pressure. Eventually, Jeff agreed.

Dad was in the living-room office, moving one pile of invoices from one side of his desk to the other, opening one drawer, shutting it, then walking across the room to open another.

'Dad, I need to speak to you.' I wanted his full attention. I wanted him to look at me, to see how serious I was, to see that this wasn't just a whim, a fantasy from a young upstart.

He continued to move around the room, not looking up. 'Hm?'

'I have an idea. *We* have an idea . . .'

'Who's we?' he asked with his back to me, thumbing through yet another filing-cabinet drawer.

'Me. And Jeff. We've been thinking . . .'

'Have you seen that old order from Arkwright's . . . the cricket shoes?'

'No, I . . . anyway, so Jeff and I think we should create another business with you, a more modern set-up, to run alongside Foster's.'

'Damn. Where would your grandmother have put it?' He continued rummaging.

'So what do you think?'

He turned around, his eyes everywhere in the room apart from on mine. 'About what?'

'About me, Jeff and you . . . setting up a new company.'

'Not interested. Besides, you don't know the first thing about running a business.' His eyes were cold, indifferent. I'd seen that look so many times as a child. Like when I'd wanted him to let me ride on his back like other boys had done, laughing with their dads on school race days. Or when my mother reminded him it was my birthday and he would mumble wishes and ruffle my hair awkwardly. He turned and continued searching for the missing order. 'Anyway, you don't need another business. You'll get this one soon enough.'

'What do you mean?' I was talking to his back again.

'Your uncle Bill won't be around for long. Drinks too much. When he's gone and I die, you and Jeff will get all this.'

I said nothing; it was futile. I knew there would *be* no business soon. I sighed and left him to his search.

By the time we inherited Foster & Sons, there would be no place in the market for such an antiquated firm. The only other options were to carry on badgering both Dad and Bill to make the necessary changes, or to go it alone. I could only bang my head against the wall so many times. But with no money and no business experience, starting a new company with Jeff was crazy, not to mention impossible. I was ambitious, but not daft.

Between Jeff and me, our only knowledge of shoemaking was what we had picked up working on the shop floor for the past few years. If Foster's did go bust, or miraculously it was still in a fit state to be inherited, we needed to know all aspects of the business, not just manufacturing, but buying stock, bookkeeping, sales and distribution, staff management, patternmaking, machine maintenance ... and a lot more besides.

There was only one way we were going to advance our knowledge and that was to go back to school, so we enrolled on a shoemaking course at a local college three evenings a week, travelling on Jeff's scooter. Walking through the college gates, it felt like I'd gone backwards, not forwards.

Alongside night school, Jeff and I carried on working as usual for the next few months, secretly mulling over ideas that we would put into action if Foster's eventually became ours. We even began to look around at new premises, ready for the day when we had grown the company so big we would need a larger factory.

Studying while working took a lot of time, energy and commitment. It also hit our pockets hard. The course had to be paid for. Feeling particularly ebullient one day, I decided to ask Dad if he'd like to pay for our fees and travel costs. What Jeff and I learned would not just be beneficial to us when we inherited the company, it would also benefit his bottom line now, I explained. I should have known better.

'You can spend your time how you like,' he said, 'but not my money.'

Jeff and I were picking up an incredible amount of useful skills and knowledge and we tried desperately to persuade either Dad or Bill to take on some of our suggestions for improvements, both in shoemaking and in business practice. There were so many things we could have done that would have made a difference, but again they refused to listen. To them we were just two young kids trying to make a mark, thinking we knew it all, that we could teach the masters.

The truth is, they didn't need us to tell them that their business was going downhill fast. They could now see it in the figures. The company still wasn't developing enough new designs, was still relying on outdated marketing techniques like continuous, weekly printed ads. Bill and Dad weren't in control of the business – the business was in control of them. We were totally dependent on existing clients and markets, and many of those customers were now being lured to Adidas, Puma and other brands that had regularly been bringing out new and better products. We needed to seek out and expand into new territory. But we weren't doing so, and I knew now that we never would. I could see the writing was on the wall. Both Jeff and I knew that something had to give. Finally, faced with steadfast rejections of any suggestions for change, I could take it no more. The decision was made.

CHAPTER 6

The Showdown

I knew that today was going to be the day. My frustration at watching Foster's fall as other companies thrived had become all-consuming. Having finally been given permission to operate the Blake sewing machine, I manoeuvred the needle around the sole of a running pump like a racing driver on a Grand Prix track. I'd never attempted to stitch a sole so quickly but, with reckless anger, I was taking risks, twisting the shoe like a steering wheel to guide the pumping needle around the tight curves of the heel. My foot pressed the speed pedal towards the floor, my teeth gritted, eyes burning with concentration. I pressed harder. The piston-like needle pumped faster, furiously clacking like the fire of a machine-gun. Then, on the last bend, I crashed, the needle tracing a perforated line across the instep, just missing my hand.

I cursed, cut the thread and threw the shoe to the floor, then marched down the bare, plaster-wall corridor to the office. Dad was sitting in the dark behind Grandad's roll-top desk, scanning a copy of *Athletics Weekly*. A brass table lamp threw scant light over his face – his greying eyebrows, cold blue eyes and sagging cheeks. His eyes flicked to me then back to the magazine as I slumped into the upholstered chair facing him. He carried on reading, said nothing.

I was in no mood to beat around the bush. 'Dad, Jeff and I are leaving.' He didn't flinch. I waited a second. 'Dad! Did you hear me?'

He spoke quietly, his eyes still fixed on the magazine. 'Why?'

'We have to. This business is dying. You won't let us help you.'

He slowly closed the magazine, placed it on the desk and looked up.

'I've told you before, I don't need your help. We're fine . . .'

'You're not fine, Dad. We're losing the market; we need people on the road finding new business. We need new designs—'

'We're doing fine,' he interrupted. 'You're young, impatient. I told you, this will be yours soon.' He gestured with his eyes and a casual flick of the head.

I stared into his lifeless eyes. I saw a man without fight, his face weary with age, hard work, alcohol. I saw a man resigned to his fate – birth, labour, death. I saw a man who believed he knew his place, that life was about working hard, providing for your family and not making waves, just another cog in a well-oiled wheel. It was a destiny he had accepted without a battle.

But it wasn't mine. I took a deep breath. 'We're leaving. Today. Jeff and I are setting up a new company. We'd like to work with you, but you said you . . .'

Suddenly he stood up; the fight in his eyes had returned.

'This is your idea, isn't it, not Jeff's?' He snatched a steel letter opener from the leather-top desk and held it at waist height, blade towards me. I jumped up, the chair scraping on the polished floorboards. For a moment I thought he'd really lost it. We faced each other, eyes wide, both waiting for the next move. Dad extended his arm, pushing the blade towards me. 'Here, you might as well stab me now.' He opened his hand, offering me the letter opener. I looked from his face to the blade, back to his face. I'd never seen such loathing.

As I turned and left, it felt like *I'd* been stabbed in the heart. Figuratively I had. Dad had severed our relationship but put the blame on me. Not me *and* Jeff, just *me*. I knew there was nothing I could do to reconcile that. In many ways, I felt like he had wanted to cut me adrift for years. Now that we were to become business rivals, he'd found the perfect reason.

I didn't walk back along the hallway. Instead, I turned right, out through the front door and stood in the sunlight. The sky was clear save for two high clouds. *Me and Jeff*, I thought, *detached, on our own*.

I took a deep breath, looked back along the road at the row of identical houses, the uniformity only broken by the slightest of variations – a potted plant on a windowsill, a darker shade of curtain, a different colour of paint on the front door. I was now liberated from the chains of convention, the mentality that because things had been done a particular way for a long time, it was the way they ought to be done for ever.

I was free to plot my own path, to reach beyond what was expected. There *were* no limits now, no rules imposed, no dreams and aspirations that could be quashed by others. It was me and Jeff, and a future of freedom.

I stared at the door I'd just come through, pictured the

queues that had once gathered on the rain-stained, two-tone grey paving slabs, clamouring for those seemingly futuristic running shoes that my grandad had created back in 1895. Since Dad and Bill had taken over, the queues had never returned. They were probably now lined up outside the sports shops selling the latest Puma Weltmeister football boots with their screw-in studs, or the Adidas 'Melbourne' track shoes with their nylon half-soles. All that was gathered on the doorstep of the Olympic Works today were windblown pages of the *Bolton Evening News*, yesterday's news, just like Foster's. I walked away, my sense of liberation shadowed by a tinge of nostalgia, like I was already looking into the past. I walked away and wondered how long the doors would remain open.

CHAPTER 7

Mercury Rises

'You've done what?'

Although I'd dropped hints at what was coming, Jean's initial reaction was not what you would call supportive. We were only two years into the mortgage on our bungalow. Bills still remained unpaid on the home improvement projects that Jean had instigated. But she knew that I had been unhappy at work for a long time, and this, combined with my enthusiastic and optimistic pep talk about our (eventual) unlimited earnings potential as business owners, managed to win her over, for now.

The silent treatment from Dad continued, however, but only with me. He saw Jeff as an innocent party. In Dad's eyes, I had cajoled my brother into setting up a 'rival' company, bullied him even. My desire to move Foster's forward caused me to be more outspoken than Jeff, and it was true that he was quieter, more of a follower than a leader. However, we'd both worked in the factory and had our eyes opened through national service, and we were acutely aware that lately it had become more than just a desire to develop Foster's; it had been a realisation that if Foster's *didn't* catch up with the 1950s, the company was doomed.

But, as usual, I got the blame. Dad and I both shared the same genetic stubbornness, and neither of us was going to concede that we were in the wrong. In reality, we were both in the right. Dad was content with not making more effort or making things more complicated; he wanted to maintain the status quo. It was the culture of his generation. It was *his* way. And if the business disintegrated because he refused to adapt to the changing times, so be it. It was his (and Bill's) business to do with what he liked, even if that meant running it into the ground.

I, on the other hand, needed the shackles on my entrepreneurial spirit taking off. I couldn't survive in a business, or even a job, where you clocked in, mechanically completed whatever tasks were asked of you without question, and then clocked off. If there were things that needed improving, they had to be improved. It made no sense *not* to follow that path. But Dad and I were vastly different people.

There was only one way to look now, and that was forwards. The big question was, how? The full shoemaking course was two years, but even though we were almost a year into it, we couldn't wait that long without an income. While Jeff continued to gain more knowledge about design and patternmaking, I dropped out, spending days scouting for machinery and premises so we could start trading as soon as possible.

I decided not to look for a property to lease in Bolton, partly out of respect for Foster's, but also because we wanted to be nearer the heart of the more established shoemaking region of Lancashire – the Rossendale Valley, 5 or 6 miles further east.

There was no shortage of suitable properties that could be home to our start-up business, but we also needed somewhere to live. Awkwardly, Jeff was still living under the same roof as Dad, even though we had now broken away from the family business. It wasn't an ideal situation for either of them. Jeff would be under constant sniping attack and Dad would be forever reminded of his two sons' betrayal. We both agreed that he needed to get out quickly, but, without funds, it was going to be impossible.

The only way of raising enough money to be able to rent a factory was to sell my bungalow. This would mean Jean and I moving back in with her parents for a while until we located a suitable factory and could find somewhere else to call home.

Lodging with the in-laws was not something I particularly yearned for, especially after getting used to cosy family life in our own home. But, again, I knew it was necessary to first go backwards before we could move forwards.

In the late 1950s, there were plenty of empty buildings in and around the Rossendale Valley, most of them completely dilapidated. We picked one that was just *mostly* dilapidated. With a little patching up and a lot of turning a blind eye, an abandoned brewery on Bolton Street near Bury town centre became our launchpad.

There were many reasons why this double-fronted, three-storey building was not ideal. These included a slate roof that leaked rain through fist-sized holes onto an unusable third floor; beams that creaked precariously underfoot; and a stinking, disused well in the centre of the ground floor that had first been a dumping ground for old mattresses discarded by the former bedding business tenants, and then subsequently became a popular meeting point for Bolton Street's local rat community.

However, there were also a few pluses:

1. An area on the ground floor had a separate entrance and opened onto a large yard at the side of the property. This could be sublet to bring in some extra funds.

2. The factory included living accommodation, which meant Jean and I could move out of her parents' back bedroom and live on-site, just like Grandad Joe and Grandma Maria had done in the formative years of J. W. Foster. Jeff decided he would remain living with Mum and Dad for the time being.

3. There was also a bus stop right outside the factory, which was convenient for Jean to travel to her place of work – the Greengate & Irwell Rubber Company in neighbouring Radcliffe.

Jean set about furnishing our new three-roomed home, buying as many comforts as we could afford with the money left over after business investment. We carried what few items of furniture we possessed through the front door, passing through glass-fronted office space and into a small living area, into which we squeezed our two-seater settee, armchair, side table and black-and-white TV set. While I shuffled things around, Jean defrosted her hands over a ring of blue flame in the adjoining kitchenette.

I climbed a wooden staircase that rose from a corner of what was to be our office space. It led to the only room that had already been decorated. I padded across the carpeted floor, yanked open a sash window and watched a gaggle of bingo ladies entering the tile-fronted Princess Ballroom, which faced us on Bolton Street.

Leaning further out of the window, I could see a trio of round-shouldered men, hands tucked in pockets, their faces drawn and bleak as they headed to the Lord Nelson pub on the far side of our adjacent yard. They ambled, almost forlornly, as if their nightly visit to the drinking hole was an obligation, just another shift. To some of the most hardened, it probably was.

I took a deep breath. This was home. This was our view on life, a life coloured for some only by a daily infusion of alcohol, by twice-weekly jaunts to banter with a saucy bingo caller, or by fortnightly pilgrimages to that green-turf altar of Gigg Lane for the home games of Bury Football Club.

Most of the local allegiance, however, was 6 miles down the road at Burnden Park, home of Bolton Wanderers. Never had the club had such a fervent following. Earlier that year, 1958, they had beaten fierce rivals Manchester United 2-0 in the FA Cup final, in front of 100,000 spectators at Wembley Stadium. Scorer of both goals was a local hero, Nat Lofthouse, wearing Foster's boots naturally.

I was in the minority, I guess, not being a football fan myself. I only had an interest in their footwear, and, in Nat's case, the advertising opportunity his performance created for the company. I didn't understand those who made the emotional investment while enduring outdoor confinement, shoulder-to-shoulder with tens of thousands of angry disciples whose mood for the coming week would be set by which team managed to put the ball in the net most times during ninety, usually rain-sodden, minutes.

Throughout a season it was a scenario played out week after week. The gain? A testosterone rush of tribal victory. The potential loss? Misery, dejection and disappointment for you and those around you, remedied only by the next once-a-week fix, administered on the concrete terraces.

And the worst thing was, it was all out of your control. No matter how angry you became, how much advice you yelled at the players or insults you hurled at the referee, no matter how much tactical planning you made with friends in the pub beforehand, or how intricate a post-mortem you carried out afterwards, it didn't make one jot of difference to the outcome. The same with bingo.

To me, your energy is better spent on things you can control, at least to a certain extent. But it had become the self-chosen lifestyle of the masses, especially in a working man's town like Bolton, and it was a life I needed to break away from. As I gazed down the street along the row of Victorian redbrick terraces, I felt the excitement rise. Now I had a factory, I had the means to begin that escape.

The factory wasn't a pretty sight, either inside or out, but it was ours, and, at the end of 1958, Jeff and I began trading under the grand plumage of 'Mercury Sports Footwear'.

The motley assortment of second-hand machinery bought via classified ads in *Shoe & Leather News* had to be positioned next to the bare brick walls as the central floorboards on the first-floor workroom were too weak to sustain such weight.

One of our first visitors, a leather salesman from Ingles of Leeds, looked wary as we showed him around the factory: 'Are you sure you've got enough equipment to make shoes?' he said, noting the sparsity of mechanics.

There were indeed big gaps between each work station, but we knew we had enough, even though it was just the bare basics. In the centre of the room, we had built a bench to hold three hand-lasting jacks, a design that the head of the shoemaking department at college had helped create. Our meagre finances wouldn't stretch to a machine, although it wasn't long before we picked up a Camborian side-lasting machine. While hand-drafting the upper, and lasting the toes and heels on the jacks, we could now use the Camborian to pull in the sides, which not only produced better contours on the shoe but also speeded up the whole process.

Next to that was a roughing machine, simply a rotating wire wheel that was used to roughen the bottom edges of the leather uppers to expose the fibres so that they absorbed the adhesive better. A polishing machine by the side of this was used to buff soles. There were also three hand-operated devices on this side: a channel machine to provide a guide for sewing around the sole; a patching machine for making repairs to the uppers; and a guillotine for pattern-cutting.

Along the opposite wall stood a double revolving scourer, used to remove blemishes and smooth the leather; an edge trimmer for tidying the sides of the sole; a bank of air pads that used compressed air to apply pressure when gluing the rubber soles of road training and racing shoes; and finally a Blake sole-sewing machine like Dad's, for stitching leather soles.

It might sound like a lot of machinery, but it was the bare minimum we needed, and was just enough for us to start manufacturing a limited line of shoes.

Although Dad hadn't spoken to me since we left Foster's, both Jeff and I still felt a sense of loyalty not to compete directly with his business. Based purely on the notion that Jeff was a keen cyclist and knew what riders needed in footwear, we began by specialising in cycling shoes and developed three models: the Challenger, the Aggressor and the Supreme. After Jeff had trialled and tweaked them for several weeks, our next challenge was to create a demand.

The budget was tight but we used some of our funds to advertise in *Cycling* magazine. Norman Kay, a local competitive cyclist who had seen the ads, called in and asked if he could be a sales agent on a commission-only basis. We told him to literally get on his bike with a backpack and carry samples to all of the cycle shops within a 50-mile radius of Bury. It worked. He was a hit with local store owners and, within a few months, demand exceeded what Jeff, I and our pitiful array of second-hand machinery could produce. Excess demand was a great problem to have for a fledgling company, but one that needed fixing fast if we were to keep our buyers happy. If orders went unfulfilled, not only were we leaving money on the table, but our reputation was doomed from the start. We needed more machinery, more materials and more staff.

Our current roster totalled Jeff, me and Joyce, a friend of my mum's who came in to help sew the uppers when we needed an extra hand. It was fairly obvious we were going to require several additional 'Joyces', but we just didn't have the money to pay the going rate in wages.

Instead, we put a classified advert in the *Bury Times* newspaper, asking for an apprentice. Our first interviewee was David Kershaw, a fresh-faced school leaver who impressed us with both his cheeky character and his eagerness to learn every aspect of the trade.

We sent him to Rossendale College once a week, partly to give ourselves a break from his incessant banter, but mostly to fill his mind with all things shoemaking.

To cover the extra outgoings, however meagre, we needed to make sure that more revenue would be rolling in, and, for that, we needed a second salesperson. We decided to try our luck in the south. It was a gamble, since it was hard enough trying to promote Mercury throughout the local cycling and retail community, but I knew that sooner or later we would need to expand our territory.

More money was spent on a classified advert in *Cycling* magazine. It didn't take long before we received several applications and appointed another freelance agent. Fortunately, he proved to be even more successful than the first.

Mr Taylor was a Scotsman who had moved to London to represent a handful of cycling products. He brought in a phenomenal number of orders, and, again, Jeff, Joyce, David and I were struggling to cope. We were now also faced with a cash-flow dilemma – we had none. It was time for a face-to-face with my first bank manager, Mr Stoppard – or Mr Stop Heart as he became known.

Mr Stop Heart, a slim, balding man in his fifties, listened to my pleas for finance for our new venture, then was quick to regale me with the story of a bank manager colleague who, in the 1930s, had lent £100 to Billy Butlin, founder of the mega-successful UK holiday camp company.

Mr Stop Heart was obviously envious of his colleague's foresight. It was evident that he wanted his own success story, and who was I to argue with him? I told him that *his* Billy Butlin was sitting in front of him right now, that I would make the holiday camp owner look like small fry, and make *him* look like a financial genius if he had the guts and imagination to believe in the story of Mercury rising from the ashes of the fated and once-famous J. W. Foster & Sons.

He listened intently, envisioning the day he could get one up on his bank friend. In truth, it didn't take much persuasion for an initial loan and he agreed to the grand sum of £200. It was a lot of money back then, but, in terms of the business, it was nowhere near enough, but at least it was a start.

It was a further loan of £500 from Jean's uncle that supplied a modicum of stability to our wobbling ship. He thoroughly believed in Mercury and was happy to provide the money interest free. Such was his enthusiasm for our exploits, and possibly also because of a burning desire to see his money returned, he would regularly turn up at the factory on his bike and ask if we needed him to do anything.

With the money, we managed to buy enough materials to satisfy the current demand and pay our other ongoing bills. Then a strange thing happened.

The flow of orders pouring in from our Scotsman in London suddenly dried up. It wasn't a gentle downturn either; more like the tap was suddenly turned off. From running at near-capacity, we were now faced with machinery sitting idle. I fired off letter after letter, first enquiring if he was okay, next offering words of encouragement, and finally, as panic set in when cash grew tight again, demanding that he resume his role immediately under threats of terminating our association. All remained unanswered.

Maybe he had gone on holiday and not told us. Maybe he had moved on to a new opportunity. Maybe he had been taken ill. It was 1959 and we didn't have a phone number or any other means of direct contact. All I could do was hope that one of my letters would trigger the orders to begin again and look around for another agent, just in case.

It was a few weeks later that a letter arrived on my desk

from a lady with a London address asking if there was any commission due to Mr Taylor. The letter went on to say that Mr Taylor owed her a few weeks' rent and she was worried that any sales commission owing was being sent to his wife, who still lived in Scotland. The letter went on to say Mr Taylor had been killed in a car crash several weeks ago.

I stopped reading. I'd realised something must have changed in Mr Taylor's life, but *killed*? I'd conjured up many reasons why this brilliant sales agent might have suddenly stopped communicating, but being killed had never crossed my mind. It seemed impossible, but there it was in black and white.

I had already come to the conclusion that Mr Taylor had deserted us, but now a feeling of guilt engulfed me after the weeks of annoyance, frustration and anger that his disappearance had caused me and our fledgling business. We would survive, but for Mr Taylor and his family, it was final.

We decided not to replace our southern rep as demand had increased dramatically, especially from local athletics clubs. The supply and delivery of local goods was by far cheaper and easier than having to send products across the country, so it made more sense in these early, economically challenged days to prioritise savings over geographical expansion.

In addition to running-club interest, we were also starting to appear on the radar of local sports shops, particularly those offering discounts for schools. We had created an affordable, spiked running shoe, which was proving hugely popular and had given our production line the boost it needed.

The shoe might have been budget, but it was far from a basic design. The leathers we usually used for lower-priced shoes were chrome-tanned (using chrome salts to preserve the skin). It was only on the more costly models that we employed vegetable-tanned leathers, a more expensive process using oak bark instead. However, our special-priced shoes used the latter, more expensive skins. We'd managed to find a way of lowering the production costs when using this type, through a novel method of sourcing the leather.

Rather than ordering through a tannery as we would normally do, we obtained offcuts from the manufacturers of car seats. There was little choice of colour – mainly red, duck-egg blue and an insipid beige – but the leather was soft, durable and offered huge savings when we desperately needed them.

CHAPTER 8

It's All About the People

As predicted, Bill died of an alcohol-related illness in the winter of 1960. He and Dad remained in conflict to the end. It was sad, but expected, and an obvious conclusion. We had all known deep down that Bill would die early, and that Foster's would quickly follow suit.

Dad became the sole owner of J. W. Foster & Sons, inheriting the only two employees remaining in Bill's hand-sewn side of the business. They made the DeLuxe shoes that were shipped to Frank Ryan in the USA but, shortly after Bill's death, both employees walked out of Foster's, and then there were none.

In his younger days, Dad would have been quite adept at making these shoes himself. He could have kept the contract alive while he sought new employees, but now, after years of animosity and disinterest, he was no longer invested in the company and consequently the USA exports stopped.

From its days of Olympic glories, J. W. Foster & Sons had become nothing more than a shell, and Dad, now in his mid-fifties, had no desire to start all over again. He had neither the energy nor the inclination to try to save the historic company that Grandad Joe had built up since the turn of the century.

He also still felt aggrieved that I had deserted him, and he blamed me for the demise of his company. Jeff and me leaving may have been a catalyst, but the company was already in a steep decline. It was sad, but predictable, to see its downfall. All of the work that Grandad had put into it; the reputation it had built as the premier manufacturer of athletic shoes; all the gold medal Olympians who truly loved the Foster's brand; and the near-monopoly it once enjoyed in the supply of British football and rugby club training shoes – all terminating in a disappointing cloud of apathy and animosity.

Dad knew he had no option but to simply close down the business, but in a stroke of good fortune at the eleventh hour, the local council handed him a lifeline and issued a compulsory purchase order for the Foster's factory. The proceeds were enough to buy a small sports shop nearby, which Dad would run for a few years.

Just before the wrecking ball began swinging at the Olympic Works, Dad offered Jeff any machinery that he could salvage. With production still stuttering following the mysterious silence of our London agent, we didn't need a lot, but decided his large sole press would save us the cost of using a local components supplier.

On a foggy Wednesday morning in December, I was awoken by the honking of a lorry on Bolton Street. Still bleary-eyed, I opened the yard gate and the truck laboured in, clutch grinding and brakes hissing with the effort of bearing the humongous piece of machinery on its back.

Jeff had joined me and the driver in the yard, scratching our heads as we tried to figure out how to get it off the lorry. The driver had assumed that we would have the necessary lifting gear in the factory. I'd bought a block and tackle hoist from a clearance sale several months ago, and an hour or so later had succeeded in setting it on a protruding sturdy beam.

We managed to offload it from the lorry and stared at the steel monstrosity slumped in the centre of the yard. Then, of course, it began to rain, heavily. We had to move it into its rightful place straight away. Only its rightful place was up a flight of rickety stairs to the first-floor workshop. Finally, and before both we and it drowned in the downpour, we cajoled it to the top of the staircase using rope, crowbars and the last ounce of strength that Jeff, David, our young apprentice, and I could muster.

We tried levering it inch by inch across the floor using crowbars but the ends went straight through the floorboards, showering us in small clouds of dust and splinters. Finally, with the aid of some makeshift rollers, we moved it into place. The three of us stood back and gazed at this thing of beauty. It had taken half a day to install, but we knew the savings from this sole press would be worth the sweat and swearing we'd invested.

As Jeff and I would be operating the sole press, we needed someone to take over as a hand clicker, placing patterns for shoe uppers on the leather and cutting out the shapes with a sharp knife. An ad in the *Bury Times* brought a flurry of applications. There was one applicant who stood out, both in suitability and in appearance.

Norman Barnes towered over both Jeff and me, and was as thin as a racing snake. He said very little, but he listened a lot.

My gut instinct told me he would be reliable and hardworking, the two assets we needed for our first full-time employee. It proved to be a good hunch. Norman would remain the backbone of our factory for the rest of his working life.

Norman was old-school, turning up for work at least twenty minutes early every day, and never having a day off sick. It wasn't long before we 'promoted' him to the big sole press. Norman was delighted with the machine, especially the sense of power he had over the rest of us. Every time he set it in motion to 'punch' a sole, the whole floor sank then sprang back up, causing Jeff, me, David and anybody else who happened to be working at the time to bounce in unison. But I knew it would only be a matter of time before the boards gave way and the first-storey workshop would plummet to the ground floor. I prayed that we would be able to afford more modern, lighter machinery before that happened.

It was a time when many footwear manufacturers were closing down, as production was outsourced to the Far East. Although it was a buyer's market, Jeff and I still had little or no money to invest in new equipment, despite the bargains around. Almost every month I was receiving an auction catalogue of yet another shoe company going into liquidation.

Most auctions were held in once-thriving factories, previously crammed with machines, but now the gaps in the row of production lines stood out like missing teeth. These were where the machines that were leased had been snatched back due to missing payments, which, when added to the accruing debts, more often than not forced a more terminal conclusion. Thankfully, due to our small size, we couldn't justify leasing anything new and had avoided such fatal debts while much of the UK's shoe production industry withered. But visions of the chunky sole press crashing through the factory floor began to keep me awake at night. Something had to be done.

Over the next few months, I attended a few auctions to gauge what machinery was on offer and at what price. No matter what that price was, though, it was always out of reach.

Having got a better grasp of how to spot the real bargains, and realising that machinery was beyond our budget, I eventually managed to buy a bundle of raw materials at well below market price. Feeling pleased with myself, I crammed the sides of veal and cowhides into the back of my rented Ford van, filling every inch.

I headed back to Bury with a smile on my face and the rear wheel arches of the van dangerously close to touching the tyres. Even with the added cost of vehicle rental, the bargain material would keep us busy for months and add more profit to every pair of shoes we produced. The smile didn't last long, however.

A few miles from the factory, a policeman waved me in and pointed to a roadside weighbridge. As I steered into the queue, he tapped a pen on the window and made a circular motion. I wound the window down and he leaned in.

'Heavy load, sir?'

I looked in the rear-view mirror at the leather jammed into the back compartment. 'Just a bit of leather,' I said, nonchalantly.

'Driving a van that appears to be doing a wheelie says to me you might have more in the back than you should have. Wait in line then drive onto the scales.'

Needless to say, my van was well overweight and a fine was issued, turning what was originally a bargain into overpriced stock. So much for my smug self-congratulations.

At the next auction, I sat next to a small, quiet man wearing a bow tie. With every new lot, his face lit up like a toddler in an ice-cream shop. His sophisticated appearance combined with his infantile glee intrigued me. We chatted, and he introduced himself as John Willie Johnson, owner of E. Suttons, a shoe and slipper manufacturer based in nearby Bacup.

John chuckled at my tale of the weighing station and generously offered to have his men deliver anything I might buy. He also suggested that we travel together to the auctions in future to save costs. I volunteered to pick him up but, having seen my van, he insisted we use his car.

I'd noticed at the auctions that John only ever bid for a few individual items, but when there was no bid for a 'lot', a bundle of varying bits and pieces, the auctioneer would glance at him, and John would duly oblige. He seemed to be the vacuum cleaner for any oddments left over at these sales.

'What do you do with all these things?' I asked him on the drive back.

He smiled. 'I'll show you.'

We detoured to his four-floor factory in an old cotton mill. John gave me a guided tour of each floor, introducing every single worker by their first name and making sure he didn't miss anyone out.

We crossed a cobbled courtyard into a sprawling, single-storey building. Inside, long shelves sagged under the weight of all his 'lots'. I wandered through this Aladdin's cave, past rows and rows of machinery. I lifted box lids, peered into murky barrels and picked through piles of hardware yet to be sorted. Then, sandwiched between a life-sized stuffed bear and a stuffed crocodile, I spotted a 'pounding-up' machine.

It was just what we needed at Mercury to smooth out the lumps on the rugby boots we were now producing alongside the cycling shoes.

'How much for this?' I asked.

'It's not for sale,' John replied.

I was confused. 'Can I rent it then?'

'Nope.'

My face dropped.

John put his hand on my shoulder: 'You can have it,' he said, smiling. 'Just give it back when you've finished with it.'

A few months later John announced he had acquired a modern sole press. I have no doubt he bought it simply to lend it to me. Finally, my nightmares about the factory collapsing could stop as we swapped the old monstrosity with this new, lighter equipment. Although our factory was still in need of major surgery, looking at the rows of borrowed equipment it already felt like we had come a long way from the antiquated world of Foster's.

I was stunned by the generosity of this stranger I met at the auctions. Were it not for the bounteousness of people like John Willie Johnson, and others similarly benevolent along my journey, especially in the early days, my business would never have rocketed to the phenomenal heights it reached. They were instrumental in providing help and support at a time when I needed it the most, and often for free. Along with luck and timing, it was the people I encountered who made the difference between moderate achievement and monstrous success, and John, along with Derek Shackleton and Paul Fireman, both of whom you're yet to meet, were crucial players in our global conquest.

CHAPTER 9

Changing Names

It was the summer of 1960, the start of the Swinging Sixties, a time of cultural change. If the post-war economy of the 1950s had ignited a feeling of hope, the 1960s brought a flood of totemism that, finally, all was well with the world. The British population seemed to be clinging to the optimism of Harold Macmillan's 'most of our people have never had it so good' speech three years previously. A technological revolution had begun, unemployment was down and industrial output was up. Conscription had ended too, and parents – along with the newly formed Beatles – encouraged teenagers to go out, have fun, enjoy the freedom.

We too became parents in that summer. On 3 July, Jean went into labour. I ushered her into our old van and raced to Bury General Hospital where she was led away, while I was told to go home and wait for a phone call. It was standard maternity procedure in those days, fathers viewed as mere hindrances while the finale of gestation was taken care of.

The following morning a voice on the other end of our

office phone informed me I was the proud father of a baby girl. It was 4 July, Independence Day, an American celebration of ending British rule. Little did the Americans know that this British businessman had intentions to conquer their country again.

I felt complete, like I had accomplished my duties as a married man, expectations of fatherhood successfully satisfied now I had produced a family. Jeff, David and I celebrated in the Lord Nelson pub that lunchtime, forsaking the usual sandwiches and mug of tea for a quick pint before returning to work.

Visits weren't allowed at the hospital, so it would be another week before I could meet my daughter. When the introduction did come, I was nervous, unsure of what to do, especially when carrying this tiny bundle out of the hospital. I was suddenly overwhelmed with a sense of responsibility, a forever responsibility.

As I crossed the car park, my pace slowed almost to a halt. It dawned on me that I was this baby's father, her protector, provider and saviour. Was I ready for that? Would I ever be? *Could* I ever be? These anxieties and more spun through my head as I drove Jean and our baby back to the factory, slower than I'd ever driven before. As I glanced at our sleeping daughter in Jean's arms, I realised success was not just about reaching my goals now; it was just as much about providing a secure and stable future for my beautiful girl.

My other offspring, Mercury, was also nearing a certain level of stability after such a rocky infancy. Locally at least it was becoming a sports-shoe brand that both athletes and retailers trusted, and, more importantly, wanted. Although far from making a fortune, we were well on the way to being modestly comfortable. As the orders continued to flow, and we were definitely beyond the point of teetering on the brink, it felt like we were on the up.

At the end of the previous year, Jeff too had wed; and in keeping with the Foster tradition of names starting with 'J', he had also married a Jean. Like me and my Jean, Jeff and his still didn't have enough money to buy a house, so they moved into a room on the first floor of our factory, sharing bathroom facilities with Jean, me and baby Kay. Thankfully, we all got on. But having the same address in Bury had its issues. There were now two Mr and Mrs Fosters, two J. W.s and two Jean Fosters. Distributing the morning post was more or less a random affair.

By the time Jeff, the two Jeans and I had established an agreeable bathroom rota, things were looking more and more agreeable in Mercury too. Noting the healthy ascent of the figures on our sales and profits charts, our company accountant strongly advised that we become a limited liability company and register our brand name, 'Mercury', to avoid any legal battles down the line.

Several days later, in the office of patent agents Wilson Gunn & Ellis, I daydreamed as I looked out of the window at a sunny Manchester city centre skyline, while Mr Ellis meticulously explained the technical ins and outs of patent registration.

'. . . and Mercury is a registered name of Lotus and Delta, a division of the British Shoe Corporation,' he said.

I turned back to him. 'Sorry?'

'Mercury has already been registered,' he said calmly.

'Oh.'

'Yes. Oh,' he repeated.

'So what do I do?'

'You have two options. You can buy the name from the British Shoe Corporation, or you can challenge their registration, because of their lack of use. They call themselves Lotus and Delta, not Mercury.'

'And how much would that cost?' I asked.

'Around a thousand pounds, either way.'

I felt the colour drain from my face. 'A thousand pounds! Is there a third option?'

'Change your name.' He said it flippantly, like the two years of goodwill and reputation we had built into the Mercury name were easily dispensable. He certainly knew his patent law, but this impassive clerk had no idea how businesses worked in the real world. 'Choose a made-up name, something that nobody else would have thought of,' he continued. 'Like that.' He pointed through the window at a billboard on the side of a tall redbrick building. 'Kodak. Means nothing, but people remember it. Bring in a list of ten possible names like that and we'll check if any are available.'

I left his office deflated. How could we change our name just like that? We'd confuse, and probably lose, our customer base, and our distributors would be up in arms. But it seemed like there was no choice. We didn't have a *hundred* pounds to spare, never mind one thousand!

I went home and, instead of checking in on the workshop, went straight to our living quarters on the ground floor. I flipped the cap off a bottle of beer and looked around the room for name inspiration – Electrolux, Hoover . . . nothing.

It was all very well being something that meant nothing . . . once it was famous. Hindsight can make any brand name seem like a stroke of marketing genius. But in the beginning, our name needed to have some relevance to what we were offering. It needed to suggest something, conjure up an image of ... of what? Winning? Running fast? Pedalling quickly? Aargh. Why was this so hard? It was just a name. A word. Think of a word. Make up a word.

I picked the first letter of each thing in my vision, 'O' for oven, 'S' for settee, 'B' for bottle, 'A' for armchair ... Osba, Sabo, Osab, Baso. Crap. All crap. How the hell did Kodak come up with their made-up name? Then I thought that maybe we could use an anagram of Joe and Jeff, but that didn't inspire anything apart from Joff or Jeffo. That wouldn't cut it.

I flopped into my armchair and grabbed the first book I could reach from half a dozen titles filed on a small bookshelf. I smiled. It was an American *Webster's New School and Office Dictionary*, which I had accepted with feigned gratitude as a prize at an annual athletics event when I was seven. I let the pages riffle through my fingers then stopped, opened a random page. I ran my index finger down the columns ... clum, clumber spaniel, clump – God no! I opened another page ... mamushi ... I mouthed the word repeatedly and looked up. It had a nice ring to it, was pleasing to say ... but people would think it was Japanese. My finger scrolled down ... mamzer, man. I took a swig of beer and riffled to another section ... redwood, redye, ree.

My finger paused on the next word. There was a vague association between athletic shoes and the definition: 'a light colored antelope; reebok'. Hmmm. Reebok. It was short, catchy, easy to pronounce. Reebok. It suggested light, but fast, agile. Reebok. Reebok. Reebok. I liked that. I wrote it down. Only nine more possible names to find ... I searched

the dictionary, wrote down nine more animal-related con-
tenders – Cheetah, Falcon, Cougar etc. – and fired off a letter
to Mr Ellis in Manchester.

Just over a week later, I received a response. There was only
one that hadn't been registered: Reebok. However – there
always seemed to be a 'however' with Mr Ellis – there were
two other potential conflicts. 'Rebow' had been registered
as the trade name of a ladies' underwear manufacturer, and
'Raelbrook' was the trademark of Tootils, a large manufacturer of men's shirts.

Damn. I'd gotten used to the name Reebok. It represented
everything we needed, and, even though I had offered nine
other possibilities, I'd set my mind on this one. I wondered
how much money I would need to put aside for a court case.

Happily, provisional funds weren't necessary. When I
returned to the patent office a few weeks later, Mr Ellis
said that he didn't think there would be any objection from
Rebow, and, conveniently, that his company also acted for
Tootils. He'd inform them that in his professional opinion
there was no conflict between the names Raelbrook and
Reebok. The name Reebok was ours. Incidentally, if it had
been a British dictionary I had won at that junior race, our
company would have been spelt *Rhebok*.

And then, of course, Mr Ellis provided another 'however'.

'This registration only covers the UK. If you're planning
on doing business in other countries in the future, you'll have
to protect the trademark for overseas regions.'

'Great. Let's do it.'

Mr Ellis paused. 'Okay, but it's quite expensive.'

'Quite expensive?'

'*Very* expensive. But less than it would cost having to fight a false registration claim, should it arise. And if you become successful' – I noticed his emphasis on *if* – 'and your trade-mark isn't protected abroad, you probably will face a fight.'

I thought for a moment. We weren't trading overseas at the moment, but it *was* my intention to do so as soon as we had the resources. If we couldn't supply shoes abroad, we'd be no better off than Foster's.

'Okay. I need to register in Europe, the USA and Japan,' I announced. It was more than a simple statement of regis-tration needs, though – it was a public statement of global intent. It was out there now. As announcements go, it was pretty bold, but there was even more dramatic news just around the corner.

CHAPTER 10

A Challenge

Although I now realised fully how far my ambition reached, what I didn't grasp, rather naively, was how much it was going to cost to achieve it. The fee for brand registrations in foreign territories was astronomical, or so it seemed to me, a shoemaker with just enough in the bank to cover costs, keep the machinery maintained and Mr Stop Heart off my back, at least temporarily.

As such, Wilson Gunn & Ellis became one of our company's largest outstanding debts, something they were quick to point out in a succession of demanding letters. I responded with an offer to pay using a series of post-dated cheques and assumed that would be the matter closed. It wasn't, but their lack of immediate response meant they were soon just another forgotten item in the bulging filing cabinet of my mind.

Life was good. The two of us had found our feet in the business, working well as a team. Jeff would do the 'clicking' – cutting uppers from the leather skins – Joyce would sew them together, and I would last them and prepare the soles ready to be attached, first with a rubber solution, and then machine-sewed. David, our apprenctice, would act as a runner and help wherever it was needed, while both Jeans would answer the phone and deal with the paperwork. It felt like a true family firm, with what I assumed was the same spirit as the early days of Foster's when Dad and Bill were working for Grandad Joe.

Orders for our cycling and running shoes were increasing steadily and it would have been easy to settle for this relatively stress-free set-up, just like Dad and Bill had, the business providing enough income to maintain our current, simple lifestyle. I think for Jeff it was tempting; he was less ambitious, less driven. But I had to see how far we could take it. I knew that it was down to me to provide for my family, but I didn't just want a wage, a comfy life and an easy path. I wanted to be challenged, to take on not just local companies, but world brands. I wanted to prove to myself that I could win.

We were certainly a long way off that at the moment, but it felt like we were on the right path. It was something I enthused about regularly with Jean, partly to keep her on side, and partly because the more I vocalised it, the more real the possibility seemed. From the moment I woke up, my mind was focused on how to sell more shoes than we sold the day before. Breakfast was a board meeting in my own head.

Jean placed a small plate of fried eggs and bacon on my knee, and a cup of tea next to a rolled, cream linen napkin on the side table next to the settee. Our usual morning ritual. Our dining arrangement at all mealtimes, actually. Despite Jean's constant reminders, I had still not bought a second-hand dining table, my recent (and quite valid) excuse being that there was no room now alongside the pram, the cot and all the other oversized accoutrements necessary for such a tiny human. Jean sat beside me on the two-seater, warming her hands around a steaming cup.

'You look happy.'

I smiled. 'Can't complain.' A shaft of morning sunshine flooded the kitchenette in soft light, illuminating the second-hand stove and fridge like they were prizes in a game show. They were small possessions, but they were ours. Just like the tiny flat we occupied in this cold factory. It was no palace, but it belonged to us, an incubator for success. Although I knew Reebok was destined to break into the overseas market, I still had no idea how. Bill's Yale University orders had been something of a fluke, something I didn't know how to repeat. I couldn't visualise that success, couldn't paint a picture of it yet. I just knew it was coming, felt the anticipation, the excitement building.

I heard the clink of the letterbox opening, followed by a flutter of envelopes spilling onto bare floorboards in the front room. Jean gathered them up, sat back down and passed me the clutch of letters. I rested my plate on the arm of the settee, dabbed my mouth with the napkin, and opened the first few. They were the normal motley collection of typed statements and bills, plus a couple of handwritten letters from customers giving feedback or complaints. I passed those back to Jean. After opening the fifth letter, I paused, reread it. Reread it again. The colour drained from my face, from the room. All I could see was black type on a white background. The black that stood out most formed the words 'winding-up petition'. The patent office of Wilson Gunn & Ellis wanted to close down our company, Reebok Sports Limited, just like that.

'What's up, love?' Jean could see the panic in my eyes.

I couldn't bring myself to utter the phrase. They were mere words typed by an anonymous secretary. She would have been completely oblivious of the devastating effect such a pattern of ink could have on someone's morning, on someone's future.

Jean put a hand on my forearm. 'Bad news?'

Aware that her dreams and hopes were reliant on mine, I didn't want her to worry. I knew that if she worried, she would make *me* worry and the vicious cycle would spiral. She would wake the elephant in the room – that although business was slowly on the rise, I was making it all up as I went along. And sooner or later, something would expose me for the fraud that I was and bring it all crashing down. And here it was, delivered in simple black and white, without fuss or fanfare, on an unexceptional Thursday morning.

I felt sick as I rose.

Jean's eyes bore into my face. 'You've not finished your eggs.'

I avoided making eye contact.

'What is it?' She stood too.

'It's nothing. I'll sort it.' I grabbed my jacket off the back of the door and hurried to our accountant's office across the road.

It was only 8.30. The door was locked. I couldn't go back to the factory, or to Jean. My face would give away the seriousness of the situation. Instead, I went to a corner café, ordered a mug of coffee and read the letter over and over again. Finally, through the steamed-up window, I spotted a fluorescent light flicker inside the accountant's office.

Peter, my accountant, took a while to answer my hammering. A man of quiet disposition, his eyes looked cartoonish as he peered around the door, a startled expression magnified in thick, round-rimmed spectacles.

'Is this what I think it is?' I thrust the letter at him.

He scanned the page. 'Oh dear.' He looked up. 'That's not good.' He opened the door fully to let me in and gestured to a chair in front of his desk.

I flopped down. 'I know it's not good, Peter. I don't need you to tell me that. I want you to tell me how to stop it.' I immediately regretted the sarcasm in my voice. Peter was a nice man, shy, but always helpful.

'You need to appoint someone to act on your behalf, a solicitor. If you don't contest it, and soon, you're finished. They'll close down Reebok and sell all your assets to pay the debt.'

I sank lower in the chair. The last thing I needed was a solicitor's fee to pay on top of the brand registration debt. Actually, that wasn't strictly true. The *last* thing I needed was to be closed down. 'Who do you recommend . . . that's cheap?'

'You don't need cheap; you need Derek Waller in Manchester,' replied Peter. 'He's a bit on the expensive side, but he's definitely your man. Just opposed us in a tricky case and got a draw. No idea how, but he certainly knows his stuff.'

I wandered back to the factory, trying to haul my focus away from any forthcoming legal battle and ensuing costs, and towards the day's tasks at hand. But first I needed to make an appointment to see the man who would try to save our company.

I wasn't sure if the rotund man at the far side of a mahogany desk was asleep. His eyes were half-closed and heavy jowls dragged them down at the corners. His mouth was set in a fixed pout like a freeze-frame of somebody sucking on something bittersweet.

I gazed at the rows of leather-bound law journals on the floor-to-ceiling bookshelves behind him, then squinted at the framed documents that were hung on the wall to my right. These were all certifications, diplomas and awards that had been bestowed on Derek Waller, intellectual property solicitor.

'Okay,' said Derek, suddenly coming back to life.

I swivelled my gaze back to his face. 'You're still awake, then!' It had been a good three minutes before he spoke after I'd explained the predicament.

'Pondering, Mr Foster, pondering. Lots to weigh up.'

'And will we win?' I asked.

'I'm sure we will get a satisfactory result.'

'Like what?'

But he was gone again, formulating an answer in silence. He was a strange man, someone who I found hard to fathom, but I guess that was part of his winning strategy, like an unorthodox chess player, unpredictable but still calculating six moves ahead. I rose to leave and waited for Derek to do the same, which he didn't, so I quietly left. Only time would tell how good he was for Reebok.

CHAPTER 11

A Spell on the Road

When Jeff and I created the Mercury brand, we knew we had to be different. And that's what we were. Aside from football boot manufacturers, there were very few UK companies specialising in sports footwear at the time. It was a market ripe for monopolising. We just needed to expand our reach by getting into more shops.

A couple of freelance sales agents had been approached to help us get our products into sports stores. One was Doug Black, who opened the door for us at a camping, climbing and ski shop on Cathedral Street in Manchester owned by brothers Bob and Ellis Brigham. Reebok made sports footwear, Brigham's was an outdoor activities retailer, not a sports shop. However, when Bob Brigham realised that we were just down the road in Bury, he asked Doug Black if Reebok would be interested in making him a customised climbing boot. He wanted to stock a lightweight boot that could grip on the rock face, something that would compete with a similar and expensive model that was made by a company in France. There was only one company in the UK making climbing boots at the time – Hawkins. Bob had been about to call them before Doug mentioned us as a local company, something that Bob Brigham was keen to support.

From this request was born the FEB rock-climbing boot. Bob was pleasantly surprised by both the design and quality of the product, as well as the speed with which we produced it. It was to be the start of a long, useful and friendly relationship between the two of us. Once again it proved that being in the right place at the right time was paramount for business success – even if you didn't know what the right time was, or where to be when it arrived. Good luck is probably a better way of putting it in this case.

Many of the high-street sports shops that our agents approached in the early 1960s were owned by retired footballers. At that time, a footballer's wage was capped at £20 per week. When they had to hang up their boots in their thirties or forties, they usually had very little in the way of savings and still needed to earn a living. The bright ones realised that, while their talents on the field had come to an end, they could still profit from their relative fame by opening a sports shop under their name, selling anything from football boots to snooker cue chalk.

At the peak of this trend, almost every town had three or four of these sports shops, and we needed Reebok to be in them. To do that, we had to expand our sales team. But at exactly the time that we needed to increase our sales force, we lost our two freelance agents. One, an international athlete from Blackpool, had moved to London to improve his running opportunities, while the other had decided to jump the fence and open his own sports shop in Southport.

I estimated that we needed four or five agents to cover the whole country. There was no way we could afford to pay them a wage, and, because we were still relatively unknown beyond the northwest of England, it was a hard slog to persuade good salespeople to work for us on a commission-only basis.

There was only one thing for it, something I had been trying to persuade my dad to let me do when I worked for him at Foster & Sons. I would have to pound the streets myself, covering as much of the country as I could while Jeff looked after the factory.

To cover the costs of travelling up and down the UK, and because I now had an extra mouth to feed, I decided it would be prudent to become a commission-only sales agent for two other companies at the same time. At least that way I'd have three stabs at bringing in an income. The other two companies were Fairbrother, a London-based business specialising in dart flights, card games and dominoes, and Louis Hoffman, a designer and manufacturer of women's tennis dresses.

This new role meant I was now working three or four days a week on the road visiting sports shops, and two or three days in the office at Reebok. Spending so much time away from Jean and Kay was tough, but I was certain the effort would pay dividends for all of us eventually.

Being on the road gave me valuable insights into the profitability of sports shops. As I waited for shop owners to finish serving customers so I could talk to them, I'd wander among the shelves, clothing racks and equipment stands, taking note of their stock. In almost every shop there was just one main sport that monopolised most of the floorspace – football – with a few token items from other sports dotted

J. W. Foster Family from the 1920s (L-R: James (my father), John (Uncle Bill), Maria (my grandma), Joe (my grandfather)).

J. W. Foster & Sons, Olympic Works, Deane Road, Bolton. No. 57 (left), was the original workshop, no. 59 was the pub next door, the Horse and Vulcan, which Joe bought.

Inside Olympic Works: Bill (far left), Jim (left), Joe (far right).

Nellie Halstead, one of Britain's greatest-ever female athletes, smashed several records in Foster's.

Letterpress advertising print of Foster's De Luxe hand sewn running pump.

WRITE FOR PRICE LIST AND SELF-MEASUREMENT FORMS.

J. W. FOSTER & SONS, Deane Road, Bolton.
Largest Athletic Shoe Manufacturers in the World.

Alf Shrubb broke three world records in 1904 at Ibrox Park wearing Foster's pumps.

C. B. Holmes (Bolton United Harriers) represented England at the 1936 Berlin Olympics wearing shoes made by Uncle Bill that were so tight they could only be worn once.

Me aged eight with my cups and silver/gold medal pinned to my chest.

Our Scouting days (Jeff – back row, centre, me – centre).

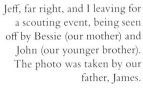

Jeff, far right, and I leaving for a scouting event, being seen off by Bessie (our mother) and John (our younger brother). The photo was taken by our father, James.

Inside our Bright Street, Bury, factory, with Trevor operating a sole attaching press.

GREAT BRITAIN AND   NORTHERN IRELAND

TRADE MARKS ACT, 1938

ReeぼboK

The Trade Mark shown above has been registered in Part ³ of the Register in the name of Reebok Sports Limited.

in Class 25 Schedule IV under No. 3.75660 as of the date 16th February 19 65 in respect of Shoes for use in athletic sports.

Sealed at my direction this 13ᵗʰ day of December 1966.

The Trade Marks Registry, Patent Office,   GORDON GRANT, 25, Southampton Buildings, London, W.C.2.   REGISTRAR.

Registration is for 7 years from the date first above mentioned, and may then be renewed, and also at the expiration of each period of 14 years thereafter. This certificate is not for use in Legal Proceedings or for obtaining Registration abroad. NOTE—Upon any change of ownership of this Trade Mark, or change in address, applications should AT ONCE be made to the Registrar to register the change.

Registration certificate of the first Reebok trademark. The centre logo (torch or ice cream cone) was the early shoe side stripes.

I recognise the handwriting, but not the drawings. My drawing did improve over time.

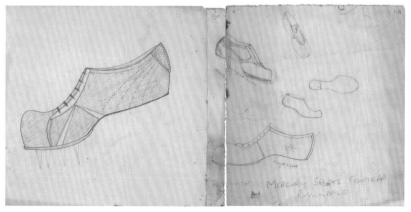

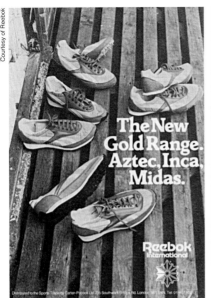

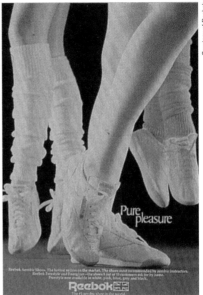

Advertising the 'Gold Range'. The Aztec was our major breakthrough in the USA, having gained 5-star recognition in *Runner's World* in 1979.

Very early US advertisement for the aerobics Freestyle shoe. It became a classic poster.

One of our early successes, the 'Ripple'. It has the early logo and our original side striping.

A great leap for Reebok, when Cybill Shepherd wore her High Tops at the 1985 Emmy Awards.

A typical aerobics workout class. They would all be wearing Reebok.

The cast of *Aliens*. Sigourney Weaver hunted down extra-terrestrials wearing a pair of futuristic Reebok 'Alien Stompers'.

Me on the right with Paul Fireman. Paul came to Bolton to see the progress of the new International HQ we were building and to join me in laying a time capsule.

Charlton Heston and Wendell Niles at the opening of Reebok House in Bolton in 1988.

Among the many stars joining us in Monte Carlo was Sharon Stone.

Presenting the Princess Grace trophy to the winners of the Monte Carlo Pro-Celeb tournament.

With some of the stars at the Monte Carlo Pro-Celeb Tennis, in our classic tennis shirts designed by Tuan Le.

Overlooking Sydney Harbour on a visit to the Hendler family, who I appointed as Reebok distributors for Australia and New Zealand.

My daughter Kay enjoying the company of Dolph Lundgren ('He-Man') at Reebok's 'Night with the Stars' in 1988.

around. It was clear that these high-street sports shops relied on revenue from football kits, footballs, football boots and shin pads. Everything else was ancillary. While Reebok still had a moderately successful line in rugby boots, we were not giving anywhere near enough focus to football.

I thought back to Foster's. They had missed a glaring opportunity too. They were in the right trade but in the wrong sport for growth. In the 1920s, Bolton Wanderers were the team of the decade and Foster's were supplying almost every team in the various leagues with training shoes, but not boots. It would have been a relatively easy step to follow up the success in trainers by also offering a range of football boots to *all* the league teams, but the family never capitalised on that advantage. I wondered why. It seemed like a huge opportunity lost. Perhaps it was because it would have needed a big investment in new machinery.

Most football boots in those days were made of a thick leather upper and a bulky sole. They had a support strap just behind the toe joint, and a hard toecap. Protection was key, attained through dense, tough materials and design. The machines that my grandad, and then my dad, owned were not set up to produce the bulky footwear demanded by the heavy, muddy pitches of the early and mid-twentieth century. The Foster's machines were set up for the lightness and agility required in running shoes.

It was only when Adidas introduced the Argentina football boot in the 1954 World Cup that the emphasis shifted from purely being protective to providing speed and agility through less weight and more flexibility. But, by that time, other companies were way ahead of the game and Foster's had missed their opportunity.

Maybe, I thought, if they had invested in the right machinery at the right time, using the supply lines they already had with most of the top-flight football teams, I wouldn't have been standing in a sports shop next to racks and racks of football boots by Adidas, Puma, Bukta, Mitre, Dunlop and Umbro, trying to sell Reebok rugby boots, running pumps and cycling shoes to a disinterested ex-footballer.

Our only football offering was trainers, and even those were more geared towards runners. The more visits I made to high-street sports shops, the more I heard, 'Why do we need Reebok when we have Adidas and Dunlop trainers?' The only thing I was managing to sell was dart flights, and that wasn't going to pay my travel expenses or further the expansion of my own company.

It was dispiriting. But, worst of all, I agreed with them. Why would they gamble on giving valuable store space to an unknown when established football brands were bringing shop owners 90 per cent of their revenue? It was a market we had missed, and one that was monopolised. There was no point in even pursuing it.

I needed to forget the mainstream and start focusing again on what we did best, and what we were known for doing best – athletic shoes. I remember closing the glass door of a sports shop in Doncaster after yet another no-thank-you, walking into the autumn sunshine and firing myself as an agent for Fairbrother, Louis Hoffman *and* Reebok. It was time to return to the factory floor and regroup.

I had to find a way of maximising our presence in the niche running and athletics shops, not the general sports shops that mainly relied on football. But how? We were already in a small handful, including Sweatshop, a specialist running store operated by Chris Brasher, one of Roger Bannister's four-minute-mile pacemakers. But we needed to be in many more, and for that we needed to create demand, but not from the shop owners. We needed to go one step back and first create massive nationwide demand from runners and athletes themselves.

We hadn't anything like the budget necessary for a global marketing campaign. We hadn't assigned a budget for *any* marketing, so whatever solution I managed to find would need to be at little or no cost. It was a challenge, but I made it my number one priority to find a way.

As is the way in all businesses, the order of priorities changed almost instantly. Jeff reminded me about the court case for our winding-up petition. I hadn't forgotten about it. How could I? It had been on my mind constantly, even while on the road, but I was determined not to waste time waiting for the outcome. I couldn't afford to. I had to assume that we were going to win and carry on as normal. What I had forgotten, though, was the date. It was tomorrow. If it didn't go well, my goal to find the perfect – and free – marketing strategy wouldn't be necessary. We'd be out of business anyway.

The following afternoon I sat behind my desk, nervously swivelling back and forth. Jean stood beside me, jiggling Kay up and down in her arms. Jeff sat facing me on the other side of the desk. I couldn't tell if it was the fluorescent strip light that had blanched all colour from his complexion or the gravity of the impending court decision. His Jean leaned on the black filing cabinet, arms folded defiantly.

'Look, it's going to be fine.' I stood and put a calming hand on Jean's arm. She smiled, unconvincingly.

'We've got a great solicitor,' I continued, with as much

optimism as I could muster. 'I've got every faith.' The others said nothing. I sat back down and we all resumed staring at the phone.

The four-week wait for the court case had taken its toll both physically and mentally. I'd envisioned a scene so many times in which I told Jean we were ruined that I almost couldn't tell if it was my imagination or an actual memory. I'd lost weight, too, probably 10 pounds. The thought of food made me feel sick. During my time on the road as an agent, I would often go full days without eating, the nagging fear at the back of my mind overriding any primal need for sustenance.

Suddenly, the shrill ringing from the phone startled us all. 'Hello?' It was Derek Waller. I nodded at Jeff. He and the Jeans leaned forward, urging good news. Derek liked to talk. Three pairs of eyes bore into me, looking for the first glimmer of expression as I gripped the phone tight to my ear and held my breath. After a minute I interrupted Derek. 'So, what's the outcome?' He spoke again. My eyes lifted to the ceiling as I exhaled loudly. I cupped my hand over the mouthpiece. 'They threw the petition out.' Jeff jumped to his feet and pumped his fists as if he'd just won the Tour de France. The two Jeans hugged each other. We were safe again.

Although Derek had succeeded in having the petition dismissed, naturally we still had to pay the money we owed. He had negotiated a deal with Wilson Gunn & Ellis that, although it wouldn't break the bank, would make our financial situation even more challenging. We still had ongoing costs, and more material and equipment that we desperately needed to buy. Not to mention that our respective wives were pressuring Jeff and me to find living conditions more convivial than sharing a bathroom between two tiny flats in a decrepit factory. But we had been spared, and, for now, we were still in business, albeit with even more outgoings than ever, including the not insubstantial solicitor's fee. However, Derek knew our financial position and it was some six months before his bill arrived. It was a magnanimous gesture and one that cemented our business relationship for years to come.

Where most people might have suggested a nice meal out or a picnic in the country to celebrate the victory and clear the mind, I suggested to Jean that we go to the Three Towers, a local fell-running event that we sponsored. I'm sure she was enamoured of the prospect.

On a damp and drizzly day, we watched club runners race up Holcombe Hill to Holcombe Tower, then across the moorland to Darwen Tower, across Winter Hill to Rivington Pike and down the muddy slopes to the finish below. It was hard to identify the leaders, their bright club colours obliterated as they scrambled through bogs, streams and furrows.

As with all social events at that time, my interest and attention were only partial. There was rarely a time when I could switch off completely, stop the neurons in my head firing as they tried to make new connections that would map out a path of further business progression.

That day was no exception. I clapped in the right places, tried to keep Jean as cheery as possible, but all the time I was thinking about how we could get more people to market Reebok across the country, with agents who were enthusiastic but who didn't demand salaries we couldn't afford.

And then it hit me. I was looking at the answer right in front of me. Each and every dirt-stained runner was a potential sales agent. They were all amateurs, so they would all be happy for the chance to earn a bit of extra money within an activity they were passionate about. And each and every one had the potential to enlist a fellow athlete as a sales agent if there was enough incentive. In fact, I thought, why stop at the runners? Why not everybody involved in running and running clubs?

I began contacting all the secretaries of the 500 or so athletic clubs affiliated to the Amateur Athletic Association and proposed that they, or one of their members, become a Reebok agent working on a commission basis. They would get 15 per cent commission on any sales they brought in and Reebok would arrange the postage and packing. The results were astounding. Within a couple of months, I had over fifty agents taking orders, the number growing every week.

I then re-targeted all of the clubs that didn't respond first time round and offered a free pair of Reebok running shoes if the secretary could find us an agent within their club. The numbers rose again and soon almost a hundred agents were talking about Reebok and selling shoes to both their fellow club members *and* at nationwide race meetings.

There were many comparisons to be drawn between this strategy and the technique that my grandad had employed in the 1890s, when he started to win races wearing his own Foster's spiked shoes, attracting the attention of his running colleagues and opponents. This was merely notching the idea up a few gears.

It seemed phenomenally easy, and I wondered why other sports-shoe brands hadn't thought of this tactic before.

CHAPTER 12

Time to Move

The year 1963 brought big changes in the cultural identity of the UK, as well as changes for the better in our own lives. It was a year remembered for many things, not least the death of Labour leader Hugh Gaitskell, which seemed to act as a final nail in the coffin of the old-school guard and a cementing of the new world order. Dreams were openly encouraged to be pursued on all fronts during this generational revolution of permissiveness. And as spring peeled away the snowdrifts of the 'Big Freeze', both a new Britain and a new Reebok emerged.

The business was growing, and so was the Foster family. Jeff and his Jean had also had their first child, Ian, but their entry into parenthood was not without problems. Ian frequently had purple spots on his skin and subsequent tests showed he had purpura, a rare blood condition. It was obviously a worry, but if it played on Jeff's mind, he rarely showed it at work.

This new arrival signalled the time had come for both

families to find better living arrangements. There were six of us sharing what was effectively a two-bed, one-bathroom maisonette in a run-down factory. Not exactly the start in life that either set of parents would have envisaged for their first-borns. We all moved out of the factory living accommodation and back to Bolton, buying modest homes in Harwood.

We still weren't at the stage where we could splash out on expensive cars, though. Jeff bought an old second-hand Jaguar, while I, much to the consternation of Jean, invested in yet another battered van, this time for the princely sum of £25. It was hardly an upgrade, but practicality rather than luxury was still at the forefront of my mind.

Having moved ourselves to more convivial premises, it was also time to think about relocating the business. We had outgrown our Bolton Street base. The year's extreme winter was the final straw. It was impossible to heat the factory in such cold weather. Operating extremely sharp and potentially dangerous machinery was not ideal when your fingers were numb. We also needed more equipment, and the one floor we could use in our present abode was already straining under its current load.

I wanted to remain in or around Bury, close enough to the heart of the footwear industry to benefit from easy supply, but far enough out not to be involved in next-door-neighbour cutthroat business shenanigans. I'd never even considered relocating elsewhere, until I received a request for a meeting out of the blue.

A few months back, I'd attempted to resurrect the export deal Bill had arranged with Frank Ryan and Bob Geinjack in America. I'd recreated the hand-sewn DeLuxe shoe and sent it to the pair at Yale University. It wasn't a great copy, but I thought it was worth a punt, a way potentially to reopen the door to distribution in America. I didn't think anything would come of it so was surprised when, a few months later, I received a request to send samples of the whole Reebok range.

This, in turn, led to an invitation from Frank for me and Jean to visit him in Ireland, where he had rented a huge manor house for the summer near Dún Laoghaire, south of Dublin.

Frank picked us up from the airport in an ostentatious Cadillac that looked completely out of place on the back roads of Ireland. Outside a restaurant in Dublin, he parked the car in typical New York fashion, bumping vehicles back and forth until there was enough space to house his shiny monstrosity. When he opened the door for us, it was so wide it completely blocked the pavement, forcing a traffic jam of pedestrians. This captured the curiosity of more people on the other side of the street, who sidled over to see who everyone was looking at. Soon the crowd spilled onto the road, causing a full-scale roadblock. As Jean, Frank and I fought our way into the restaurant, someone shoved a pen and paper into my hand and asked for an autograph. They had no idea who we were but assumed that some Hollywood stars had arrived in town.

After lunch, we drove down country lanes barely wide enough for the Cadillac, let alone any oncoming traffic. Thankfully, we met no other drivers and pulled up at the entrance gates to his rented holiday mansion, where he got out and instructed me to manoeuvre the beast up the half-mile driveway.

The following day, without my knowledge, Frank had arranged a meeting with a government official back in

Dublin, at which I surprisingly received an invitation to move our factory to Ireland, along with the offer of a comprehensive package of financial incentives and assistance. I declined, and consequently Frank declined our shoes, or rather I didn't hear from him again, which amounted to the same thing. Still, it had been a memorable trip for many reasons, including a visit to the remains of Tara, an ancient burial ground.

Back in England, I contacted my old auction friend, John Willie Johnson, to see if he had any leads on factories for sale. He knew of a mill owned by Bury Felt Ltd. At the time, the felting business was shrinking as rubber underlay was becoming the more popular option for carpets. One of their units at Bright Street in Bury had been closed after they scaled back production.

I looked out of the passenger window as Jeff drove us in his Jaguar through a sprawling council estate. Women hung out washing and chatted over garden fences, while groups of children played street football or peered into prams pushed by their teenage peers. The women paused, cigarette smoke wisping into the April air. Their heads followed our slow route, whispers exchanged as we passed in our *posh* car.

One of the things that had sparked my interest in this particular factory was its location. Surrounded by terraced houses and other factories, it neighboured this housing estate, an industrial hub nourished by a reservoir of ready workers within walking distance of work. Some would already have shoemaking experience through employment, both past and present, in the nearby Parker's shoe factory. Many of those living on the estate would surely be keen for the chance to earn a few extra pounds during the times when we needed to boost production in the factory.

The mill itself was huge, far too big for Reebok, but we were offered just the ground floor at a very affordable rent. The open work floor provided enough space to accommodate the three new clicking presses, the lasting machines and conveyor system production line that we needed in order to progress. It was almost perfect, and over two months we built a small raised office overlooking the work floor, and, perhaps more importantly, installed a gas heating system.

Having physically helped us to move, John Willie Johnson also continued to keep an eye out for additional machinery that would help improve our efficiency. Although it wasn't new, we now had most of the equipment we needed, and, fortunately, one of the units in the Bright Street factory was occupied by a small engineering shop. Any repairs to our aged production line were quickly seen to, thus keeping maintenance costs and machine downtime to a minimum.

For the next few years, sales charts would show a consistent upward trend. The rise of Reebok was modest, but we'd had to double our workforce from ten to twenty to handle the production of our track and field, cross-country and road-running shoes, as well as a line of rugby boots.

On the business front, we couldn't complain. On the personal front, though, my brother and his wife were becoming increasingly worried about their son. The purpura had not abated and Ian's doctor was concerned that, as he started walking, his propensity to bruise and bleed profusely would become a real issue. The advice was to remove Ian's spleen, and, in February 1965, Jean and Jeff's little boy was admitted into hospital. He never came out.

Tragically, Ian died due to complications during surgery.

Jean and Jeff were too distraught to formally identify his body after the operation, so I volunteered.

I can safely say that it was the lowest point of my life so far. I stared at a closed door in Bolton Royal Hospital, steeling myself before entering. There was nothing unusual about the door, its dull, painted surface like any other along this fluorescent-lit corridor. Behind other doors lay store cupboards packed with everyday cleaning materials, some concealed rows of medical supplies. But I knew that, by putting my hand on the cold steel handle and pushing open this unexceptional rectangle of wood, I would be left with a vision that would scar my mind for the rest of my life. I took a deep breath and stepped in.

The room was small, the lighting dimmed to blunt any sense of sterility but bright enough to avoid having to stand too close to the raised bed for the identification. A cotton sheet was tucked under Ian's chin, his blond hair neatly combed. His face was ghostly white, colourless apart from violet pennies of purpura on his cheeks and forehead. My heart sank as I was consumed by sorrow and grief for Jean and Jeff. *How do you cope with losing a child?* I thought. *How do you ever find happiness again?*

Nineteen sixty-six was a memorable year for the right reasons, two of them. The late Martin Peters *et al* showered us all with glory when England beat West Germany 4-2 in the World Cup final at Wembley Stadium. And Jean and I had a second child, a son, David, five and a half years after the birth of Kay. Sports fans might shout, 'Back of the net!' for both occasions, but my mind was a kaleidoscope of emotions after the birth. Our family felt complete. We now had a girl *and* a boy, the full set. But, on the other hand, it didn't feel right to revel in our good fortune while my brother and his wife were still reeling from the death of their only child just twelve months previously. Parental joy did infuse their world again, however, when Diane Foster was born in 1968. The following year they would go on to have another child, Robert. On the surface, they seemed like the happiest parents in the world, but I knew that inside they were still suffering.

By the mid- to late 1960s, road running was growing rapidly in the USA. We had to find a way to become part of this new revolution. It offered the opportunity for local club runners to race alongside some of the best athletes in the world over distances of 5,000 metres (3.1 miles), 10 kilometres (6.2 miles), a 21-kilometre (13.1-mile) half-marathon, and a 42-kilometre (26.2-mile) full marathon. *How could we take advantage of this surge in popularity?* I mused.

Until now, the big-city marathons like Boston, Fukuoka and Kosice were largely invite-only, forcing those passionate about road running to either run unregistered, enter under false pretences or watch from the sidelines. The 1967 Boston Marathon hit the headlines for all the wrong reasons when an official tried to manhandle a female runner from the circuit. Although women could run the circuit unregistered and without official bibs, Kathrine Switzer had entered officially using only her first initial and surname. The ensuing media coverage captured the attention of the masses, both male *and* female, helping to ignite an explosion in road running.

This popularity had also turned the heads of Reebok's business competitors in the UK. Tiger (later to become Asics) running shoes were being imported from the Onitsuka company in Japan and sold directly to athletes. The man behind

Tiger imports in the US was Phil Knight, better known as the founder of Nike, but it was Stan Eldon, a top long-distance runner, who was bringing Tiger to the UK. Chris Brasher, my friend at Sweatshop, had also become the sole importer of, first, Nokia orienteering footwear and, later, New Balance shoes.

But it was Tiger who was proving to be our biggest competition. They were offering road-running shoes with canvas uppers, much cheaper to produce than our own leather and suede versions. We had to move fast before Reebok was completely swept out of the market by this new trend.

Fortunately, as we were within the heart of the textile industry, it didn't take long to source canvas, but binding the cut edge of this heavy twill fabric without it fraying was a challenge, and required new machinery and expertise.

Finally, the Reebok Fab-Road trainer jumped from the drawing board to the marketplace, competitively priced to rival Tiger's canvas shoes. To boost initial sales and to get the word out quickly, I ran a launch promotion in *Athletics Weekly*. A pre-paid envelope was attached, which readers could simply tear out, insert cash or postal orders, and send to us without having to write out an address or buy a stamp. Then we waited.

One day, a few weeks later, I arrived early at work. Norman was already there, of course; he always was.

'Joe,' he shouted from the tea room. He nodded at a tray set in front of him. It was stacked with pre-paid envelopes. 'Must be over fifty,' he said calmly.

I was stunned. I took the tray to my office, beckoned Norman to follow, and tipped the envelopes onto my desk, many rattling with loose change.

Norman smiled. 'Can't beat that sound, eh?'

We spent the next ten minutes opening envelope after envelope, each revealing cash or postal orders for the Fab-Road. We were nearly finished when Jeff walked in. He stopped and stared at the desk. 'What the . . .?'

I held out the last two envelopes. He ripped them open, still with a look of disbelief on his face.

'Right,' I said, rubbing my hands together. 'I've done my job. Now it's down to you to make them.'

Over the coming months, hundreds of new orders flooded in. Flushed with the success of our first canvas shoe, we decided to do battle next with Nokia's new plastic shoe that Chris Brasher had begun importing. Later the same year we developed the Fab-XC, a specialist version for cross-country, fell and orienteering races. For this, we introduced a nylon fabric that was coated in plastic, the same material that had replaced the tarpaulin seen on the back of open-top lorries.

The Fab-XC also proved to be a hit. Its lightweight form and improved waterproofing prevented it from becoming heavy with water and dirt absorbed from running through mud and streams. We didn't know it at the time, but we were at the forefront of a new running trend in the UK, and our initial efforts meant Reebok was already well placed to take advantage of our pole position.

With so many runners as our agents, it was hard in the late 1960s for amateur athletes *not* to come across the Reebok brand. It was also obvious that we were appearing on the radar of other sports-shoe brands. I was flattered that the likes of Tiger importer Stan Eldon and Chris Brasher of Nokia shoes were now sitting up and taking notice.

However, I was soon to discover that popping your head

above the parapet in business also had negative consequences. Adidas had been watching us, too, waiting to pounce.

Our Reebok design incorporated a T-bar and two side stripes on our running shoes, as well as the 'Winged Messenger' logo that we carried over from the days of Mercury. In 1968 we received a letter from Adidas to say they considered it was an infringement of their trademark three stripes. We had to take a pragmatic approach, mainly because we didn't have any money to fight them.

With the creative suggestions of local athletes, we changed the markings to an arrow and lateral striping, a design inspired by the tail markings on British Airways planes. I'd also been thinking about the letter 'R' in our logo. It was directional, which meant that on the left shoe it pointed backwards. I decided to drop the initial altogether and drew the arrows into a circle. It seemed to work, and when the man who created all my graphic designs suggested the Motter Tektura font, I knew we had finally achieved the unique Reebok identity – the Starcrest.

It had been a pain to change our silhouette again, but I was pleased with the outcome, and it was reassuring to know that Adidas was thinking about us! It felt like we had entered the arena, admittedly as rank outsiders, but at least we were now in the game.

CHAPTER 13

America on My Mind

Being in the game was one thing. Winning was another, and to do that we needed to take on the big boys on their own turf, the USA. We were still a relatively small company, yet now with a good share of the UK athletics market.

Although cracking the American nut was my main aim, there was also, of course, a fairly big territory that was closer and in the opposite direction, so in 1967 Jeff and I decided to take a week out to evaluate the European market across the Channel.

In late September we drove through France, Belgium and into northern Germany on our way to SPOGA, the International Sports Goods, Camping Equipment and Garden Furniture trade show. We knew that the sports shoes market was completely dominated by Adidas and Puma – we were making a few hundred pairs of shoes a week, while the Dassler brothers must have been manufacturing thousands – but it was a good opportunity to experience an international sporting goods exhibition.

It was late afternoon when we pulled up opposite the

twin-spired cathedral in Cologne, still showing damage from the Second World War. We presented ourselves at the desk of an accommodation-finding service in an office set up by the show organisers opposite the cathedral, but the news wasn't good. We were told that there was nothing left in Cologne, but if we returned to the office at 5pm that evening a bus would take us to the nearest available hotel.

Our 'hotel' turned out to be a dark and decrepit boarding house on the banks of the Rhine in Königswinter, a one-and-a-half-hour bus ride from Cologne. With continental breakfast the only food on offer, we tried to ask the house-keeper directions to the nearest restaurants. Jeff had done most of his national service in Germany and, although his German wasn't perfect, it was certainly passable to most, except this housekeeper. Seemingly, she couldn't grasp even a sense of what Jeff was asking and I was doing my best to mime. After much tutting and sighing, she relented and pointed us in the direction of the town centre, where, after a forgettable dinner and a couple of steins of *Weissbier*, we were ready to tackle the housekeeper again.

Sour-faced and begrudgingly, she showed us to a dingy room occupied by one double bed and an army of spiders. It had been years since I'd shared a bed with my brother, let alone a dozen scuttling arachnids. Needless to say, sleep was hard to come by. At some point, I must have dropped off, though, as I was startled awake by the housekeeper as she banged on our door and yelled in perfect English that it was 6am and breakfast was being served.

The rest of the day Jeff and I made our way around the exhibition stands, bumping into one or two fellow Brits. By late afternoon we decided that we'd seen enough and, not wishing to take advantage of the accommodation service again, we found our car and headed to France.

A few months prior to our trip to SPOGA I had contacted Opal, a company selling mobile homes in the south of France. One of their sites was in Argelès-sur-Mer in Languedoc, and I decided it was a good opportunity to make a detour south so we could find out more about their products. As prospective buyers, we were given a tour of their site and offered an overnight stay on their static caravan park. Twenty-four hours later we drove away clutching ownership papers. I'm still not sure how we ended up buying a mobile home in France that day, but I remember at the time it was something to do with a lot of red wine, a conviction that we needed a place to relax, and the justification that we could use it as our 'European office' despite having already decided that we were going to focus only on the UK and the US.

Europe, it seemed, was even harder to break into than the US. As well as the market being saturated by Adidas and Puma, there wasn't as much disposable income floating around, plus there was no common language. There was no doubt that America was where the true riches lay, a country of 350 million, the vast majority speaking the same language as us – more or less. Here, track and field was still a niche, but it was a huge niche compared to the UK, and a serious business from college level up.

There were other reasons it was so important. America was the trendsetter. Other countries around the world looked to it for innovation, new styles. There was also a culture of disposable commerce. The level of income, and the lifestyle this afforded, enabled people to take greater risks when purchasing something. They weren't like Europeans, who thought twice, three times about buying shoes and clothes. The Americans were more impulsive. If they liked it, they bought it. If it proved to be a good purchase, they'd buy it again. If they didn't like it, they moved on to something else, no refunds, no fuss, no hard feelings.

For now, there was only one goal, and soon an opportunity arose that would eventually get me a Reebok-clad foot in the door.

I was an avid reader of all the sporting goods magazines. I had to be. It was the best way of keeping up with the latest trends. In one issue of *Eurosport*, I came across an advertisement by the British Board of Trade. They were offering sponsorship for sporting goods manufacturers to participate in a joint British stand at the NSGA (National Sporting Goods Association) exhibition in the USA in February 1968. Use of the stand was included, as were return flights, and 50 per cent of all hotel and other expenses. It was a no-brainer for Reebok and a great way for the UK government to encourage British companies to export.

Bob Brigham, who had asked us to produce a rock-climbing boot for his outdoor activity store in Manchester, wanted to go too. He suggested that we register as a joint venture with his new MOAC (Mountaineering Activities) company. Neither of us had ever been to the USA before, so a bit of comradeship seemed like a good idea, and one lunch-time we went to a Manchester tailor to have matching suits made for our Reebok/MOAC American expedition.

Although the exhibition in Chicago's McCormick Place was only a four-day event, it was cheaper to buy a ticket for a two-week return, so Bob suggested we spend a few days in New York first, attend the Chicago event, and then take a side trip to Bermuda to stay with some friends he knew. Who was I to argue?

The date of the show coincided with the second birthday of my son, David, but, without hesitation, I had confirmed our participation in America, plus a few days extra for a little fun. I'd like to be able to say that I made that choice purely to reap the rewards that would later benefit my family. But, being perfectly honest, that would not be true. As with my dad before me, and his before that, work and family were separate entities, linked only by the one providing necessities for the other. Business gain was my driving force, or rather my obsession.

It was the Foster culture, a misnomer if ever there was one. The only 'fostering' done was to look after the wellbeing of my business. The nurturing of my family had become secondary. It was the way it had been with my own dad, whose priority had been his social life at the pub. Now I was following the same path, the price of which I had yet to pay.

Our bags crammed with samples and point-of-sale material, we boarded the flight at Manchester airport and spent most of the journey drinking and smoking. I was thirty-two, on a flight to America! As we descended towards JFK airport I felt like a seven-year-old on Christmas Eve with one visual gift coming after the next: the New York skyline, the Empire State Building and the Chrysler Building – all iconic images that I had seen on TV or cinema screens, and now, here I was, about to experience this thrilling world first-hand.

New York flashed past the windows of our yellow cab on the ride to our hotel in Times Square. It was all that I imagined it to be, all that I'd seen in movies and TV programmes. Horns blared, neon flashed and steam poured from manhole covers. It was bright and brash, its occupants striding purposefully and its buildings tall and proud.

For the next few days, we braved the freezing streets of Midtown New York, visiting as many sports and outdoor activities shops as possible, to soak up the store layouts, the pricing, the variety, and to actually pick up and feel the weight and cushioning of shoes that I'd only ever seen on the pages of magazines. Eventually, the February wind whipping between the skyscrapers would defeat us, and we'd retire to enjoy huge steak dinners at Tad's, a cosy downtown restaurant.

If there was one other thing that confirmed my preconceptions of America, it was that everything was larger than life, including those restaurant meals. We would stare down in awe at monstrous steaks spilling over the sides of dinner plates and accompanied by fist-sized Idaho potatoes slathered in a quarter pound of butter. And all for a dollar!

Then, stepping outside, my neck would crane as I peered at the colossal architecture. The people too were larger than life – bold, loud and confident, every taxi driver, waiter or hotel receptionist like a melodramatic character in a TV series.

Even the temperature was extreme, a sharp cold that cut through the skin like a blade. But if we thought New York was freezing, the biting temperatures of Chicago were off the scale. Heavy snow was falling and jagged chunks of ice poked from the surface of Lake Michigan like frozen shark fins.

The night before the NSGA exhibition, a reception was held for our UK sports industry group at the British consulate. Nibbles and wine were provided, along with stern warnings not to venture out at night alone and to keep to major, well-lit streets. With or without Bob, I had no intention of late-night wandering. Frostbite or stab wounds were not the kind of souvenirs I intended to take back to England.

Like everything else on this trip, Chicago's McCormick Place on the shores of Lake Michigan was enormous. It was (and still is) the largest convention and exhibition centre in North America. It has a roof long enough to land a light aircraft. Inside was a battalion of stands exhibiting everything commercial that is remotely connected to 'sport', including hunting, shooting and fishing paraphernalia.

For a sporting exhibition, there were a heck of a lot of smokers in attendance, me included! During the exhibition, I sucked on cigarette after cigarette offered by the many delegates who visited our stand. They were the extra-long (of course!) 101 cigarettes, and while I, British and not prone to wastefulness, smoked them down to the filter, the Americans would take two or three drags then stub them out. It was my first face-to-face experience of the throwaway, disposable culture that existed on this side of the Pond.

At the exhibition, although Bob picked up a small order for his FEB climbing boots that Reebok was manufacturing, I picked up nothing more than a hacking cough. I had a lot of interest in Reebok shoes from retailers, but when they asked where they could get them from and I gave them my business card they would peer at it with confusion.

'England? What state is that in?' they'd enquire in all earnestness.

'England,' I'd start to explain, 'in Britain.'

Eventually, the penny would drop. 'Ah ... England, near London.'

'Yes ... near London,' I'd repeat wearily. I couldn't be bothered to explain.

At this stage they'd usually hand the card back: 'Let me know when you've got someone that we can buy off here.'

All wanted to buy in dollars from a USA-based supplier. They didn't want the hassle of having to import products. They didn't need to. There were already plenty of other suppliers in the country. It became obvious that we needed a distributor based in the USA, just like Foster's had in the 1950s with their contacts at Yale. Adidas had three or four distributors covering North America. I guessed we needed the same. And thus began the start of a very long search.

By the end of the NSGA show I was coughing incessantly and, after we touched down in Bermuda, I dumped what was left of my cigarette stash in the nearest bin and vowed never to smoke again. Thankfully, the coughing cleared up almost instantly, which was as much of a relief to Bob as it was to me. We were sharing not just a room but a bed at his friends' bungalow just outside Hamilton.

Awkward sleeping arrangements aside, the laid-back atmosphere and balmy heat of Bermuda was the perfect anti-dote to the mania and cold of the past ten days. Hamilton's colonial tea shops were a genteel substitute for Manhattan's late-night diners; and, in contrast to the constant sirens wail-ing in Midtown, here a solitary policeman dressed in shorts calmly directed traffic in the tranquil town centre.

Bob and I toured the island on hired mopeds, visiting the governor's residence and the old naval shipyard. As we raced through citrus groves, I closed my eyes for a second, feeling the warm breeze on my face, inhaling fragrant wafts of orange blossom, and allowing the Bermudan heat to ease taut shoulder muscles. In two days' time I would be back in Bury with the smell of diesel from my van, the windscreen wipers angrily swatting raindrops to allow glimpses of the rain-stained, two-tone grey that painted the roads, buildings and townsfolk throughout late winter.

Ordinarily, it would have depressed me, but I was looking forward to seeing Jean and Kay, and giving David his birthday present. I was also yearning for the familiar surroundings of the factory – the smell of old leather, the whirr and clunk of hole-punching machinery, and the excitement of each new day's business challenge. I was ready, and I now knew what we needed to do to break into America. Exciting times lay ahead. I could feel it.

CHAPTER 14

An Opening to the World

The Board of Trade must have deemed the USA venture a success. They continued their support for businesses like ours for many years. Although Bob never returned after that first visit, I made representing Reebok at the NSGA an annual event. However, finding an American distributor proved to be somewhat more of a challenge than I'd imagined. We were too small, too underfunded and a complete unknown.

Despite this, I *had* been approached by Rolf and Peter Martin of Fred Martin Agencies, a sports agency business set up by their father in Winnipeg, Canada. They were already agents for Puma but had come across the 'Prefect', our special spiked shoe for schools. It was something that Puma couldn't match for the price.

The Martins placed some exceptionally large orders for our small production line, which entailed many late nights at the factory, with us desperately trying to meet the shipping deadlines. But I was more than happy to put in the extra hours – we now had a distribution deal across the Atlantic, albeit on the wrong side of the 49th parallel.

At that time, large orders such as this were shipped in wooden crates. After racing to Liverpool docks to have the crate loaded, we breathed a sigh of relief as we watched the ship sail off. It was the last of a batch of big orders from the Fred Martin Agencies so, at last, we could go back to normal(ish) working hours.

A couple of weeks later, however, we received an urgent request to repeat the order and ship it as soon as possible. While unloading in Canada, the crate had fallen into the water, consigning dozens of pairs of Reeboks to the murky depths of a Canadian port.

Sunken shoes apart, the Martins had success with the Prefect, and actually provided a pair to Canadian high jump athlete Debbie Brill, who as a schoolgirl developed a technique that would later become known as the 'Brill Bend'. It was similar to the innovative Fosbury Flop, and involved jumping the bar with your back parallel to the ground. Debbie went on to set several world records for her age, some of which still stand today.

Sadly, news of Fred Martin Agencies buying from Reebok eventually reached the ears of their biggest client, Puma, who were not impressed, to say the least. They threatened to oust the Martins as their Canadian distributors if they continued working with us. They didn't, and thus our Canadian contract came to a grinding halt.

In 1969, however, my prayers for someone to offer us international distribution were answered when we caught the attention of Lawrence Sports, a major manufacturer of football boots in the UK.

Soccer, as our American cousins prefer to call it, was starting to take off on the other side of the Atlantic, and the company's sales director, Derek Shackleton ('Shack'), had convinced the owner, Harold Lawrence, that Lawrence Sports needed to be a part of it. Shack figured that a link with Reebok and our broader range of sports footwear, in particular our trainers, would give them a better chance of gaining traction in the US.

Shack casually put it to me that it would be mutually beneficial if Lawrence Sports took over as worldwide distributors of Reebok. Looking back, I guess Reebok at the time still had some of the same mentality as Foster's when it was run by Grandad and we missed a glaring opportunity. Maybe if I had been brought up with a different outlook, I would have approached Lawrence Sports and suggested that, while they distributed our products, they might also manufacture a line of Reebok football boots.

Alas, I didn't. Partly because in those days Lawrence Sports was a much bigger company than Reebok and we didn't have the authority to dictate to them, but also because at that time I was swept up in the euphoria of thinking we had found our access to the American market. *Was that it? Was that how easy it was to get global distribution, to get us into America*? I thought. Wow. We were there with just one phone call.

The deal seemed too good to be true. Lawrence Sports would buy all our annual production, currently around 12,000 to 15,000 pairs in the track and field, cross-country, road running and rugby sectors. I would become part of the international sales team. It was a good offer, ensuring our staff, numbering twenty by now, were assured full employment, while Reebok was guaranteed maximum production and timely payments from Lawrence Sports. The only downside was that we now had to stop supplying direct to the massive team of athletics club agents that we had built up over the past seven years. I'd spent a lot of time and effort recruiting agents, and to stop working with them was a huge gamble, but this opportunity was too good a chance to miss. Overseas distribution was the biggest hurdle to overcome. This deal would alleviate many headaches. I agreed and signed on the dotted line. It was a decision that nearly cost Jeff and me our company.

With Shack buying up all production and handling the distribution, I now found I had time on my hands to explore other avenues for Reebok. A leather clothing line seemed like one of the obvious choices. We already had the contacts for material suppliers, plus a production line that could easily be replicated to stitch garments. Plus, it was a fun time in the fashion industry, an era of leather and suede hot pants and skirts.

Although Reebok financed the operation, Jeff didn't want to get involved in Leatherflair, my new fashion business. He did, however, help me paint our first retail shop in Bury in brand colours – principally a garish purple that was a distinctly 1960s and '70s tone. He also helped install a workshop at the back, where I employed a materials cutter and two women to stitch the pieces together.

Another girl was taken on to manage the shop and choose the fashions from a London design house. This store was quickly followed by two more in Blackburn and Southport.

Jean also took an active interest, and, apart from giving her opinions on what to buy and stock, she became involved in delivering finished items to the other two shops.

Along with advertising in local newspapers, we paid Miss Blackburn to model our clothes at fashion shows, including a soft wedding dress trimmed with a feather boa that always grabbed the spotlight on catwalks. It was showstoppers like this that kick-started our supply chain to leading department stores. There was no denying it was a fun business that provided a relatively easy additional income stream.

As well as dabbling in ladies' wear, 1969 saw the launch of what in my opinion was one of Reebok's greatest-ever shoes.

We were heavily involved with Bolton United Harriers just down the road from the factory, sponsoring many local athletes. One, Ron Hill, was already a successful international runner, having gained medals in British, European and Olympic long-distance events. Jeff was also a member of the same club, and, as the two of them talked one day after a training run, Ron revealed his vision of the 'ultimate' running shoe. He was talking to the right man. The next day, Jeff and I threw ideas back and forth based on Ron's suggestions.

When someone like Ron Hill came up with ideas for improvements, you didn't ignore them. Ron had run at least a mile every day of his life since December 1964 (this 'streak' would last until January 2017, a total of fifty-six years and thirty-nine days). Some would say it was an addiction, but if you knew this intelligent family man from Accrington, you knew it was pure passion, and an extraordinary pursuit of perfection in mind, body and equipment.

Unlike most elite athletes, who land on their heel when running, Ron was what you would call a 'floater', always landing on the ball of his foot. This technique forces more forward momentum, as well as reducing stress on the knees. If you run barefoot, your body will naturally favour landing on the midsole or ball. Ron wanted natural; in fact, he would often race without shoes, even in cross-country and road races. He wanted that same barefoot feel. His vision was for a minimalist road-running shoe but based on a track and field design. As well as being ultralight, it had to have virtually no heel. The way he ran, he didn't need one, so it would just be extra weight.

What we eventually came up with was way ahead of its time. The trend at the time was for thicker midsoles to give extra cushioning, but Ron didn't want padding either. The new shoe had just an eighth-of-an-inch layer of cushioning, and an eighth-of-an-inch outer sole made of hard-wearing gum rubber. The upper was made of washable suede, which is reversed kid hide, so the flesh side would take the adhesive without us having to do any preparation on the leather.

It was a special glove leather made by Pittards of Yeovil. I had called in on them while on my way to the rubber company that moulded soles for our cross-country shoes. I thumbed through a swatch containing an extensive selection of incredible colours and decided on a striking burnt amber with the reference name Snazzy Fox.

Ron loved the shoes, so much so that he never let them out of his sight. He inflicted very little wear on his shoes anyway, but when the sole did become worn, rather than have a new pair, he would bring them back to the factory and sit watching as they were re-soled.

With its distinct colourway and Ron's endorsement, the World 10 shoe soon became the Aston Martin of road racing, both in looks and performance. In his full career, Ron would clock up 115 marathons, winning twenty-one, and would set four world records at four different distances. In 1970, he became the first-ever British athlete to win the Boston Marathon, beating the course record by a full three minutes, despite the cold and wet headwinds. That win alone brought huge awareness and subsequently hundreds of orders for Ron's World 10 shoes.

We had been lucky in having such a prolific champion in our local athletics club, luckier still that he shared with Jeff his suggestions for improvements. Without such timely good fortune, Reebok may not have arrived onto the world stage so quickly – if at all.

CHAPTER 15

A Near-Death Experience

Lawrence Sports continued to honour our agreement through the first year and into the next, exporting Reebok to Australia, New Zealand, Canada and South Africa. Frustratingly, though, despite Shack's insistence that it would come soon, they still hadn't succeeded in finding that holy grail – a US distribution channel.

I tried to remain patient, confident that America would come online soon. I had the utmost faith in Shack. He was a man of his word and he knew how important a stateside supply chain was to me.

Then, in 1971, just short of twenty-four months into our contract, I received a call from him to say he was leaving Lawrence Sports. The owner, Harold Lawrence, was now in his seventies and had passed most of the decision-making to his son-in-law. This had caused a clash of personalities, and Shack had decided he couldn't work there any longer. I felt physically sick, despite receiving reassurances that his leaving wouldn't in any way jeopardise the partnership that Reebok had with Lawrence Sports.

Sure enough, though, as soon as Shack left the company, things began to go rapidly downhill. Firstly, payments to Reebok started to get delayed after Lawrence Sports began sending shoes back to us citing issues over quality. I was mortified. We'd never had problems with the standard of our Reebok output before. I asked Jeff to bring samples of the shoes we were making for Lawrence Sports to my office for inspection.

Both Jeff and I scrutinised them for errors, turning them over and over in our hands, looking for scuff marks, creases in the leather, adhesive overuse, our fingers tracing the stitch-work. We both agreed there was absolutely nothing wrong with the quality and I demanded they release our withheld payments. They refused. We were reliant on Lawrence Sports. They represented almost 100 per cent of our revenue. Their lack of payment meant our cash flow was more or less cut dead. If the bank found out, we'd be in serious trouble. We had to find some cash, and quick.

I spent endless, fruitless hours talking to Harold's son-in-law, and, when he wasn't available, his department managers. It was here that I found out the truth about why we'd suddenly been cut off. When Shack left, he'd taken a lot of his sales staff with him to Bata, and Lawrence Sports were struggling to replace them. The knock-on effect was that orders were starting to thin out, and they had to slow production down, ours included.

At around the same time, football boot technology had moved on. Traditional sewn or glued-on soles were being replaced by injection moulding. Lawrence Sports were forced to invest heavily in a new, multi-station injection moulding machine, only available from Germany. It was supposed to be delivered in January 1971, in time for the standard football boot production run – January through June – but it wasn't. While they waited, their football boot production came to a halt. Which is pretty serious for a company that only makes football boots.

When the injection moulding machine eventually turned up in April, the installation crew discovered it was too large to fit into a new building that Lawrence Sports had built specially for it. It took another month for the building to be enlarged. Finally, it was ready to start production. Then the moulds were found to be faulty and needed to be remade.

By the time this great lump of a machine was ready to start churning out injection-moulded football boots, pre-season orders should have already been delivered. The peak period for football boot retail sales is small, July and August, with small repeat orders through to December. Consequently, as the football season neared kick-off, all of the retailers cancelled their orders and Lawrence Sports began to haemorrhage a huge amount of business. Inevitably, cash-flow problems followed.

It was obvious they were going into liquidation, and, because of my decision, Reebok was chained to their sinking ship. They had 2,000 pairs of our trainers in their warehouse. We couldn't afford to lose both the payment *and* the actual stock. It would be our final death knell.

Apart from the specialist climbing boots we were still making for Bob Brigham, we, or rather I, had made the unbelievably naive mistake of putting all our eggs in one basket. It was a stupid error to make. My overriding need to find a way into the US market had blinded me to the potentially fatal dangers. 'Stupid, stupid, stupid,' I kept berating myself. To avoid bankruptcy, it was time to think positively. I had to take responsibility, cut costs and hopefully grind our way out of trouble.

I gathered everybody together on the factory floor. It was a beautiful day outside. Shards of sunlight beamed through the factory windows like theatre spotlights, illuminating the faces of the twenty or so, white-coated workers staring at me.

I felt awful, sick with guilt. They were a loyal crew who worked together as a family. Even though Lawrence Sports cutting production was the catalyst that caused the problems, it was my fault that I'd put my company in the situation where we were totally at their mercy. I was responsible, the captain that had plotted a bad course and run the ship aground. I deserved any hostility that would surely arise.

'We've hit a serious cash-flow problem,' I began. There was no point beating about the bush. I noticed a few of the workers folding their arms defensively, expecting the worst. I explained about the problems at Lawrence Sports and how their difficulties had wrecked our finances.

'So,' I continued, 'starting from tomorrow, we're going to have to reduce production and temporarily lay some of you off.' 'Some' meant just over half, though I declined to say this at the time. Then the questions started coming thick and fast.

'How long for?'

'Who's staying on?'

'Will we get paid for this month?'

I answered them all completely honestly, emphasising that it was a stopgap measure while we put in motion a recovery plan. I guaranteed that every one of them would be taken back on as soon as possible, but that we just didn't have the money at the moment to continue employing everybody.

We were always the last two people to get paid – it was and always had been our owner ethic. We were responsible for the welfare of our staff, employees who were perpetually loyal and hardworking. The buck stopped with both Jeff and me if a decision was made that would affect their livelihood, for good or for bad. I hadn't foreseen Shack leaving Lawrence Sports, which made my decision to tie ourselves to the company a bad one, and our staff were forced, through no fault of their own, to suffer the consequences.

Perhaps it was my straightforwardness, or just that they were such an incredibly allegiant team, but not one member of staff showed any of the animosity that I deserved or expected. Some offered to carry on working for nothing to ensure Reebok's survival, others insisted they would return when things were better. I was truly moved.

To get 'better', we had to move fast. We needed cash. The failings of Lawrence Sports had killed my Leatherflair business too, as we could no longer afford to run both Reebok and the fashion sideline. We closed the shops in Bury and Blackburn, but couldn't cancel the remaining two-year lease on the one in Southport.

There was also the small issue of the 2,000 pairs of Reebok stock sitting in the depot at Lawrence Sports. It was only a matter of days before Lawrence Sports would go into liquidation, at which point our shoes would be lost as part of the forced sale. I needed to get them back, now.

On the same day that I announced the lay-offs, I rented a large van, drove 150 miles to the Lawrence Sports depot in Stanwick, Northampton, and flung all our shoes in the back.

Now we just had to find a way of selling them, to bring in some quick money.

We'd always had a factory sales outlet where we sold seconds, rejects with slight flaws but still of very good quality. Our reject bins in Bury were regularly raided by young lads who scaled the walls to rummage for matching pairs. Sometimes even *slightly* matching would do. More than once I'd noticed local boys on the streets or in the pub wearing either two unmatched sizes on their feet, or a pair of similar but not identical styles of trainers.

But even the 'looters' and bargain-hunters wouldn't be able to make a dent in our stockpile of 2,000 leftovers. Jean stepped up to the plate and put the message out to friends and contacts at schools and clubs, saying we had bargain seconds for sale at half-price or less. Even at a 50 per cent discount, we were making more money selling direct than we would have by selling them to Lawrence. Between us, we managed to scrape enough money together to be able to pay our immediate debts. But, equally importantly, I saw Jean in a new light. I had a newfound respect for her after she had shown she wasn't afraid to get her hands dirty when the going got tough and, were it not for her actions, the going would have got a whole lot tougher.

CHAPTER 16

New Openings

As is often the case with doors, when one closes, another one opens. Sometimes several doors. Although initially we might have lost a little nerve when all production ceased, the actual thought of complete failure wasn't something that Jeff and I had ever considered. It was more of a reset.

It was an old acquaintance who opened the first door. Shack heard that we were in trouble and managed to persuade his new employers, Bata, to add a 'Ripple' (sole) trainer alongside their line of Power brand football boots, resulting in an immediate recurring order of 100 pairs per week for our factory. This was the only other regular order we had in addition to the weekly fifty pairs of climbing boots for Bob Brigham, apart from a handful of custom, hand-made running shoes for individuals.

To help with our cash-flow dilemma, Shack also arranged for us to buy leather and some of the other components we needed for this trainer directly from Bata with very extended credit, and made sure that Bata paid for the trainers within seven days of us having made them. In reality, this meant that they were effectively buying back the leather and components three months before Reebok had to pay them for the materials.

This proved to be a real lifesaver. In addition to the extended credit I renegotiated with our other suppliers, I could finally go to the bank with a viable survival plan. We were still nowhere near in the clear, but I could see a way forward, a light at the end of what had been a very dark and long tunnel. We just needed to get more orders now.

Although the Lawrence Sports debacle had nearly killed the company, taking the reins back from them was actually a relief. It had been great having extra time to pursue other business lines, but this was always tempered by a nagging doubt that I wasn't in full control. Freeing Reebok from the near-monopoly that Lawrence Sports held over us meant other companies were able to come to us, and I was able to promote our business to them. Word travels fast in the relatively small world of sports shoemaking. Interest in us from other companies soon surfaced once they heard that new deals were being made.

On the back of our Bata arrangement, I then received a call from Stylo, a chain of shoe shops owned by two brothers. With the growing influence that sport was having on the high street, they were converting some of their footwear outlets into sports shops and wanted us to make them a line of trainers. Again, Shack had Bata agree to supply the leather on the same extended line of credit.

Then the German sports brand Hummel were in touch. They had a UK distribution centre in Bristol and wanted us to manufacture a budget-price black trainer. It was an easy shoe for our factory to produce and their regular order of 200 pairs a month meant that I could contact most of the staff we had let go and bring them back to work. Production was now back up to around 80 per cent of where it had been before we'd had to reboot after the Lawrence Sports letdown.

During this recovery period, we diversified again. Cash-flow generation had to take precedence over everything, including my plans for expansion of the Reebok brand. That seemed like a luxury right now. What was imperative was to increase production however and wherever we could. With this in mind, we started to manufacture rowing shoes, parachute boots and skateboard shoes alongside our existing lines. Our emergence in this field led to yet another door opening – a big door.

Finn Aamodt from an Oslo-based sports company had seen our product and was looking for a factory to make 20,000 pairs of trainers for the Norwegian army. Although we were nearly back to full strength, this was well beyond our capacity of 2,000 pairs per week. We would have to subcontract some of the work to competitor companies if we were to achieve that kind of volume. Fortunately, several members of our staff had previously worked for the Parker Shoe Company and offered to put me in touch with their general manager.

Parker's was a local manufacturer of traditional street shoes for high-street brands. They were once thriving, but orders were now beginning to falter as big brands started to buy from the Far East. Because of this, they had spare production capacity, so we agreed a price and Jeff sent them the patterns and makeup details. Although Parker's did a good job, and we had an amicable relationship with them, the end product was not up to the standard of Reebok. Consequently, we didn't get any repeat orders from Finn Aamodt.

Reebok made high-performance sports shoes – light, with a flexible and aggressive design. Parker's was set up to produce street shoes. They used lasts that didn't have the shape and toe spring of our own, plus their machinery used nails. This required a sturdier, heavier insole, whereas our insoles were lightweight and would adhere with glue.

The Norwegian army order was a nice earner at a time we needed a boost, but it also taught me a lesson about outsourcing. It wasn't enough just to work with someone who had the production capacity; we also had to consider whether their production methods, their machinery, their last shape and their materials were conducive to making high-performance, lightweight footwear. If not, and the output was satisfactory rather than exceptional, it could damage our reputation.

With production back to full capacity and cash flowing again, it was time to concentrate on promoting Reebok as a brand again. Over in the USA, the road-running 'niche' was starting to go mainstream. This, in turn, was beginning to spill over into the UK, where the demand for road-running shoes was growing. Distribution was key to get our name out there, not just in America but also in the UK again now. When Lawrence Sports collapsed, so too did not just our hopes of US distribution, but also our UK national distribution channel.

At least we could now start supplying direct again to the dozen or so sports retailers who specialised in athletics. But without reps the only way to increase our distribution to non-specialist shops was to send letters and prices, and hope that they would reply with an order. As far as Reebok being a known brand was concerned, we were pretty much back in the position J. W. Foster & Sons found itself before Jeff and I left, and so trying to secure orders via correspondence was futile. I had to remind myself that sometimes taking a step back enabled you to see the path that could move you forwards in the future.

It did seem at the time, however, that we were taking many more steps back than we were forwards. But the important thing was not to lose faith. Right now we were busy and productive again. I would have to be patient with my dreams of expansion. Fortunately, I was a born optimist and I knew there would be more opportunities to get Reebok into America, and the brand wider known in the UK. That's the excitement of business – you never know what's waiting around the next corner.

CHAPTER 17

A Key to America?

In 1972 an envelope dropped through the letterbox of our Bright Street factory. It was from a fitness runner in Philadelphia who had seen our products advertised in *Runner's World*. Shu Lang was his name, and he had boldly suggested that *he* would like to be considered as a distributor in the USA.

According to his letter, he had somehow got hold of a pair of Reebok running shoes and had noted three things: the quality; their lack of availability in the USA; and the absence of an American-made equivalent that could compete with the German, Japanese and Finnish imports of Puma, Adidas, Tiger and Nokia respectively.

He was convinced that, with an aggressive sales and promotional campaign, he could tap into the thousands of high-school and college cross-country and indoor and outdoor track teams, together with the growing number of people who were running for fitness, or competitively in 5k and 10k road events.

I was impressed with his enthusiasm and flattered by his comments, but I had reservations. After some back-and-forth correspondence it became clear that, although Shu had plenty of local connections in the northeast, he had very few that could take us countrywide. But there was no doubt he was keen and, more importantly, we had no one else.

I decided to take a punt on him, but encouraged him to work with additional distributors in other regions across the States. While Shu began his own round of networking, I dipped into my Rolodex to see who I could connect him with in other parts of America.

First on the list was a Californian company called Sports International, run by a couple I had met at an NSGA exhibition. Like Shu, they were keen to work with us. After brief negotiations, they set up Trans World Sports to handle the Reebok distribution for the west coast.

Things seemed to be falling into place, perhaps too easily. First Shu's letter out of the blue, and then a simple conversation with someone I'd once met at an exhibition, both leading to distribution potential on both the east and west coasts. Maybe I'd been overcomplicating matters. Could it be this easy?

The short answer was no. Just weeks before Trans World Sports was due to launch, I received notice that they had decided to pull out, claiming they'd now decided to focus their funds on other interests. I never did find out why.

Oh well, we still had Shu on the east coast. I dipped into my contacts list again and made arrangements to meet with the CEO of Total Environment Sports, which, going by what he'd said to me at the NSGA, was a huge sportswear outfit.

I flew up to Detroit after an NSGA event in Chicago and

was picked up at the airport by the owner, Jimmy Carter. So far so good – a US president and a major sports supplier. Only they weren't. The Jimmy Carter driving me through thick snow to the company headquarters worked on a production line at General Motors, and the executive office turned out to be his kitchen dining table.

It was a long way from what I was looking for, but he was a nice guy, and who was I to be choosy? I agreed to supply Jimmy Carter until I had to pull the plug after Shu informed me that Total Environment Sports was violating our verbal agreement by advertising our shoes at discounted prices.

As another one bit the dust, I became discouraged and scaled back my efforts to find someone else. It was proving too difficult to identify the right distributor who could work with Shu to expand our territory in the States.

Over the years that followed, Shu, my east coast and only distributor, became more and more demanding. Almost every postal delivery would contain a ranting correspondence from our man in America complaining that I'd been too slow to reply, hadn't replied at all, or that the order contained the wrong sizes or the wrong type of shoes.

When I refused to take him on, Shu shifted his attention to Jeff, urging him in letters and telegrams to dispatch specific styles 'without delay'. One of his letters began:

Dear Jeff
As they say, why do you need a wife when you have someone like me to nag you?

Although Shu wasn't making many inroads into selling Reebok, it was useful to have someone based in the US who could keep us in the loop about how the industry was developing. He also kept an eye on the competition, sending us samples of other brands and pointing out how he and his customers thought they could be improved upon, such as adding vent holes or eliminating heel tabs to save money. It was interesting to hear that the larger brands had become arrogant towards their dealers. They either demanded a minimum cost per order or dictated what the dealer could stock and to whom he could sell. However, because of the popularity of these mega-brands, the dealers were putting up with it.

Shu also provided useful feedback from college coaches and athletes on the performance of Reebok shoes and where they needed tweaking. Some of these ideas Jeff took on board and incorporated into the designs. Others were filed in the bulging Shu folder alongside his less constructive criticisms of our ongoing partnership.

Through Shu, I was beginning to realise just how difficult it was to break into the US. The big four of Adidas, Puma, Nike and Tiger had a virtual stranglehold on the retail market, with the B-list picking up a few orders on the back of strong advertising, but with no shops keen to stock them. What chance did we have?

The retailers weren't runners, they didn't read running magazines. If they read anything, it was just trade journals and sports magazines. They were blinded by brands. To them, there was no point in stocking unknown shoes when others on the shelf sold themselves. For unknowns like Reebok, our only option was to either embark on a sustained and costly advertising campaign or focus on those retailers who couldn't get all the name brands for whatever reason.

In the meantime, we would continue approaching schools,

colleges and track and field clubs, and pursuing mail-order sales. As Shu realised, there would be no quick and dramatic success. All we could hope for was a slow, steady build, but even this was causing frustration both here in the UK and with him in the US.

In the spring of 1974 Shu and his wife came to England to visit us, and to try to reconcile some of the problems in the way we were working together. From the gist of his more recent letters, he implied that the main difference was that *we* weren't working and *he* was, just not with our help.

After a day sightseeing in London, I showed the Langs round our Bright Street factory in Bury. Shu immediately pounced on some Mustang shoes in our packing area. He held a pair aloft, eyebrows raised. '*These* are what I've been waiting for. Why wouldn't you send them?'

It was true we'd been a bit lax with shipping the orders that Shu needed. It wasn't personal, just that there was so much else on my to-do list and sending shoes to Shu didn't seem to be having any impact on my aim of conquering the American market. Item forty-seven – *ship forty pairs of shoes to Shu* – kept getting put to the back of the queue. 'It's just been a bit crazy,' I offered apologetically.

'Crazy? CRAZY? If you want to see crazy you should be in my shoes when I have to keep telling the coaches the same thing week after week. THEY'VE NOT ARRIVED YET.' He was in full-on attack mode now, his wife's attempts to calm him completely ignored. 'You want me to build the brand in the States, Joe. How am I supposed to do that with no shoes? Or the wrong shoes? Or the right shoes but in the wrong sizes? Tell me, Joe, how?'

I tried to placate him and privately berated myself for my

shoddy responding. The problem was, I knew that for every communiqué I sent to Shu, he would immediately send two or three back. I just didn't have the time to spend half of my days writing. But it was like months of pent-up frustration were flowing out of him.

'You seem to think that if problems are ignored, they'll go away,' he continued. 'Don't get me wrong, Joe, I'm not questioning your sincerity about expansion into America, but I am beginning to doubt your ability to do it. I've created enormous local demand in this year and a half but we still don't have a definite line of shoes you want to promote; you send irregular shipments and you won't respond to our enquiries.'

'I know,' I said calmly. I could tell he hadn't finished and decided the best tactic was to let him spill it all out, and mop up afterwards.

'We've put a lot of time, effort and money into this and we don't have very much to show for it. You hold the key. If we're really going to do anything with this distributorship, we can't keep lurching from crisis to crisis.'

I tried to play down his annoyance and frustration. I'd almost become immune to it now. But was he right? Was it down to me? Had I thought that because I had a distributor in place, I could ease off on that area of the business and focus on other pressing matters, like expanding the UK side of things, when, in fact, the opposite was true? For nearly five years I'd been actively chasing a way into the US. Now I had a foothold, I needed to make the most of the opportunity, no matter how slow a slog it seemed.

What were we doing wrong? Only the future would provide the answer. What Shu needed was for Reebok to supply him with shoes to meet his orders, but for this to work it would require Reebok to manufacture and hold huge stocks of either finished shoes or materials.

It took a few more lessons for me to realise this could never work. Neither Shu nor Reebok had sufficient financing. Reebok had positioned itself among the leading performance brands in the UK and, like Foster's before, we had a niche in a small market that was suddenly becoming mainstream. The brand was in demand but I was failing to grasp what was needed. I had been dealing with enthusiastic individuals, runners, good people with ambition, but none had the experience required and, most importantly, the funding to achieve the result.

What I didn't realise was that we were part of an industry that was still 'growing up', getting big. As a small brand, it was not possible, or cost-effective, to produce and hold a stockpile of every model to await a retailer order. This was the lesson I was slowly learning: that if Reebok was going to succeed, we had to think big, but at that time I didn't know how to achieve 'big'. I also realised that becoming a 'larger brand' was extremely difficult when the financial requirement was beyond the capabilities of both Shu and me. We just weren't in that league. One thing I wasn't going to do was give up, though. I would have to find another way, somehow.

I vowed to Shu that I would make it my priority, and the Langs left feeling slightly more positive – or at least the next four letters that Shu dashed off to me made me think that.

For a few months, I made time to answer his enquiries promptly, and Jeff double-checked the shipments we sent. Shu was finally happy, for a while. 'I'm very pleased with the way things seem to be improving. For the first time in living memory, I may even be complaint-less!' said one of his letters.

But gradually other business matters demanded my full focus and my attention to Shu's demands diminished. I knew at the back of my mind that the wrath of Shu would return soon enough. It always did!

CHAPTER 18

Dad, Death and a New Distributor

It's not always true that *all* publicity is good publicity, especially when the subject is poor business practice. Sometimes your reputation can be damaged for good. Fortunately for us, in the case of Reebok being mentioned in stories about the demise of Lawrence Sports, it turned out to have unexpectedly positive consequences.

Carter Pocock, a sports goods wholesale distributor in London who represented Dunlop Green Flash among other brands, had been following our progress since we appeared in trade publications alongside Lawrence Sports in the aftermath of their collapse. Rather than us being guilty by association, they saw it a different way. Their man at the top figured we must have been a brand of note to be working with what was deemed, at the time, to be a hugely respected company.

Reebok was the only British sports-shoe manufacturer

with any credibility in the expanding road-running niche. Widespread awareness of our brand at this vital point only came about because we were mentioned wherever news of Lawrence Sports' failure appeared. It was a perfect example of a bad situation morphing into timely good fortune.

The London company needed to jump on the bandwagon and figured they would benefit by working with the only British company that had any traction in this sphere. It came by way of a phone call from Len Ganley, the managing director of Carter Pocock, who asked if I would be interested in discussing the distribution of Reebok in the UK.

By now I was a little more experienced in what we needed from a distributor thanks to our dealings with Lawrence Sports, and also to some extent with Shu. It wasn't just someone who would carry our full range of shoes to a widespread audience; we also needed a commitment of funds, an advertising budget.

I needed to do a bit of research. I knew Carter Pocock as wholesalers rather than distributors, so if I was to meet Len, I needed to be asking the right questions. The UK market represented 85 per cent of our business: could I once again commit so much? I decided there would be nothing lost in at least meeting with Len at their premises near the Elephant and Castle, London.

I was happy with what I saw and heard. They had a large number of reps travelling the country, which meant our product would get widespread exposure. We would also be appointed an exclusive Reebok brand manager, plus they would commit 5 per cent of their revenue from Reebok sales to a marketing budget. I thought for a moment, then, in a spirit of cavalier optimism, shook hands on the deal, subject to the paperwork being drawn up by my ever-reliable legal aid, Derek Waller.

I was wary, but I figured I'd learned enough from the previous calamity to be able to spot any warning signs that might bring our distribution to a juddering halt. At least I hoped I'd learned enough.

I needed to keep a close eye on the distribution set-up, so at 4 a.m. every other Friday I drove from Bolton to London to monitor their sales and future orders. I was also ensuring that they were maintaining their commitment of resources to Reebok, and watching out for any telltale signs that might jeopardise the chain of production. I'd then jump back in my car and drive four hours back to Bolton in the evening, my head spinning with new ideas for increasing our own sales and boosting our name in the UK, and waded through the correspondence and telegrammed orders from Shu in America.

On the weekends when I hadn't been driving south, Jean and I would take Kay and David to the Lake District, where my parents now owned a caravan and a small boat on Lake Windermere, or on seaside day trips to Blackpool or Southport with Jean's parents.

My relationship with Dad had returned to near-normality by now – normal being, we spent time in each other's company in the Lakes or occasionally in the pub, but we had little to say to one another. He was still running a small sports shop on Mornington Road in Bolton, and, during my sporadic visits, we would have a few superficial chats about business, but I was aware that this was territory best left untouched. Whenever Foster's was mentioned, I could tell from the tensing of Dad's jaw muscles and the slight curl of his lip that not all of the ill-feeling had dissipated.

It was a shame that he still harboured a grudge. Perhaps Jean and I would have spent more time with my parents rather than hers if things had been different. Who knows? I guess I would have liked Dad to have had more interest in Reebok, but that would have meant showing more interest in me and, at sixty-eight, why would he suddenly change the habit of a lifetime?

He wasn't in the best of health, having already had a minor heart attack the year before, and carrying this grievance would have done nothing to reduce his stress. So it came as no major shock when I received a call from Mum one morning to say that Dad had suffered another cardiac arrest in the night. This one had been fatal.

Just as I'd often felt like an inconvenience to Dad, it was ironic that the time of his passing proved 'inconvenient' to the rest of the family. The wedding of our younger brother, John, was to take place in five days. Suits and top hats had been hired, dresses bought, the venue paid for and the catering arranged. But Mum insisted the wedding went ahead despite Dad's death, and so, two days after the celebrations, me, Jean, Kay and David, along with Jeff, John and the rest of the family, all huddled together at Bolton Crematorium to say goodbye, deep in sombre, private thoughts.

On the bench next to us, Kay and David watched dispassionately. They hadn't spent much time with either of my parents. Mum never voiced any interest in having them round, either to give Jean and me a break or because she wanted to be a doting grandparent. 'I never had help when you were growing up,' she would tell me on numerous occasions, 'so why should you?' Dad must have held a soft spot for his granddaughter, though, even if he didn't show it. He'd named his boat on the lake, *Kay*.

Although I was sad at Dad's passing, the grief was more for Mum's loss than my own. Dad and I had never been close, never held any strong bond. It was a relationship that I'd gotten used to, more like the kind you have with a rarely seen uncle. You know they're family, but they have very little bearing on your own life. It was a way I was used to, a way my dad was used to, and probably a way that Grandad Joe was used to before that. Now he was gone, it had no great effect on either my emotions or my way of thinking. It was just simply a shame for my mum. She had lost her life partner; I had lost the chance to prove him wrong. Life would carry on as normal, as would business.

At the end of 1976, some twenty-four months into our collaboration with Carter Pocock, confidence in each other was complete and they asked if they could expand on our agreement. They wanted to include a range of apparel in the distribution contract, which was good in that it entailed more money for Reebok, but it would also demand more of my time, a commodity that was in short supply.

I could see the logic and potential benefits of my involvement, especially considering my previous experience with Leatherflair, but it was another project that took me one more step away from my number one aim of cracking America. After much discussion, we agreed that it would be better to outsource manufacturing under a separate licence agreement.

Carter Pocock appointed an apparel product manager (the owner's daughter, Christine Pocock), whose job it was to oversee the whole line, thus, in theory, reducing my workload. In practice, however, it didn't quite work like that. Any outside manufacturer had to obtain a licence to use the Reebok name and logo, which I needed to approve. To protect the Reebok brand, it was also necessary for me to give my personal approval for each garment in the apparel range. The only way to achieve this was to increase my trips south, and so the fortnightly, 4 a.m. Friday drive south became weekly.

With all the end-of-week travelling, I was often too exhausted to go out with friends to a local pub on a Friday or Saturday night, preferring to spend my time gardening, or completing the list of DIY tasks that Jean had compiled over the previous week and stuck on the fridge door. This solitary time enabled a modicum of physical relaxation, but mentally I was still working at full pace, my mind fully on Reebok, trying to unlock the conundrum of Shu and his extremely limited American distribution.

Jean was supportive and knew I needed time alone to think. She knew our bigger aims and understood how much effort it was going to take to get there. When she could see I was deep in thought, she would take David and Kay, now nine and fifteen, on family outings alone. My thinking time at weekends was essential for Reebok's progress, but it was a sacrifice of family time that, although of my doing, meant it was Jean and the kids who suffered the most.

There's no denying that I was preoccupied with a business that consumed every waking moment, often while asleep as well. That's not to say I'm defending my actions; it was just the way the company had grown and was still growing. I was juggling so many balls that, if I lost my concentration for just a second, I feared it would all come tumbling down. I was already a prisoner of my own rising success, a real danger for any flourishing entrepreneur.

*

In light of our experience with Lawrence Sports, it now made sense to separate the manufacturing from the distribution. With the help of our solicitor, Derek Waller, I set up a new company, Reebok International Limited. Aside from safeguarding the factory, I figured it was a name that had more gravitas, more clout to take on my increasingly regular, distribution-hunting missions overseas.

I knew that Shu was doing his best, given the limited resources, but it seemed like we weren't getting anywhere. It felt as though he was just an importer whose sporadic orders needed filling, but one who would kick off when faced with the slightest hiccup. I began to push his needs to the back of the queue yet again and, unsurprisingly, the flow of belligerence spiked once more. It was as if he knew when I took my foot off the pedal, even by the slightest of margins.

His latest bugbear was the lack of a catalogue. 'You're probably the only manufacturer around that hasn't a single piece of literature for their product,' he ranted quite rightly in one, particularly long and drawn-out letter. 'I told you *I'd* prepare brochures,' he continued, 'but on further consideration, I feel this is your responsibility, not mine. I think back to the $200 we spent last year on photographs and artwork, only to find out a month later most of the models we'd used in pictures were being dropped or changed. I'm not prepared to go through that time and expense again.'

His final line in one particular letter hit home though: '... much more is required than just building a good shoe and letting the world beat a path to your doorstep, Joe.' He had repeated the grievances I'd harboured while working for my dad and Bill. Was Shu just like the frustrated 'me' in the 1950s, unable to move forward fast enough while the man or men in charge dawdled?

It made me wonder if Dad really didn't want to expand his company, or whether, like me, his time and attention were always dedicated to sustaining the current level of business and he had no time to pursue progress. Perhaps I had got him wrong. Either way, I was not going to fall into the same trap. I knew what rich pickings lay in America and it was a reminder not to get sidetracked, even if that meant pandering to the demands of Shu. He was my only hope at the moment. Without my support, he, or I, had no chance of establishing a nationwide distributorship in the US. Again, I wrote to apologise and to commit my support. Only this time I truly meant it.

I promised that Shu would remain as our exclusive USA distributor and that any enquiries sent to me from others in his region, the northeast of America, would be passed on to him. I told him that for dealers outside this territory, I would give them the option of trading direct with us, but at 25 per cent above Shu's prices. Promotional tactics *I* committed to would involve marketing direct to athletes and schools, plus regular advertising, paid for by me, in the UK's *Athletics Weekly* and *Runner's World* in the US, but Shu would be expected to pay for his own adverts. He seemed happy, and we were both ready for a 'fresh start'.

With the cash-flow situation improving in the UK, I also undertook an image-building programme, incorporating printed polythene shoe bags, display advertising, newly designed shoe labels and printed leaflets to showcase our range. My confidence in the company's chances of breaking into America had returned on turbo-boost. I knew that with this renewed vigour and effort it surely was only a matter of time.

CHAPTER 19

Back to Square One

Shu continued to bang on doors and spread the Reebok name to *segments* of the American market, but it was obvious, as the months passed into a year, that we still weren't making very much headway. Tiger had five distributorships in the US, Adidas had four; even smaller brands like Brooks had at least two. We needed to add more distributors to double or treble the flow of shoes across the Atlantic if we were to ever start making an impact. That would take money for advertising, a huge chunk of our already depleted cash. Plus, we would still need those distributors to open doors, get new dealers to commit to an unknown brand. We'd already seen how difficult it was to persuade dealers to take a shoe that wasn't already known to the customer. In fact, Shu had recently resorted to having 'customers' call a store to soften them up to the brand a month before he approached the owner.

Alternatively, I thought, we could set up Reebok International in the USA, to give us the gravity of having a company in America. This would require an immediate cash injection if Reebok UK was to have 100 per cent ownership. That was doomed from the start. We just didn't have that kind of money.

So, I put it to Shù that either I had to seek out more distributors or, better still, that he, Jeff and I should form a joint ownership of Reebok International USA. I explained how the latter proposal had many advantages: 'This would bring marketing security to you, to Reebok UK, and the factory. We wouldn't need to sell in a small way through dealers under the guise of different names. We would go direct as Reebok to schools, clubs, dealers and through mail order.'

Shu was interested. I could sense it in his silence down the phone. Silence was rare with Shu. He had an immediate vocal response for everything, a counterargument for most ideas.

'All the problems we've been having with advertising, catalogues and building the range would be gone,' I continued. Those three aspects of the business would be handled by Shu in the States, without the need for my input – or total funding from my end. 'We'd be in it together, under one name. What do you think? A partnership?'

There was another pause. I began to think my luck was in, that Shu was going to go for it. Pooling our resources and, more importantly, our finances seemed to be the only way forward. Then came the inevitable challenge. Or should I say challenges? Lots of them.

'There are not many distributors who would have put up with your antics, Joe,' he began. 'I've been in marketing for eighteen years now. There have been lots of times where a distributor or importer would have justifiably withheld payment from you for things like shipping wrong or defective shoes or having to wait seven months, yes seven months, Joe, to receive $2,000 owed by you.'

I tried to placate him but he continued talking over me.

'How many others would have spent the time and effort, and at their own cost, to repack three hundred pairs of defective shoes and mail them back to the factory? Who else would have gone to the trouble of stamping "Made in England" on over 130 pairs because Jeff or someone else in your factory had forgotten to do it, then trucked them 60 miles to customs for reinspection and repacking?'

I couldn't deny that I'd put Shu through some difficult situations, most of my own doing, but I'd never promised him it was going to be easy. We were still a fledgling company, winging it as we went along. What did he expect? Nike hadn't just sailed smoothly to the top of the pile without similar, unforeseen setbacks. 'We're pioneers,' I told Shu, 'exploring new territories. We have to expect the unexpected. Nike made mistakes, but they got there. Look at them now.'

'Nike spent tens, perhaps hundreds of thousands of dollars on advertising to pre-sell their product,' he argued. 'That's why they're where they are now.'

It seemed I'd misinterpreted Shu's silence. Perhaps his initial reticence was just shock at my audacity to even suggest such a thing. It certainly sounded as though he was fed up with the whole thing. It was time to bring the conversation to a close if that was the case. I had a million-and-one other things to do besides justify myself to a distributor who wasn't distributing. 'So, I take it you're not interested, then?'

'I'd be interested in a joint venture if I thought I would benefit. But the conditions and climate would have to be right, and it would probably take around a year for that to happen.'

He then listed his conditions for a partnership, including a proven and stable line of shoes. It was true that we had developed then dropped too many models over the past few years. We needed to put all our efforts into a smaller range. Shu also insisted on a continuous advertising and promotional campaign, and a more appealing catalogue. And he wanted me to bear the costs of it all.

'My idea was for a *joint* venture,' I said, stressing the word 'joint'.

'Every other manufacturer pays for marketing and display ads,' he said. 'They all bear the costs, *and* they list their dealers or distributors on their ads.'

There were more 'basics' he demanded, including better quality control at the factory, more price stability, and more help to make sample shoes available to prominent athletes and coaches. These were all things I knew we needed to do, but there was only so much I could manage at one time. Sales in the UK were improving rapidly and we were making progress against Adidas and the others. Our success on this side of the Pond had convinced me we were doing the right things here, but the more I learned about America from my visits and from Shu, the more I realised those same fruitful tactics didn't necessarily work in the US. It was a very different playing field and I still didn't know the full rules, which is exactly why I needed someone like Shu.

We continued the discussions to and fro over Christmas in 1976. I was keen to find a way to make it work. Shu was a good man, honest and loyal. I needed him with me. I had nobody else in America.

We agreed to talk again in the New Year but, in the end, it was me who made the decision. I'd had second thoughts about a joint venture. It was going to be essential for Jeff and me to maintain complete control, plus I knew that Shu just didn't have the resources necessary. He was a one-man band, working from his basement, and with no access to extra financing for warehousing and distribution. Instead, we reached a new agreement whereby we more or less retained the status quo; that is, I would still cover the costs of advertising. I'd also decided that, to help our own cash flow, Shu's payments to us would be due with each order he placed, not on a credit arrangement. Additionally, I told him I'd be looking for four other distributors across the USA, but until they were in place I would advertise Shu as our exclusive distributor for the first three half-page ads in *Runner's World*.

Although we had the usual teething problems with new distributors – mainly, getting the shoes to them – our advertising campaign, combined with editorial recommendations in *Runner's World*, created national interest in America and sales began to flourish. After seeing the uptick in demand, Shu asked if he could expand to take on distribution for the whole of the US. It was something I thought about long and hard. I liked Shu, but I knew he didn't have the funds necessary to run a national operation. I figured it was better that I dealt directly with the other distributors, with Shu acting as co-ordinator.

As can be the case when you bring more people into the equation, this eventually created more problems than it solved. If I'd thought dealing with correspondence and orders from just Shu was a headache, the constant communication from a handful of eager importers became a barrage of noise. Territorial disputes turned into mediation exercises, and keeping tabs on equal pricing was almost a full-time job in itself.

In one instance, I seized on an opportunity that presented itself in Accrington, just 10 miles from our Bury factory. A young American lady visiting her mother called in to ask if she could take some trainers back to California for herself and her boyfriend. After a lengthy conversation, it transpired that she lived in Los Angeles. I spotted an opening.

For the first time, I had been considering sending some models to Joe Henderson, the editor of *Runner's World*, for evaluation in their influential shoe ratings, but with all the extra work of liaising with individual distributors in the USA it had slipped my mind and I hadn't got around to posting them. The deadline was looming and I was pretty sure that, even if I sent them now, I couldn't guarantee that they would arrive in time. Kindly, the lady agreed to personally carry the samples back to California for us and have them delivered to Joe's office.

Subsequently, Shu received a letter from *Runner's World* confirming their delivery by a man who he'd assumed to be Reebok's new west coast distributor. The man was actually the lady's boyfriend who had simply done us a favour, but Shu thought that we had engaged the services of a distributor in California without telling him. He was fuming.

On top of all that, my advertising costs had gone through the roof as I tried to support each territory's campaign from the east to the west coast. Only Adidas were spending more on advertising to athletes. I also had a serious problem with the customs duty in America, plus Jeff had revealed we had a new trademark dispute to contend with as Puma were claiming our stripe was too similar to theirs.

It felt like I was being tested to see how much pressure I could handle. Jeff was doing his best to take some of the strain, but most of the problems were issues I needed to deal with. I'd managed to create a perfect, perpetual circle of stress. More advertising brought more interested distributors, who brought more work (and problems) before they brought more sales. It got to the stage where it felt like my job was more firefighting than shoe manufacturing, and, every time I put out one flaming feud, another fire would start behind me.

I no longer had the time, money or patience to continue with my string of distributors. One of them had stopped corresponding and owed my company almost one thousand dollars. Another had simply pulled out of our deal without notice. I cancelled all advertising in *Runner's World* and offered Shu the whole country on the proviso he was responsible for everything from pricing to advertising.

From Shu's side, he saw it as he'd sell our shoes but get no help from us. It wasn't far from the truth. It was obvious I didn't have the resources to crack the USA. If Shu wanted to try, using our product but *his* money, he was welcome to it. As it was, he didn't, and subsequently, in December 1977, after five years of trying, we closed the US operation down. As far as breaking America was concerned, we were pretty much back to square one.

CHAPTER 20

Fated

I could never understand why the NSGA show was held in Chicago in February. I mean, Chicago? In February? I guess it was because most of the sports retailers were based in the northeast, so it was easier to get to, but there can be very few cities in America that are less conducive to hosting an international exhibition at that time of the year. It's always bitterly cold, bone-chillingly breezy, and often involves doing battle with blizzard conditions. I doubt any delegates armed with samples looked forward to trundling their wares to the Windy City for the world's biggest sports trade show.

Naturally, the weather presents all kind of challenges to exhibitors who want a hassle-free journey involving nothing more than setting up their stand in a warm hall, making a bunch of new deals, then getting the hell home. My attendance was rarely without drama.

During my 1977 trip, the bus returning me to my hotel came to a halt in a traffic jam, its windscreen wipers struggling to swish the snow from the driver's view. For half an hour my fellow passengers and I sat in silence, watching the wind build drifts against the still wheels of the cars in front. It was obvious we were going nowhere fast. Eventually, the driver stood and announced that there was no way we were going to travel any further. The door hissed open and he gestured for us to leave.

I raced through the blizzard into the lobby of the nearest hotel and asked the porter how far I was from my own accommodation. It was too far to walk, especially in the current minus-15-degree temperatures. Through the hotel's steamed-up windows I watched a taxi pull up outside and one of my fellow bus passengers jump in. From the shape of the luggage he was carrying I assumed he was an exhibition delegate. I decided to try to jump in on his ride – fellow sportspeople and all that.

Turning up the collar of my sheepskin jacket I raced through the revolving doors into an icy blast just as his taxi pulled away. As I stood peering at the traffic jam on the other side of the road, another taxi pulled in, offloading a group of Japanese businessmen who blocked my way, bowing incessantly as I tried to climb into the cab. I made a joke of the situation but the driver was in no mood for chit-chat. It was only when I eventually got to the warmth of my hotel room and turned on the TV that I discovered why there was such traffic chaos. On the screen, the flashing lights of ambulances and fire engines danced manically over mangled wreckage. A sombre news reporter described how a train on the overhead loop line had derailed in the bad weather. By morning, eleven people had died and over 180 had been injured. Chicago in February was not just a challenge, it could be a battle for survival.

Some respite was offered every three years, however, when, inexplicably, the show moved to Houston. It was the same time of year but the conditions were much more amenable. This should have led to a less troublesome experience, and probably for most attendees it did. Not for me, though. My NSGA participation seemed to be cursed, no matter which city was the host.

On my first visit to Houston, the second leg of my flight – JFK to Texas – was cancelled due to fog just after I had checked in. Reliably informed that my cases full of exhibition essentials would be on the next plane to Houston, I was put on an overnight flight that involved no fewer than five stops on the way to my final destination. The hope was that, by the time the flight arrived in Houston, the fog would have cleared.

Despite a lack of sleep, I managed to keep my spirits high – thanks to a few double spirits in the sky – and we eventually began our descent to Houston. Five minutes later we began our ascent from Houston as the pilot announced the airport was still too fogbound and we would be returning to Dallas-Fort Worth.

I looked at my watch as I sat in the airport lounge. I should have been setting up the stand by now. It was valuable time lost. After two hours I boarded the plane again, having been told that the poor visibility had improved.

It had, but Houston airport baggage hall was a disaster area. The airport had been closed for seventy-two hours, with only errant luggage arriving. With no passengers to collect them, all the bags had been thrown in the middle of the hall, resulting in a 20-foot-tall mountain of cases to sift through. Where do you start with that?

I joined the circle of despairing passengers searching the mountain. Fortunately, with their bold white Reebok lettering on black leather, my four bags were easy to identify. I grabbed them and headed to the exit.

I shared the story of my epic journey with the driver of the shuttle constantly ferrying show delegates from hotels to the NSGA. He listened, nodding and raising his eyebrows in the right places as we weaved through the downtown traffic. As I alighted, he bade me a cheery farewell, then lifted his trouser leg to reveal a handgun. 'Y'all be careful now, y'hear?'

With my anxiety well and truly heightened, I then learned that half of the British contingent still hadn't arrived at the Astrodome exhibition hall, presumably because they were still scaling the baggage mountain in search of their samples.

The next Houston show was no easier. During a rare few hours off in the UK, I managed to rupture my Achilles tendon playing badminton four days before I was due to travel to the NSGA. I was determined not to miss the exhibition, though, and, after some emergency treatment via a friend of a friend, I boarded my flight to Texas with my leg in plaster and a pair of crutches jammed under my armpits.

Even though I spent much of the show hobbling between meetings, I managed to have several interesting tête-à-têtes, including one with Brian Fernee, an expat who had set up three local radio stations in Los Angeles. He was eager to work with me, and over lunch he came up with a plan that involved setting up a new company called California Runner to take over our USA distribution. He certainly knew his stuff and was extremely persuasive, in a Californian kind of way. Had I found my white knight?

Back home, Jeff and I spent months working on a shoe that we named the California Runner. We figured it would help Brian if he had a signature start-up model. I then spent some time in Los Angeles helping with launch plans. I even signed up for welfare, something that Brian said would be useful if I ever wanted to emigrate in the future. It wasn't in my sightline at that moment, but who knew what the future might bring? By now I'd spent a fair amount of money putting all the pieces in place, travelling to and fro, and using our production resources to design his launch shoe. Everything was ready, west coast distribution plans looking rosy. As it was, I didn't emigrate, and nor was Brian successful with his venture. Despite my investment of time and expense, the arrangement collapsed almost as soon as it launched. Brian was a nice guy, and a runner. He also had enthusiasm, but he had no experience of distribution. Once again, just like my Achilles tendon, my hopes of US success were shattered.

CHAPTER 21

Finding Fireman

As is the way with many quests in stories, fables and folklore, the journey along that winding road often involves encounters with gatekeepers, people who hold the keys that enable you to continue towards your destiny. Without these people, the road becomes a never-ending circle, like a roundabout without exits. The challenge for protagonists along this journey is that, although they meet a lot of people, they don't know which ones hold the keys. They don't know what they look like, or where they're based. It's often fate – or good fortune – that enables the encounter.

Even then they don't know if they're false guides, ready to lead them along the wrong path even if they have the best intentions in mind. There are endless obstacles that could derail the protagonist, so it's a minor miracle when everything comes together and the next door is opened.

There's only one way to find the right key holder, and that's to put yourself in as many situations as you can, where you get to meet as many people as possible. Networking can be a numbers game. Sometimes you're lucky and meet the right person at the right time within minutes. Sometimes it can take years. But you have to fully believe that the gatekeeper is out there somewhere, and it's your job to find him or her.

I first met Paul Fireman at the 1979 NSGA show in Chicago. I couldn't have known it at the time, but that one, seemingly inconsequential coming together of strangers among the thousands of other tradesmen attending that February exhibition was all that was needed to set in motion the wheels of fate that would shape my life and eventually change the global landscape of sportswear for decades to come.

Paul was attending with his company, Boston Camping. I was there as part of the British Board of Trade contingent again. David Jenkins, Britain's 400-metre star, was part of our group and brought Paul over to our stand to make introductions. He had a youthful face and a quiet manner, and I could see from his large-set frame that he was not a runner. Paul was very easy to talk to and we chatted for over half an hour, during which I found out he was a college dropout and had tried to make professional grade on the golf circuit.

The conversation was interesting yet unproductive, but something at the back of my mind told me there was more to our small talk than just business etiquette. Paul had expressed a real interest in the market, in us. It was obvious from the questions he asked that he was smart and genuinely interested in Reebok and our market. His business was in the outdoor adventure niche, though, not sportswear, and his experience of distribution was limited to just one region of the US, the northeast. *But there was something*, I thought, as I watched him disappear back into the crowds. That something made me leave the stand to catch up with him and suggest we meet again, as I had an idea. I hadn't, but I did have a feeling that something good might come from another get-together. We arranged to meet at his office and showroom in Boston that coming spring.

Although we still weren't getting orders from these NSGA events, we were definitely attracting interest. But our lack of a permanent presence in America had always been the stumbling block, until now. The meetings and introductions I had usually involved small to medium retailers, so I was taken aback when an executive from Kmart visited our stand and seemed genuinely curious about our product. He asked a few questions, examined our samples and requested a meeting. Kmart wanted to see me. Kmart!

I could have conducted meetings with both the executive at Kmart and Paul Fireman over the phone after I returned to the UK. It would certainly have been a damn sight cheaper than flying back across the Atlantic, but both were potentially immense turning points for Reebok. Securing a deal with Kmart would be huge. And with Paul? I wasn't sure, but my instincts told me that I may have met my gatekeeper. I needed to show my commitment, and also to see how committed each of them was to working with Reebok, and there's only one way to do that – face-to-face.

In May of 1979, I was buckled into a British Airways transatlantic flight, America-bound again. It was to be the second of four trips I made to the US that year. I needed to satisfy my curiosity about Paul Fireman and hopefully secure a life-changing order from Kmart. Paul was interested, that was certain, and I had the feeling that he could build the bridge we needed. But that was all it was, a gut feeling.

The engines roared and we tore down the runway. I closed my eyes and dared to imagine that this journey would be the one, that when I returned through the clouds into Manchester we would not only have a distribution deal in place, but we would be supplying one of the biggest department store chains in America. If so, the glass ceiling on Reebok's success would be smashed for ever.

The first leg of my trip was to Detroit, where I had an appointment with a buyer at Kmart's head office. In the plush reception area, a young girl pointed to a nondescript building across the car park. It looked like any standard warehouse. 'Go through the green door at the side and find row F, desk 35. Have a nice day.' She smiled, teeth perfect, eyes sparkling, everything about her immaculate and shiny, but lacking individuality and character.

I looked again at the warehouse, then back to the smiler. 'Over there?'

She nodded, still smiling; 'F, thirty-five.' She wrote it on a yellow Post-it Note and extended a slender finger crowned with scarlet nail varnish. I presumed the nails were fake too.

On the other side of the green door it was indeed like a warehouse. A battalion of desks was lined up in regimented rows all the way to the far wall. Each had matching accessories – plastic white in-/out-trays and pen holders, blue and red ring binders stacked neatly between grey metal bookends. At each desk sat a suited man or woman. All were either clutching phones to their ears or tapping furiously at typewriters. I looked down at the Post-it Note then up at the solitary black letters on the squares of white that dangled on chains from the high, false ceiling.

At row F, I turned right and marched to desk 35. The buyer gestured for me to sit as he finished up a phone call. I looked around, mesmerised. I'd never seen anything like it, so clinical, sterile, like corporate battery hens.

He noticed my gazing. 'It saves space, and seems to work well,' he smiled. We indulged in the usual small talk for a while, a ping-pong game of superficial exploration, before getting down to business.

'We like your product and we'd need at least 25,000 pairs for the initial delivery.' He paused, maintaining eye contact. 'But your price is way too high.'

I ignored the price comment. It was the scale of production that worried me more. The price we could negotiate. 'Twenty-five thousand?' I repeated, trying to sound calm.

'Yes, just the first order. Don't worry, we always go small with the first batch.'

Our small factory was only producing around 2,000 pairs a week at the time. There were other factories in the valley that could help, like Parker's, but even if they all had the time and space to accommodate our order, there was no way we could currently supply that quantity. No way!

'No problem,' I said.

'And the price?'

I knew where our profit margin lay, but the gap between the price they were prepared to pay and the price we could charge and still make a profit was too tight. Our production costs allowed very little wiggle room. Besides that, although being stocked in Kmart would give us more exposure, they wouldn't necessarily promote our brand. It would be just another shoe on a shelf for them.

Retail outlets such as Kmart were all about sales per square foot. If the profit they made from our allocated shelf space proved to be acceptable, they would commit to a subsequent order and we would retain our real estate within the store. If the profit didn't match or better other items on the shelf, they wouldn't order any more. Even if we could find a way of lowering our costs, it wasn't the deal we needed at the time. Sure, the revenue would be useful, but, to move forward, we had to find someone who would actively promote our brand, not just stock our shoes.

Nike's shoes were coming from the Far East, so their costs were already considerably cheaper. Most street-shoe manufacturers were also now shifting their production to Southeast Asia. We needed to look into it. Doors were being opened, like at Kmart, but it was obvious Reebok wasn't ready to step through … yet. To deal with the big boys we needed to *be* one of the big boys. We needed the manufacturing resources, low-cost bulk-buying power, and a huge credit line in place. We weren't at that point.

Next, it was on to Boston to meet Paul Fireman at his Boston Camping office and showroom. It couldn't have been more different in both looks and ambience. I was immediately struck by the warmth and authenticity of the company, if not the scale. It was professional, and as far removed from the sterility of my Kmart experience as it could be. Surrounded by fishing rods, tents and camping stoves, Paul introduced me first to his partners, namely his brother and brother-in-law, then the other members of his staff – a head of sales and two admin girls.

It was a small set-up, way smaller than I'd imagined, and certainly far smaller than the picture Paul had painted of his 'organisation' at our first meeting in Chicago.

My ego bloated by the interest from Kmart, I didn't disguise my disappointment at the limited scale of Paul's business. But despite what must have come across as arrogance, it was Paul who had doubts about getting involved with me. Firstly, he wanted to come to the UK to see how visible Reebok was at road events. Also, the new *Runner's World* shoe ratings were due in a couple of months and he, like me, wanted to see which brand would have the edge. It would probably be Nike again, but at least we could try.

Runner's World was first published in 1966 under the title *Distance Running News*. Back then it was nothing more than a simple, folded black-and-white newsletter dominated by three brands – Nike, New Balance and Tiger. Now it was a full-colour glossy magazine with immense influence on both sides of the running world – trade and consumer. It was considered the bible for runners and retailers, particularly in the road-racing niche.

Bob Anderson was the publisher. I suspected that Bob's personal relationship with Phil Knight of Tiger and then Nike, just down the road in Oregon, provided more than a little help in their phenomenal growth at the time. But it also gave other brands the chance to be seen through advertising, as well as in their yearly shoe rankings.

Initially, the charts operated like this: manufacturers sent their shoes to the magazine to be road-tested. Each was vigorously inspected before one pair was crowned number one in the magazine. Readers loved it.

However, because of the influence of *Runner's World*, this annual partisan endorsement had been causing all kinds of problems for the manufacturers and retailers. Any shoe voted number one immediately became a runner's must-have.

Retailers would immediately order as many pairs as they could from the manufacturer, who in turn would have to shift production to accommodate this sudden demand. If a brand had its own factory, it was almost impossible to gear up in order to satisfy the clamour. The time from the initial reaction to actual production could take up to six months. For companies like Nike, who imported all their shoes from Japan, trying to arrange additional production and shipping from overseas caused huge headaches on both sides of the world.

A year later, when a new shoe hit the number one spot, the retailers would be left with boxes and boxes of last year's top model, and the manufacturer would have to scramble around for extra production again. And so the problem was perpetuated, year after year.

After lots of grumbling from the industry, Bob agreed to change the format so that running shoes were given a star rating from one to five, which allowed at least two or three shoe models in the different categories to be simultaneously top of the charts. It lessened the sudden monopoly and spread the supply and demand across a range of running footwear.

Reebok needed to be top of the charts. Paul needed us to be top of the charts, or rather a chart-topping shoe that he could promote. But how? In a field of giants, we were a relatively small player, providing a small line of shoes to a small number of companies. Plus, we were outsiders, the only British sports-shoe manufacturer that advertised and was evaluated in *Runner's World*. We were punching above our weight, but now we had to punch even harder. The time had come to enter the ring with the big hitters.

But first, I had to impress Paul with our professionalism,

our efficiency, our scale. And I had to do all this by bringing him to our modest, redbrick factory in Bury. What could possibly go wrong?

At the time, *Runner's World* wasn't available in the UK, so, on the morning of publication, I went straight to my office, phoned a half-awake Paul, and told him to get a copy of the magazine as soon as it hit the stands.

He called me back an hour later. 'The Aztec got five stars,' he said calmly.

I tried to retain a modicum of British reserve. 'That's great. Now—'

Paul interrupted. He articulated every word slowly. 'All three Reebok shoes got five stars.'

My British reserve flew out the window as I yelled in celebration down the phone. I knew we had finally crossed the line. It felt like receiving the keys to the Magic Kingdom. 'Then I guess we're in business now?' I said.

'Welcome to America, partner,' said Paul.

The Aztec had received a number one ranking for sole traction and rear-foot control, and immediately generated huge interest. We received a few orders from private individuals that we were able to supply and ship ourselves, but the incoming enquiries from the trade had begun to snowball. That five-star rating would prove to be a game-changer for Reebok.

The market I had been chasing for over ten years had suddenly turned its attention to Reebok for a product that excelled. Nike was still the leader, but we were now hot on their heels, if you'll excuse the pun.

It seemed such a long time ago that our solicitor Derek Waller had steered us through the winding-up petition from the patent office of Wilson Gunn & Ellis, but I now called on him again to draw up an agreement with Paul whereby he would have 95 per cent of the newly created Reebok

International Limited Inc (Reebok USA) and I would hold the remaining 5 per cent. The agreement also provided a royalty for Reebok International Limited (Reebok UK), as the early shoes would be bought from Bata until we could source them from somewhere else.

We also agreed that, because of the proximity and ease of cross-border shipping, Paul would have both Canada and Mexico within his licensed territory. I figured I would still have more than enough on my plate looking after the UK and the rest of the world!

It felt like a massive weight had been lifted from my shoulders. I no longer needed to focus on breaking into the US – I was convinced that Paul could do that for me now that we had the five-star rating. In truth, the 1970s had been hard going, like trying to run through mud in poor shoes.

Politically, the country had been volatile for a decade. Inflation had reached a whopping 22.6 per cent at its highest point in 1975, and this, combined with public sector pay limits, had reduced retail spending. The streets of Britain had been littered with rubbish for weeks on end as dustmen joined the nurses and ambulance drivers striking for higher wages.

The election of the UK's first female prime minister offered some hope. Margaret Thatcher came to power in May 1979 and immediately went to war on inflation, state spending and the unions. My optimism for positive change was confirmed when one of the first things she did was to remove exchange controls. Before that, there were limits on how much money you could take out of the country. The eradication of those restrictions meant that it was much easier to spend money abroad, and thus do business overseas. This made a big difference for Reebok at precisely the right time, now that we were ready to expand. On my travels, I could take as much money as I wanted without having to negotiate my way through reams of red tape to transfer funds from back in the UK. American Express really did become my flexible friend thanks to Mrs Thatcher.

The turmoil of the 1970s harmed all manufacturing industries, including Reebok. I knew that, at the time, our factory would never cope with the extra production we were now facing. Perhaps if it had been a decade of smooth sailing, we would have been able to expand quicker, increase our machinery and our staff, but it hadn't been, and thus we weren't set up for the sudden change of fortune that a five-star rating and a US distributor in place brought. It was a reminder that, no matter how well you plan and make contingency plans, external factors could easily derail you at any time.

With everything else falling into place, now was the right time to make a trip to Southeast Asia to scout manufacturing sites for Reebok. Here, as many other footwear companies had found out, factories could make shoes in huge volume and at a price much lower than in the UK; and, whereas in the past quality control had been an issue, now the production standards couldn't be faulted. They had been driven up by those companies that had made the switch earlier, and the factories that had been used to making low-quality shoes knew that if they didn't up their game, the foreign industry giants would simply go elsewhere. It was great timing again. We were ready to enter the game after others had struggled through the clean-up.

I'd already seen this for myself. When the idea first surfaced to move production to that part of the world, I was put in touch with a factory in Taiwan by a contact who said we could get our shoes made for a third of the price they currently cost us. I was dubious. The only place that I thought could make quality products overseas was Japan. Phil Knight had proved that with the Tiger shoes he was importing; plus, imported Japanese cars had earned a good name for themselves. It was evident that you could get good, cheap products from Japan, but South Korea and Taiwan? Everything I'd seen from those countries was just cheap, not particularly good.

With some hesitation, I pushed my doubts to one side and put in an order for two hundred pairs of a high-tech running shoe based on detailed specifications. The shoes they sent back were of the quality you might expect to find on a market stall. The Taiwanese factories weren't ready to supply high-performance sports shoes, but, in truth, at that time we also weren't ready for switching our manufacturing to overseas.

If I'd been put off by the quality offered in Taiwan, South Korea seemed one step down again. At the time the country wasn't known for producing anything, either high *or* low quality, but I'd been sent a set of particularly good samples by Malcolm Nathan, the UK agent for the HS Corporation, the largest shoe manufacturer in South Korea.

Malcolm had been watching the rise of Reebok and contacted me to suggest we look at what his company might offer. Even though the samples were of high quality, there was a chance they could be one-offs. Maybe they had made these shoes in a side room, a special production for naive foreign investors like me. What would they be like from a production line? I still wasn't convinced. I needed to see for myself, to have first-hand knowledge of their methods and abilities.

By my estimates, from visiting the factory to setting up a

production line and receiving the first shoes was going to take around six months. We didn't have half a year. Once orders started coming in, they were going to be in bulk, I was sure of that, so I needed an interim plan.

Once again, I approached Shack at Bata. Bata certainly had the capacity to accommodate our needs, but I wasn't convinced they had the 'feel' to produce the 'state-of-the-art' shoes we needed for the American market.

However, Shack was keen to work with us again and, being the persuasive character that he is, he convinced me that they were more than capable of producing the high-quality, innovative shoes that we needed. So, while Paul negotiated prices with him, Jeff spent time setting up their production line and transferring components and patterns, while I made plans for the trip of a lifetime.

My primary goal was to meet Alan Nichols, Malcolm Nathan's partner in South Korea, after a stop-off in Hong Kong. From there I would fly to Tokyo to meet a new contact, before linking up with a sportswear brand in Los Angeles, then travelling on to Boston to spend time with Paul Fireman and see how he was getting on with the distribution.

I was booked on Pan Am 2, a jumbo jet that flew continually eastwards around the world. As long as I was travelling east all the time, it was like a hop-on hop-off service. For the first time in my life I treated myself to first-class travel. I'm not a big believer in paying way over the odds for short journeys, but this was no light hop and a little luxury goes a long way on a long-haul flight. It wasn't an all-out first-class ticket, though. That still seemed too ostentatious at the time. My ticket was first-class *standby*, which meant that if the first-class section was already full on any of the legs, I'd have to downgrade.

For the first two legs – London to Frankfurt and Frankfurt to Tehran – I struck lucky and revelled in the luxuries of first-class travel, making the most of the 747's upstairs lounge and bar. In Frankfurt, the vacant seat beside me in first class was occupied by a large German man who flopped down wearily, closed his eyes and crossed himself with a whispered prayer. I guess those prayers for a smooth flight were answered as he barely opened his eyes again until we started our descent. And then things started to unravel.

As the plane touched down at Tehran airport it veered violently and came to a juddering halt far away from the terminal building. The cabin lights dimmed and an announcement warned us to stay in our seats, not to move about. I peered into the darkness as a group of vehicles approached – a fuelling vehicle, a support truck, a passenger bus and, more ominously, an army lorry loaded with uniformed military. The plane door opened and two soldiers appeared, machine-guns at the ready. There were gasps from some of the passengers, eyes wide with fear. I swapped anxious glances with the German man next to me as one of the soldiers raised his gun, scanning the first-class section with nervous eyes as if he was looking for someone in particular.

A Middle Eastern man in front of me caught the attention of one of the soldiers and gingerly pointed to the locker overhead. The soldier's eyes narrowed. He swung the barrel of his gun in our direction then nodded curtly. The man rose slowly, lifted down his case and, clutching it to his chest like body armour, scurried up the aisle and off the plane. The two soldiers followed. Through the window, I could see a handful of passengers being marshalled into the bus before it drove, lights off, towards the passenger terminal. The plane door was shut quickly and within minutes we were airborne again.

The flight from Tehran to Delhi was eerily quiet, as was the next leg to Hong Kong. Those passengers who spoke did so in hushed tones. What had we just witnessed? How close to danger had we been?

I later learned that a few days after we had touched down, hundreds of Iranian students had stormed the American embassy in Tehran and taken sixty-six American diplomats and citizens hostage as a show of support for Iran's Islamic revolution. All US airlines and their passengers were considered to be in imminent danger, as rage against the American presence in the country spread quickly. Despite numerous diplomatic attempts to secure their freedom, it would be 444 days before most of those poor hostages were released.

CHAPTER 23

Hong Kong and Beyond

The 747 dipped a wing as we swooped between apartment buildings to line up for landing at Hong Kong's Kai Tak airport. I was here to meet André Blunier, the Swiss-born editor and publisher of the *China Runner*, who also happened to sell Reebok from his small sports shop in Kowloon. We'd been supplying him with shoes for a couple of years.

The magazine was no *Runner's World*, catering only to a pocketful of expats, and André himself was little more than a simple sports shop owner. But, to be honest, I was there mainly because I wanted to see Hong Kong. It was more a personal choice than a business necessity, a place I'd wanted to visit for years. It would have been a crime not to stop off on the way to South Korea.

This densely populated mass of vertical concrete has one of the busiest ports in the world and is also the city with the most skyscrapers. It's not the sort of place you visit to relax, but it was all I expected it to be – an explosion of organised chaos thrumming with commercial opportunity, and far removed from the relative austerity of Bury.

Compared to the drama in Tehran, it was a quiet and low-key visit, terms you don't often see in sentences about Hong Kong. It turned out to be the calm before yet another storm!

After André had given me a few copies of the magazine and filled me in on the state of the athletics market in Hong Kong, I returned to my hotel for an early night before my next flight. South Korea wasn't on the Pan Am 2 schedule so I was using one of my open tickets.

A message awaited me at the hotel reception. It was from Alan Nichols: 'Please call this number urgently.'

Alan's voice was panicky. 'Thank God I caught you.'

'Why, what's up? I'll be seeing you tomorrow in Korea.'

'That's the point.'

'What?'

'I'm not in Korea. None of us are.'

'Why, where are you?'

'We're all in Taiwan. President Park was just assassinated. They declared martial law. We had to get out quick.'

'Hell. What should I do?'

'Stay put for now, or come and join us in Taiwan.'

I put the phone down thinking this trip was fated from the start.

After an early flight to Taiwan the following day I hopped in a taxi on my way to meet up with Alan and his team in Taipei. They had been told that martial law was still in place in South Korea, but there had been no violent reaction to the president's assassination. They were going to return the following day but advised me to wait a further twenty-four hours, just to be safe.

President Park had ruled with an iron fist for the previous eighteen years and, under his military dictatorship, the Korean Central Intelligence Agency (KCIA) had brutally arrested, tortured and executed anybody opposed to his regime. I can't imagine many genuine tears were shed by ordinary Koreans after he was shot under the instructions of the KCIA director while at a dinner party at a KCIA safe house.

Going through security at Seoul airport, I was told to empty my pockets into a tray, my passport and other personal documents included. I was hesitant. I had no idea who or what lay on the other side of the narrow slot that the trays were pushed through. I waited outside a closed door for what seemed like an eternity, wondering what I would do if my possessions weren't returned. Without a passport or any identification documents, I was a nobody. As far as the KCIA was concerned, I would have no identity, I'd be a non-entity, just another unidentified foreigner who had mysteriously vanished. I looked over my shoulder, hoping to find a friendly face I could ask for advice. A stony-faced soldier stared back, his hands clutched around a semi-automatic rifle.

Beads of sweat rolled down my face as I waited ... waited ... Why was it taking so long? What were the security forces looking at? What had they found? Then the door opened and I was beckoned through. My eyes darted between the four stern faces watching me. I opened my mouth to talk, to explain who I was, why I was here, why I was no threat. One of them pushed the tray towards me and nodded towards the exit door. That was it. Nothing. No interrogation, no suspicion, no withholding of my passport. I was me again.

It was dark as I was driven out of the airport. We passed

through a ring of tanks, drove by gun emplacements and were halted at several armed checkpoints. The military police and armed forces vastly outstripped the number of people on the road, and each one threw me glances of both suspicion and fear. The nervousness was palpable. It felt as though the merest misinterpreted look could result in a hail of bullets, questions to be asked after. Who knew selling shoes would involve such danger?

The taxi stopped at a huge wooden gate, with heavily armed guards stationed at either side. One peered inside then nodded to his colleague, who pushed a button enabling the gates to slowly swing open. We drove into what can only be described as Shangri-La. Everywhere there were bright lights and music.

I was relieved to be met by Alan at reception. 'How was the journey?' he asked, smiling.

'Erm ... eventful,' I replied.

My hotel room overlooked a torch-lit beach. I opened the window expecting to hear the gentle rush of waves, but I was taken aback to hear an overriding soundtrack of wailing from a group of mourners marking the death of the president. Maybe he had been more popular than we in the West had been led to believe.

After a fitful sleep and a quick breakfast, I arrived at the HS Corporation factory and was greeted with a 'Welcome Reebok' banner. It took me by surprise but was a nice touch and the first time in what seemed like days that I had been made to feel welcome. After lots of head-bowing from a dozen or so managers and executives lined up to greet me, we wandered inside en masse.

The interior was thrumming with activity. I watched one

operation that reminded me of my early days in Foster's, when safety was secondary to efficiency and machinery wasn't designed to be finger-friendly. Three men stood together punching lace holes in a leather upper. One held the upper on a wooden block, which looked nothing more sophisticated than a tree stump; another held a tool with punches spaced where the holes were required; the third man brought a large hammer down on the punching tool. I winced. There must have been a lot of trust among that team. A good bonding exercise for the staff at Bury, I pondered.

They were a dedicated lot, I had to give them that, and the rate of production was impressive, to say the least. There was no doubt the quality of shoes coming off the production lines was excellent and the samples I was given were as near-perfect as I could have expected. Shack had been a great help and had proved a valuable friend, but what Alan and Malcolm were offering here was a better product at less than half the price Bata were charging. I knew it didn't look good for our factory, or any factory in the UK, but this had to be the way forward. All I needed now was to figure out a way to finance South Korean production to meet the demands of Paul's fledgling USA company.

I had to make sure that Paul, and America, would have all the supply they needed. If Reebok took off in a big way, the last thing we wanted was to be unable to satisfy the demand. Malcolm, Alan and the HS Corporation factories were capable of mass production, but Paul would have to place orders covered by a letter of credit, from a bank, which meant he needed a credit line, which I'm fairly sure he didn't have.

I would also need Derek Waller to do the paperwork that would give HS Corporation a licence to produce shoes with the Reebok branding, as in the current agreement Paul only had a licence to distribute and sell Reebok shoes in the USA, Canada and Mexico. He didn't have a licence to actually make the shoes, which would be transported straight from the factory in South Korea to Boston. The agreement would mean that Reebok in the UK went from selling a product at a profit to receiving a royalty on every pair. It all sounded good ... if I could get it to work.

Next, it was on to Tokyo, where I stayed at the fabulous New Otani hotel, built within the original grounds of the Imperial Palace for the 1964 Olympic Games. Donning my Reebok Aztecs, I prepared for each day's meeting by doing laps on a running track which led all the way around the palace. I'd like to think it helped shed a few of the excess pounds that are unavoidable on a first-class, round-the-world trip.

The air was fresher than any I had ever experienced. As I jogged past manicured lawns, bursts of golden forsythia and scarlet bridges over trickling streams, each breath filled my lungs with the aroma of pine and cherry blossom. I wasn't trying to break any records – not that I was capable – but the mechanical repetition and highly oxygenated air provided an extraordinary clarity of mind.

As I ran, I thought of my dad forcing me to endure endless practice starts in the rain during weekly training sessions in Bolton, all so he could win money on the bets he'd placed. By the time I was eight I refused to go. I think he never forgave me for giving up running. That may have been the point when he gave up on me completely. For me, this was what running was all about – freedom, expunging stress, clearing the mind – not pushing yourself past your limits in the pursuit of victory, especially when that win was more for someone else.

After my meetings with potential distributors in Tokyo, I travelled to Hawaii for a weekend of simple rest and relaxation. It was the first leg of my journey where first class was full. The departure lounge was packed with doting Japanese couples, presumably going to Hawaii for a romantic break or honeymoon – *a bit more exotic than the week in Blackpool I'd enjoyed with Jean after our wedding*, I thought. Being demoted to business class wasn't exactly a hardship, but it did prove a pain when I reached Los Angeles airport and had to queue for hours at US immigration while dreamy-eyed lovers glided through the first-class priority lanes.

I was smartly dressed in comparison to the throngs of recreational travellers so I thought my attire, along with my British passport, would ensure a quick and easy passage through the immigration control. I was wrong. The officer demanded to know how much currency I had on me and asked me to open my briefcase. He immediately grabbed the *China Runner* magazines that André had given me.

'Where did you get these?'

'From a friend in Hong Kong.'

He stared at me for a moment then disappeared for a full ten minutes.

'What were you doing in Hong Kong?' he snapped on his return.

I tried to explain that I was the owner of a running-shoe company, but once again he marched off, presumably to seek advice from a superior.

When he returned, he had more questions. 'What's the name of your company?'

'Reebok,' I answered as patiently as I could.

'Never heard of it,' he said and disappeared again.

I looked back at the queue and offered an apologetic expression. This time the officer bounded back, thrust the magazines at me, stamped my passport and waved me off like swatting a fly. *Welcome to paradise*, I thought.

Things didn't get much better at the reception desk of my hotel. The room I had booked was unavailable. Exhaustion was kicking in and I just needed to lie down, to close my eyes and to stop thinking for a few hours. I sighed, placed both hands on the counter ready for an argument. But before I could say anything, the quietly spoken girl said they had a better room they could offer, a free upgrade.

The new room was huge, housing two king-size beds, a three-seater sofa and a coffee table. I swished open the heavy floor-to-ceiling drapes and a glory of gold illuminated the room from the red orb sinking below the Pacific horizon. The white sands of Waikiki were striped with long shadows from the tall palms that stood guard between the low white wall of the beachfront dining terrace and the gentle hush of shallow surf.

Having left Tokyo on Saturday, I'd crossed the international dateline, which meant I'd travelled back to Friday and had the bonus of a full weekend to enjoy this Honolulu paradise. I was determined not to work, or scheme and plan. Both mind and body were telling me I needed a break, a reset. And what a place to do it!

My mornings entailed late breakfasts, ankle-deep paddles in the warm water out to the reef, then long, lazy lunches of fresh scallops and sautéed island mahi-mahi under the shade of hau trees on the dining terrace. After a long siesta, I walked along Waikiki beach to the Hawaiian Village market and bought souvenirs of scrimshaw and ivory carvings before returning to the hotel for a spectacular teppan-yaki dinner that involved a lot of blade flashing, flame inducing and ingredient juggling, as well as my first sampling of delicious Kobe beef.

I caught my Monday morning flight, and gazed down sadly through the aeroplane window as the kaleidoscope of gold, emerald and turquoise grew more distant. Hawaii had been the paradise I had always imagined. Beauty was everywhere – the beaches, the forests, the food, and most especially the girls. If the trip had ended right there, it would have been the perfect finale, but I had more glamour to come in Los Angeles.

At the airport David Perry met me with a firm handshake, the kind of handshake you'd expect from the athletic, 36-year-old son of a tennis legend. David was managing the Fred Perry sportswear brand from his home in Beverly Hills. There was no hint of a British accent, despite his dad hailing from Stockport in the north of England. Born and bred in Los Angeles, he was American through and through, his rugged college looks straight from a Hollywood casting directory.

David drove us down Sunset Boulevard to his favourite restaurant, where he told me about his plan to add a footwear line to the Fred Perry brand. He had seen and heard of Reebok through the large expat community in Los Angeles, and also through trade publications like *Runner's World*. Being a fellow British company, he wanted to try to help. As our meal came to an end, he agreed to put together a business plan, which he would send to me in the UK. We left the restaurant and, rather than return me to the hotel, he invited me to his home.

The house was enormous, originally built and designed for Ginger Rogers. Stepping through the entrance, I was first struck by the depth of the carpets. It was like striding through sand. I followed David down a wide curved staircase to what had been Ginger's 'party' room. Panoramic windows provided a breathtaking view of Los Angeles, and there was a mural of the city titled *Painting the Town Red*, which featured scarlet marks indicating the dancer's favourite night haunts. At the back of the room stood two carbon arc film projectors that she had used to entertain guests with her films. Outside was a dance studio made of wood and glass, and with a beautiful, polished sprung dance floor. I pictured Ginger waltzing here with dance partner Fred Astaire in the Hollywood heyday.

David told me that Fred had had his feet and legs insured for $150,000, a big sum in those days. Feet were his lifeblood. In a way, the same was true for me. Not that my own feet were valuable, but all my eggs were in one basket – Reebok. If the company fell out of favour, or we missed the bus on the latest trends, we were finished, *I* was finished.

At that moment, standing in the former home of a Hollywood legend while on a round-the-world trip, I knew I'd already come a long way, but there was no looking back. I had to do everything in my power to increase demand and decrease costs so that I had negotiating room when it came to the likes of Kmart and other big-league players.

Maybe it was the power of Hollywood, the influence of Ginger Rogers. There was no middle ground between success and failure. The greatest gave everything, left nothing behind. I had to do the same. It had to be all or nothing from now on. I didn't want to be chasing the pack, I wanted them to be chasing me. It was time to be the reebok – nimble, streamlined and adaptable, always setting the pace and forever elusive, keeping one step ahead of competitors.

In my mind, I was laser-focused. I could see the success, feel the glory. On paper, though, my plan was still just a notion, an image of a destination but with no road map of how to get there. I knew how to join the dots to get from A to B, but no further. I had Paul in place, cheaper manufacturing on the horizon and a five-star product, but it was still going to take an extraordinary amount of luck and good timing to make sure all my ducks were in a row at the same moment in order to make my brand number one.

Jeff had always shared my dream, and the two Jeans had been fully supportive when Reebok was striving for local, or even national greatness. But now … I felt they didn't have the same vision as me, couldn't see how far this company could go, its global potential. Or maybe they didn't want to. Maybe that scale of success scared them. Either way, it had come to the point where every major decision that I believed would benefit our expansion, or every trip I made overseas in pursuit of progress, was being met with negative and con- trary arguments. 'It costs too much', 'There's too much risk', 'We're out of our comfort zone'. I'd heard them all recently, plus dozens more.

I was beginning to feel alone in my passion, in my aspi- rations, in my belief in what we could achieve. I needed the enthusiastic support of someone with a similarly ambitious nature, someone experiencing the same excitement that we were on to something big. I needed to be in the company of Paul Fireman in Boston, my next and final stop.

CHAPTER 24

Back to Boston

Paul didn't disappoint. Boston was freezing in November but he was on fire. We made a little small talk about the flight, our families, then Paul suddenly steered the conversation on to the subject of business. I gazed out of the window during the twenty-minute drive to Boston Camping, heartened by his enthusiasm and optimism. He was a true American in his positivity. *I need to surround myself with more people like Paul*, I thought, as I took in the crisp urban landscape.

The autumnal hues on Boston Common were being veiled by winter, the reds, greens and browns bleached under a bruised grey sky. Icy wedges clung to shaded corners on the doorsteps of brownstone houses along Back Bay, while the window mannequins of Newbury Street boutiques were swaddled in layers of wool and cashmere.

It reminded me just how different Americans and the British are. Here in icy-cold Boston they embraced winter, rejoiced in the change of seasons. November brought new offerings to all the senses, with special tastes, sounds, smells and activities. Back in Bury, and the UK in general, winter was dreaded. When it arrived, the population hid behind closed doors, cursing the cold, wishing the time away. And when they had to emerge in public, they would moan, whine and dress in greys and blacks as if mourning the death of summer cheeriness.

It wasn't just attitudes to the weather that marked the difference. In business, too, there was a feeling of anything is possible in this land of opportunity. Maybe it was my upbringing, but it always felt like there was a lid on success, a moral barrier to stop you reaching too far. Aspiring for greatness was frowned upon, discouraged almost, like it was arrogant and conceited. Striving for average was more the British way; attain mediocrity, be moderate, remain middle-of-the-road. Know your place. Those three words again.

We arrived at Boston Camping, only it wasn't there any more. The sign, the stock, the business had gone, as too had his partners. He told me his brother had left to set up a company that made Velcro wallets, while the brother-in-law was now the owner of a second-hand car lot.

There was no doubting he was now 100 per cent Reebok. I couldn't knock his commitment, but at that moment I also felt a pang of anxiety for him. Like I had with Lawrence Sports, he'd pinned all he had on Reebok USA.

Paul wasn't wealthy by any stretch. Boston Camping had been a reasonably successful company at a local level, steady you might call it. But Paul was like me. Steady would never satisfy. He could have carried on making average money. He could have tagged Reebok on to his existing business, but the financial, physical and mental demands would probably have been too much and, like my doomed distributors before him, it would in all likelihood have led to failure. But now, with the decision taken and his Boston Camping a thing of the past, he had no option but to make it work. It was all or bust. The same for me. In fact, at that time Paul was earning almost no income at all. His wife was earning more money selling hand-made trinkets at craft fairs. Now there was only one thing on both our minds – making Reebok big in America – and, for that, he had plenty of ideas.

One in particular caught my attention. He'd been thinking about the 'window box', the area on the side of our shoes that framed a woven label embroidered with our new Starcrest logo. It was a recent development and one that had come about in the most unlikely of circumstances.

Jeff and I had splashed out on new cars. Trading in my second-hand van and his old Jaguar, we had first bought two new Ford Escorts and then, as business boomed, we had moved up to Saab turbos.

We'd developed a good relationship with the Manchester Saab dealer, and, while I was browsing for our next pur-chase, he approached me and asked if I could make a pair of shoes for Sebastian Coe. Saab sponsored Seb and, as part of the contract, he was due to make an appearance at the dealership soon.

I was always happy for the chance to work with a world-record holder, especially one as popular as Sebastian Coe, but I smiled and reminded the dealer that Seb was a Nike athlete. He was contracted to them. It wouldn't have gone down too well if he was photographed gratefully accepting a pair of shoes with Reebok emblazoned all over them.

'Is there any way we can leave them unbranded?' he asked. 'Or, better still, attach a Saab logo?' He disappeared into his office and came back with two woven clothing labels. 'Like these.' I saw no reason why not and figured we might get a favour for a favour next time Jeff and I came back for a new car.

Although the letters in 'Saab' were taller than the Reebok logo, the word itself was short, and could probably fit on the wing side support of our shoe. Even then, it wouldn't have looked good just stitched on, but we found a way of integrating it by cutting out a 'window' and sewing it in like a picture in a frame.

The Saab window box added another novel dimension to the already unique Reebok silhouette, and Jeff and I decided that it should be integrated into the design of all our shoes. Reebok became framed by the window box, with the Starcrest logo alongside. Paul loved the window box too, but he thought we could improve on it.

'I like the Starcrest,' he said. 'Reminds me of the Union Jack.'

I told him that's where I got the inspiration.

'But it's going to cost a fortune to get it to the stage where it's recognisable. How about we replace it with something instantly distinguishable to everyone in America?' He held my gaze rather longer than I was comfortable with considering he was the driver.

'Like what?' I said, watching the road for him.

'An actual Union Jack!' He smiled, palms up as though it was obvious.

'Watch where you're going!' I shouted as the car veered towards the crash barrier. 'I'll think about it.'

I pondered the idea some more on the last part of my round-the-world trip. I wasn't aware of just how many people would recognise the Union Jack in America. Paul told me that number was *everyone*. The more I thought about it, the more I considered it a masterstroke for the US. In business, you have to use all the weapons you've got when you're going onto the battlefield, even if they're not strictly your own.

I still had reservations about the UK market, though, especially with production now moving to Korea. There was a lot of unionism in Britain. I was worried that if someone picked up on the fact that our shoes were made in South Korea, not Great Britain, they'd give us some trouble.

It was somewhat of a gamble, but we would argue that the product was designed in Britain, the company was owned in Britain and all the royalties went to Britain. Besides, most of our sales would hopefully be in America. We could handle any problems in the UK as and when they arose.

It was decided, and, within nine months, every Reebok shoe would not only carry the Union Jack but would also be packed inside a Union Jack box.

The troubles *did* come over the ensuing years. We were prosecuted half a dozen times when local Labour MPs representing areas of high unemployment grassed us up to Trading Standards. But they were costs we were prepared to swallow. The fines were small, but the benefit of having such recognisable branding proved to be priceless.

As I landed in London and was about to board my flight up to Manchester, I phoned Jean to tell her what time I'd be at the airport. I sensed immediately that all was not well chez Foster.

'I'll be busy,' she said, 'it's my local art group night.'

I'd flown right around the world in twenty-five days and now I had to take a train to Bury and then a taxi back to an empty house. The gap between Jean and me had definitely widened over the past year or so, which was understandable considering I'd been travelling so much. Jean and the kids had noticed the benefits of the business starting to do well again, but they'd hardly seen me. My absence from the family home had become normality. I was just 'that man' who paid the bills and appeared at the front door now and then. But in my mind, I had no choice. I was in too deep with Reebok, too close to breaking into America, too engrossed in seeing how far the company could go to be able to step back now. Unfortunately, it had to be business or family, one or the other. I simply didn't have time for both.

For the next few months, there was a constant four-way discussion involving me, Shack, Paul Fireman and Jeff. We still needed to finalise the details of production and marketing for the Aztec and our other five-star shoes, building up to a launch at the forthcoming NSGA in February.

There was also a never-ending ream of papers to be signed, courtesy of Derek Waller and Paul's American lawyers. Another flight to Boston was needed in January, pen in hand, and the latest tweaked version of the Aztec packed in my case.

Paul didn't want to showcase a range of products at the exhibition, although one or two models would be on display. Instead, he wanted to focus on just one product, our golden boy, the Aztec, offered as the British '25-pound' five-star shoe. The *Runner's World* rating now included the weight of each shoe in their specifications, which in the USA had taken on some significance. Paul and his agent decided it would be a good ploy to play on the price we were charging in the UK in pounds sterling and the 'pound' weight. His selling price was the equivalent of £25. He wanted to price everything in the range the same way and needed the weight specs of each shoe. I didn't have that information to hand, but told him that I could fly back to the UK, buy some scales and get the measurements to him in forty-eight hours. He was surprised I didn't already own any scales. He left the room and returned with a set wrapped in a plastic bag.

The following day I took my usual overnight flight on TWA, arriving in London early in the morning, passed through immigration without trouble, then headed to the shuttle lounge for the leg up to Manchester. From the airport, I took a taxi straight to my office. Paul was adamant that he needed the weights of all the shoes as soon as possible, so I took the scales out of the plastic bag, then did a double-take as a fine white powder fell onto my desk. I feared the worst. I phoned Paul in Boston.

At first, there was silence. Then he laughed, awkwardly. 'One of my friends is on the police narcotics squad. He has lots of confiscated scales. He gave me a set.'

I tried to remain calm, but it wasn't easy. Of course, Paul was completely innocent – he had never had anything to do with drugs, but I had to tell him. 'Do you know what could have happened to me at Boston or Heathrow airport? I could have been arrested, Paul. *British Reebok owner held on drug-smuggling charges.* Can you imagine that headline! It would have been the end of me *and* you.'

Paul paused. I could tell he felt reprimanded, for a millisecond. Then his enthusiasm burst forth again as he laughed it off. 'Anyway, you're still here. Did you get the weights? This is going to be great, Joe, I can sense it.'

It was always hard to stay mad with such an affable person, no matter what catastrophe he'd almost caused.

CHAPTER 25

My Brother Jeff

I'd never known Jeff to be ill. He was always the epitome of fitness, a competitive cyclist who trained during the week and, even now, in his mid-forties, he raced most weekends. He was always sick after the races from the sheer effort of pushing his body beyond its healthy limits, that was normal for my brother. But the day I was leaving for the 1980 NSGA event, I could see he was ill, not sick. The suffering was plain to see in his face. He had severe pain in his back, and his wife, Jean, insisted he went to hospital for tests. I asked him if he wanted me to put off my trip, but he was adamant that I carry on and told me not to worry, it was nothing, and to let him know how the show went.

It was the first time Reebok had attended the NSGA show in Chicago on its own, separate from the British Board of Trade contingent, and Paul wanted us to stand out. He'd decided to play on our Britishness, with a stand set as a cosy English lounge complete with a fireplace, armchairs and a display cabinet. For a dynamic company that sold running shoes to competitive athletes, to me it seemed to suggest cosiness and lethargy, the opposite of athleticism, but, hey, what did I know about the American market? I was just there to answer questions about the product. With the focus on just one shoe, both Paul and his sales manager, Jim, had everything under control and I could see I wasn't needed.

I traipsed round to the British Board of Trade stand and sensed that some of the participating delegates were more than a little envious now that Reebok had its own US distributor. Little did they know just how much of a knife-edge our business was teetering on. Although improving, Reebok in the UK was still in recovery mode, while Paul was spending every last penny going for broke with Reebok USA, and I mean *every* penny.

By the end of the show, Paul had a fistful of orders, plus a couple of agents willing to sign up. Now it was up to me to get the shoes to him. I'd arranged for Shack from Bata to pick me up at Heathrow so we could finalise production as soon as possible. Before I left Paul's office, however, I phoned Jean to tell her I'd be stopping off in London for a meeting before coming home. She didn't sound at all surprised that I was going to be later than planned; she was used to such messages by now. I also asked about Jeff and she told me there was no news, which was a relief.

Finally back home, I found out there *had* been news, but Jean had decided to wait to tell me in person. Jeff had been diagnosed with stomach cancer. He was having an emergency operation the next morning. In the meantime, he'd arranged for a friend to run the factory in his absence. If I was floored from jet lag, I was devastated when I got the news. How could someone as fit and healthy as Jeff get cancer?

I visited him in hospital over the next few evenings. He was always heavily sedated and looked gaunt, ashen-faced, like life had already left him. I filled him in on how it had gone in Chicago, told him about the new orders that we had coming in, about the white powder from the Boston police department's scales. He smiled weakly, eyes closed. I felt helpless. I could see my being there was an effort for him, a strain, and he needed to rest. I kissed him on the forehead and left.

I never saw my brother again. A few days later, Jeff died from complications following the operation. His funeral was on 10 March, just eight days before his forty-seventh birthday. His Jean, and their two teenage children, Diane and Robert, cried throughout the service, understandably heartbroken. I couldn't hold back the tears either. I felt my whole life had just changed.

How we were running the business, who we were working with, how we shared our successes – they had all ended in an impersonal, whitewashed room in Bolton Crematorium as the door behind us closed to the fading echoes of polished shoes on a tiled floor, and commiserations murmured by the gathered few.

Nobody could have envisaged how far both Jeff and I would come, and although Reebok was still relatively small and fragile, and Jeff wary of too much expansion, we both harboured hopes of a brighter future. Our initial dream that our company would mature into a global business that would stand up to the likes of Nike, Adidas and Puma was still alive, but now Jeff would never see if it became a reality.

Jeff and I had been a natural team. We had both taken the hard decision to leave our family business, J. W. Foster & Sons, twenty-two years earlier. We had created Reebok from nothing, in a run-down factory in Bury, and although it was still struggling cash-wise in the UK, we had finally got a foot in the door on the other side of the Atlantic, where the pot of gold at the end of our rainbow lay.

Together we had educated ourselves for it, worked long and hard, suffered when seemingly insurmountable obstacles had arisen. We had both battled legal challenges, sales drying up, and the collapse of our revenue provider, but as brothers and partners we had always found a way through and Jeff deserved to see the outcome. I needed him there to share the successes, mourn the losses. I needed him to run the factory, to find remedies when spikes in demand put impossible strains on the production line, then subsequent lulls forced even more pain on the staff who had to be laid off temporarily. I needed him to be the anchor while I was away, the voice of reason, the practical problem-solver. But, most of all, I needed him to be my brother, my rock. And now, without him, I felt fearful, like a tightrope walker without a safety net.

Amid the overwhelming sense of sadness, I knew I faced a decision. I could sit around with my head in my hands for ever, or I could get on with it. It wasn't just my future I had to consider, it was my family's – Jean, Kay and David – as well as that of everybody involved in the company who relied on my propelling the company forward. There was no choice but to step up and take control of the situation despite my overriding grief.

Naturally, Jeff's wife inherited his half of the company, making us 50:50 business owners and partners. It was no secret that lately his Jean and I hadn't been getting on. Admittedly, I had been the impetuous one in the partnership with Jeff, it felt to me that his wariness about my desire and actions to drive Reebok to a global brand was being fuelled by his wife. It felt like she had no trust in me and thought I was manipulating her husband. The tension that this caused meant we hardly ever spoke to each other. Naturally, it would have been impossible for us to work together, to have equal say in major decisions. Partnerships don't work in those circumstances. I'd experienced first-hand what a toxic relationship could do to a business, with Dad and my uncle at Foster & Sons.

Foster's potential had been manacled by their mutual animosity, which no doubt contributed to its ultimate demise. How would we be able to move Reebok forward trapped in a similar, miserable working relationship? Who would want to continue in such an environment? Business is supposed to be fun and enjoyable. There's no point in doing it if it's not.

I knew Reebok had the potential to go far, I always had, and, with a bit more of the good fortune and timing that we'd recently experienced, I was sure we could make it. But at that moment in time we were still in a very fragile state. We needed every ounce of effort, luck and co-operation to succeed. Any more friction along the path to success could have easily derailed the momentum and potentially tipped us towards the same fate as Foster's.

I explained to Jean that there were only two options: either we liquidated the company there and then, making it virtually worthless, then I would buy it back for a small fee; or I bought her current share at the market value. Thankfully she agreed that the latter course was preferential. We weren't making that much profit yet, and I had no guarantees that we would. It was the same for Paul in Boston – no guarantee of success. Distribution hadn't worked with Shu Lang, and there was no way of predicting it would work with Paul. All I knew was that we had a start, an opportunity to try, and, until I'd exhausted every possibility, it was full steam ahead.

I now owned 100 per cent of Reebok UK (Reebok International Limited – the distribution and marketing arm) and Reebok Sports Limited (the manufacturing side), and, as the sole owner of both, my first task was to find someone to take over the production line. I soon realised just how much responsibility Jeff had been carrying while I was on the road. To allow me to carry on the task of working with Bata in the south, and with Paul in the USA, it was obvious that three people were needed to cover what Jeff had been contributing.

The first appointment was Norman Barnes as foreman production manager. Norman had been a loyal worker since our Bolton Street days and he knew the staff and machinery better than anyone. I then called in Linda Rothwell, who had headed up Leatherflair, to run the factory logistics and office. Finally, we needed a head of design and development. I didn't have to look far. Bata had a large design team and Paul Brown had been assigned to work with Reebok. He was bright and young, and oozed character. I must have been quite persuasive as it didn't take long for him to trade his modern, open office for a dingy room in our run-down mill in Bury.

It was a huge relief to have our new team in place, but taking on three extra staff also aggravated our cash-flow problems. We now had even more money flowing in the wrong direction, but what choice did I have? There was no turning back now. I just hoped that a reversal of flow would happen before we ran out of money.

CHAPTER 26

A Major Fault

Apart from having to recruit a new production management team, all of the problems I had faced to date, I had faced with Jeff. The first solo battle was a big one, and one that Jeff probably would have picked up on and averted before it became an issue.

While waiting for South Korean production to come online, Paul had placed first orders for the Aztec with Bata. These shoes were then manufactured in the UK and shipped directly to him in Boston, from where he would then forward them to customers throughout the States.

Shack had made sure everything had gone out on time, but Paul had started to get returns. Not one, but hundreds. Our flagship Aztec, which had received so much hype following the five-star rating and the showcase at the NSGA, had a problem. A serious one. The midsoles were collapsing.

I jumped on the next plane to Boston and, in Paul's office, compared the returned shoes to those samples we had displayed in Chicago at the NSGA. I couldn't believe what I saw. Not only was it true that the midsoles were failing, but there were also physical disparities between the two shoes. The shoe manufactured by Bata looked different from the shoe we had displayed at the NSGA. The facing, where the lacing goes, was supposed to be cut as a rectangle, but on the returned shoes they were rounded. There was only one reason for this – the factory wanted to speed up the sewing time. Suddenly, from being a state-of-the-art design, the Aztec now looked very ordinary. Someone somewhere had altered the patterns at Bata.

Jeff would have insisted on samples from the factory floor before they were sent to Paul. There's no doubt he would have noticed the design difference and halted production, but even Jeff wouldn't have been able to foresee the bigger problem.

The changing of the pattern was bad enough, but it wasn't the reason for the midsole collapse and subsequent returns. That was down to the EVA midsole that Bata had used from their rubber factory. While Bata had been producing their own rubber for many years, EVA was a fairly new development. I was unaware of just how new this was to the Bata technicians. It became apparent that they had never worked with EVA before.

I'm no scientist, but did have an inkling of why the midsoles were failing. I was sure the mix was right, but I suspected the curing time or temperature of some of the sheets of EVA had been wrong, resulting in the bubbles in the under-cured sheets collapsing, effectively eliminating the shock-absorbing properties. After just a little wear, the shoes became flat and lifeless. They also looked run-of-the-mill with the rounded facing. I phoned Bata and stopped production immediately. But that didn't remedy the problem we still had, namely that

many of the 20,000 pairs that had come off the Bata production floor were now already in circulation.

If we did a recall, it would probably put Paul out of business.
Admitting our shoes had a problem would have been a public
relations disaster. The only thing we could do was replace
with minimum fuss all the shoes that had been returned, but
we still needed to find out how all this had happened in the
first place, and, for that, we needed to travel to the source.

Shack at Bata was horrified. He arranged a meeting
between me, Paul and John McGoldrick, the top man at Bata
in London. Bata brought their rubber factory manager into
the meeting. He immediately went into great detail about
the chemical mix, the optimum temperatures and the setting
time, presumably to try to baffle us with science. Paul and I
were having none of it and, eventually, he confessed that the
EVA they used hadn't been sufficiently tested. The manager
promised to have six new pairs of samples ready for us before
Paul went back to Boston.

At least we'd found out how the midsole problem had
occurred and could stop it happening again, but the change
of sewing pattern was down to someone at Bata conduct-
ing a time and motion study and deciding that it would be
more efficient to 'adapt' our shoe pattern slightly. For this,
all John could do was apologise and promise that it wouldn't
happen again.

We were confident that the manufacturing problem had
been fixed, but there was still a small financial issue. Twenty
thousand pairs of faulty shoes had already been delivered to
the Boston warehouse. Fortunately, Paul hadn't paid for them
yet. Bata first offered a 50 per cent discount on the delivered
shoes, plus an extended credit line of three months. Paul

refused. They then offered a 75 per cent discount, but again Paul shook his head. He had no intention of paying anything for a product that didn't match the sealed sample that we'd given to Bata.

These sealed product samples are insurance that the shoemaker makes the model exactly to order. When a factory makes a sample pair, the left and right shoe are, once approved, sealed in separate polythene bags along with the technical specifications. One set is given to the factory, the other to the client. This ensures that both parties have physical evidence of how every shoe should look. In practice, this enabled us to compare our sealed sample with the shoe they had put into production, and, of course, they were different. Bata had no defence.

It took a few more hours of heated discussions, but, eventually, Bata agreed to write off the 20,000 pairs and accept the loss, and Paul returned to America with six pairs of 'genuine' Aztecs to test.

Although we were able to replace the faulty shoes that were returned to Paul in the US, I was more concerned with the shoes that weren't returned. I knew that any brand loyalty we were managing to build up in the States could be destroyed. When the midsole problem surfaced in their shoes, Aztec owners would just move on to Nike or Adidas and we would have lost a lot of repeat custom. Paul didn't agree. He had a better understanding of the consumer culture in America and their readiness to forgive. Thankfully, he proved to be right and sales continued to pick up, regardless of the initial faults.

That same year, 1980, there was another problem – isn't there always! Paul had taken on Steve Liggett to be his production manager and duly dispatched him to oversee the set-up of our production line in South Korea. The factory had decided that they weren't prepared to dedicate a production line exclusively to Reebok until they knew that the demand was already there. This meant that any orders placed could take weeks before they were manufactured as they had to be slotted in among other smaller batches from different companies. If the factory was busy with a large order, we would be put to the back of the queue. Ensuring timely deliveries to retailers was proving to be impossible.

Not only that, to get the shoes out of the country we needed proof of payment. This was usually in the form of a letter of credit, normally from a bank. But Paul had the same problem in the US that I had in the UK. Growth was stripping all our cash and the bank wouldn't supply a letter. We needed an injection of funds, which meant Paul had no choice but to find an investment partner. In the meantime, manufacturing would still have to take place at Bata, at the higher cost.

Paul moved fast. He had to. Within weeks he introduced me to his new partner, Dick Lesser, a local businessman in Massachusetts he knew from his local Jewish community. Dick owned a huge warehouse, which he leased out to a major beer company. Let's just say that money was not in short supply for Dick.

Soon after that, Paul was approached by a large company in Paris who manufactured tennis, badminton and squash sportswear. They were looking for a distributor in the USA and Paul, now with funding from his new partner in place, thought it would be financially useful for Reebok USA to offer their services. Negotiations were made and contracts flew back and forth between lawyers.

With the hunt for funding over, the green light was given

for production to start in South Korea, and with a new distribution deal for Paul on the horizon, it was time to celebrate.

But as soon as we all relaxed, the deal with the Paris company fell through. And with it went Dick Lesser, who, after nearly twelve months partnering with Paul, realised just how much cash was needed to launch a new brand in the States. He had a lot, but nowhere near enough for such a huge challenge, or at least not the amount of credit he was being asked to provide. Along with Dick went the funding. It was stress time again.

I was in the Bury factory in 1981 when I received a frantic phone call from Jim Barclay, Paul's sales manager in Boston. Paul had been rushed to hospital with a suspected heart attack. It was probably an accumulation of worry – the faulty shoes from Bata, the dilemma of needing a credit note to get shoes out of Korea, and then the strain of Dick Lesser pulling out. Fortunately, he made a complete recovery and after two weeks was back at work.

Several meetings with other potential partners proved fruitless. One potential investor with an office in the Empire State Building already imported shoes from the Far East and so he had an understanding of the business. It wasn't enough, though. He told us that he had been approached by Nike in their early days and had kicked himself for turning them down. He believed there was no room for another Nike in the sports-shoe sector and he didn't want the embarrassment of having picked the wrong company. He too was out, having turned down the chance to invest first in Nike, and then Reebok. I'll leave it to your imagination how he would eventually feel about turning us both down!

Time was running out. Without a continuing credit line,

our supply from South Korea was going to run dry very soon, and, once the tap was switched off and orders were left incomplete, we would be dead in the water, bankrupt. It was *that* serious.

The only thing that was keeping Reebok USA afloat at that time was the faulty stock Paul had been sent from Bata, which he was able to sell off at a discount, despite the defects. Having agreed to write off the payment for those shoes, it was free money for Paul. Without it, he would have run out of cash. I guess it was another case of timely good fortune – in this case, ironically, provided by the errors of others.

Back in Boston, an anxious Paul and I had a meeting with Bill Marcus, head of the American Biltrite rubber company. It transpired that Bill had a friend and colleague in the UK who sourced footwear from Korea and it was possible that *he* might be interested in an investment partnership.

Paul rushed over to London to meet the CEO of ASCO, the Associated Shoe Company, a subsidiary of the Pentland Group. His name was Stephen Rubin, a smartly dressed man with a bow tie and impeccable manners. This silver-haired Samaritan turned out to be the saviour that Paul had been looking for.

During the meeting, it was obvious that Stephen could see the potential in working with Reebok. He was, as they say in America, one helluva smart cookie. At the age of just twenty-one he had stood for parliament as a Liberal Party candidate, then, like me at Foster & Sons, he joined the family business, the Liverpool Shoe Company.

By the time Stephen had reached his mid-forties, he had turned the company, now renamed as the Pentland Group, into one of the largest sportswear and footwear companies in the UK. This success was partly due to Stephen's remarkable foresight. He was one of the pioneers who spotted the potential of relocating footwear production to low-wage regions overseas, and in 1963 he became one of the first in Europe to source shoes from Asia.

Stephen offered to invest $77,500 in the company. In return, he would take a 55 per cent share of Reebok USA, plus ASCO would have the sole rights to source sports shoes for the US company. For Paul, giving up shares in the company was negligible. The real value of the deal was in the availability of a credit line. Without it, Reebok USA was dead in the water. It had been six months since Dick Lesser left and we were at the eleventh hour. We didn't have much choice. We had lots of orders starting to come in, but no money to actually make the shoes.

Paul phoned me after his initial meeting with Stephen. 'Joe, to get the financing I've got to give up 55 per cent of the company. That only leaves me with 40 per cent unless you're willing to give me your 5 per cent back?'

It didn't take me long to think about it. The brand was still small. In reality, we had no more than a small toe in the door of the American market, and if I'd learned anything from my ten years of trying to break in, the one thing you needed above all else was money. You could have all the product you wanted in the world, but, without the money to make it, you were going nowhere.

The retailers would order the product on thirty or sixty days credit. But if you'd got to fund it from the Far East – ship it, warehouse it, distribute it – then wait for payment, you were talking six months before you could even cover the money you'd already paid out. It takes millions to run an operation like that. I didn't have millions. Paul didn't have millions. Stephen did.

I'm sure Paul would have done the deal without me giving up my remaining share, but I saw it as an act of good faith. We had both given up everything to make Reebok a success on both sides of the Atlantic. Paul had given up his other business and remortgaged his house. He had put everything on the line.

After so many years of trying, financial support seemed to be the final hurdle. I didn't want it to be the stumbling block. Besides, I still owned the brand, had the final say on all new designs, and would be receiving 5 per cent royalties. But if Paul and Reebok USA failed now, I'd be getting 5 per cent of nothing. And we'd be finished in America. In August of 1981, I got Derek Waller to draw up the necessary paperwork.

Paul now had all the ingredients to succeed in the US. Jeff and I had provided the name, a recognisable silhouette, a brand-identifying logo, a unique outsole profile and three five-star shoes in *Runner's World*. Now he had the means to finance it properly. Finally, everything was in place.

Having said that, the involvement of Stephen Rubin created many headaches for Paul over the years to come. Stephen wasn't in love with Reebok as a brand; he merely saw it as a way of expanding ASCO into America by using Paul's salesmen. He wanted Paul and his team to call on department stores and other large footwear retailers to offer them products from the Far East at a lower price than they could obtain locally. Paul had other ideas. For him, ASCO was his sourcing agent for Reebok and he had set up his sales team to do just that. He told Stephen in no uncertain terms that Reebok would not be acting as an agent for ASCO and that ASCO had better start behaving more like an agent for Reebok. On more than one occasion when Stephen had tried telling Paul what to do in his most gentlemanly manner, the fiery Paul would scream back at him, reminding him that he was his partner, not his boss.

Despite Paul's loss of patience with Stephen, he knew that he was the provider of the cash, and, without him, we were doomed. He would always urge me to 'treat him like royalty' despite our frustrations. Although Paul would offload his grievances about Stephen onto me, I had learned to not get involved. They were both from the same culture and religion, a community to which I didn't belong, and if there was a fight between the two of them, it was only me, the outsider, who would end up with the proverbial black eye.

CHAPTER 27

Our Angel

Later in 1981, out of the blue, one of the sales agents that Paul had appointed in California emerged as the next gatekeeper for Reebok. Neither I, Paul or the sales agent himself knew it at the time, but he held the key that would propel Reebok from underdog to champion in record time.

Angel Martinez came to America from Cuba in 1958 with his relatives, the same year that Jeff and I left the Foster family business. Like most kids in the US, he dreamed of playing professional baseball, but his five-foot-three frame meant it was a dream that was literally and figuratively out of reach in a game where the average height of a baseball pro is six foot one.

Angel did have another talent, though – running, especially long distance. He aspired to compete in the Olympics and took his sport very seriously, buying the best specialist shoes available at the time. Usually, he bought them direct from a garage in Oregon, from a man who was importing them from Japan. The shoe brand was Tiger, and that man was Phil Knight, before he founded Nike.

However, Angel saw more in Phil Knight than just his great shoes. He saw a man making a living out of his passion and Angel wanted the same, so he applied for a job running a retail store for *Runner's World*, a new venture the magazine had entered into. Angel got the job, and when *Runner's World* had a change of heart and decided they didn't want to be in the retail business after all, Angel bought the shop from them, then subsequently opened a second store and started a mail-order sideline.

His company did reasonably well, but, for Angel, the correlation between the hard work – ordering and maintaining stock, managing the staff and dealing with the reps – and the profits and his quality of life didn't stack up. When two reps from Reebok walked into his store, in his mind he began to question why he was working such long hours trapped in one or other of his two shops. The reps he saw daily all drove nice cars, spent most of their time taking store owners to lunch, and had generally finished their work by mid-afternoon. He wanted that lifestyle. It was time for a change.

Angel liked Reebok shoes. He'd once bought a pair from us by mail order when he was at high school in the early 1970s, but he was sure he could do a better job selling them than the two clueless reps who sauntered into his shop every week. It was clear to him that neither had the faintest idea about athletes and their needs.

He contacted Paul Fireman, brought in managers for his two stores and was appointed as the tech rep for the region of Northern California, Washington and Oregon. Angel soon found out life on the road was no piece of cake either. He would be travelling almost constantly, only spending one week a month at home, much to the annoyance of his wife,

Frankie. In that week he would make sure he spent all the time he could with her, including joining her at the gym during sessions of a new exercise trend – aerobics.

While sweating and stretching, Angel made a couple of astute observations. Firstly, there was a distinct style of clothing common among the women in the class; it seemed they were all trying to copy the instructor. Secondly, they were all either barefoot or wearing clunky trainers. At the end of each session, both Angel and Frankie had sore, aching feet. He decided they needed specialist shoes.

Angel called Paul Fireman and suggested that, if the demand for running shoes started to decline, Reebok would need something else. 'Why don't we look into developing a new line,' he said to Paul, 'a women's shoe for aerobics?'

'Aerobics? What the hell is that?' answered Paul. He wasn't interested.

Angel knew he was onto something, though, and wouldn't give up. He took the idea to Steve Liggett, head of Reebok production, along with a napkin sketch and a pair of his own soft, spiked running shoes that he thought could be adapted.

He explained that, for aerobics, they needed to be heavily cushioned like a racquetball shoe but with the pliability and look of a dance shoe. Angel wanted to use kangaroo leather, the softest and lightest leather around, but at that time in 1981 kangaroos were still listed as a protected species and importation into America was restricted.

Behind Paul Fireman's back, they decided to make a few hundred pairs using soft glove leather made from goat-kid skin. Like Paul, I was unaware of the developments going on behind the scenes, and later I would voice my scepticism about the use of such a flimsy material to create a workable volume product. At just 0.5mm thick, glove leather would rip under the slightest of stress. We'd used the material before on our lightweight running shoes, like the World 10, but then we had used the suede side to take the adhesive for the sole and had added nylon strips to reinforce the upper.

Angel and Steve tried the same on the aerobics shoe, lining the upper with adhesive nylon. This retained the softness and flexibility but killed the leather's natural ability to breathe. To overcome this, they perforated the top of the upper with a small pattern of holes. At last, it seemed they had a workable prototype, from which they produced a small batch of shoes.

Angel spent a week touring the gyms and aerobics studios in his sales territory, gifting the shoes to instructors in the area and explaining the technical benefits. But none of the recipients were bothered about the source of material or the science behind the perforated holes. They were more impressed by the dance-shoe look, the comfy towel lining, and the fact that it was the first fitness shoe specifically designed for women. Every one of the instructors promised to try them out and report back to Angel when he next visited.

As Angel had hoped, the next time he called into the studios, the instructors already had a class full of women immediately wanting the same shoes. It was obvious there was a demand. With the backing of Steve, Angel went back to Paul to try to convince him of the potential.

Paul listened as Angel delivered his best sales spiel. He told Paul that aerobics was not just a new trend, it was a women's movement. Until then, women weren't supposed to be seen to sweat, or to have defined muscles. Through communal fitness classes, women like his wife were becoming empowered through physical activity. It wasn't just about exercise; it was about mental fortitude spurred on by peers in like-minded, female-only groups.

Angel also cited the lack of competition. New Balance was the only other brand that had cottoned on to the women's fitness revolution, but all they'd done was make a white version of one of their coloured, nylon road-running lines and called it an aerobics shoe. It was a no-brainer, continued Angel, a niche waiting to be tapped by a company like Reebok, a niche that could possibly go mainstream.

At that moment in time, Reebok was perfectly positioned to offer a fitness shoe designed specifically for women. Nike and Adidas were both sparring for the top spot in the men's running market, blinded to the rising demand for a woman's shoe. Also, unlike the big two, Reebok wasn't seen as a 'sweaty' brand. Our two biggest competitors were all about muscle, grit and perspiration, marketing shoes to those grunting and grinding their way to victory at all costs. Reebok was known as a specialist low-key footwear company making quality, high-performance running shoes. We weren't established enough to be associated with anything sweaty and mainstream yet; we hadn't reached the point where consumers had us branded. Our image 'colour' in the US was secondary, not primary, and, for once, that tone gave us the advantage.

It took some months, but eventually Paul relented and, in typical Paul fashion, when he made his mind up on something it was never half-heartedly. Just like he'd gone all-in with Reebok in 1979, selling his existing business and remortgaging his family home, he went full throttle with this new shoe and decided to start with an initial production run of 32,000 pairs. Even Angel raised an eyebrow.

Back at Reebok manufacturing, the challenge was to produce thousands of pairs based on the prototype. We needed to act fast. If Angel's assessment turned out to be true, and we couldn't supply the market fast enough, other brands would jump in and catch the wave before us.

Fortunately, Steve Liggett had foreseen this problem and acted on it the moment Angel had approached him. Unfortunately, he nearly got fired for it.

As the man in charge of production at the South Korea factory, Steve had secured exclusive use of an entire production line, without the authority of Paul Fireman. It was well in excess of demand at the time, as we were only ordering around 400 pairs of shoes a week. To gain exclusivity, Steve had guaranteed the factory that Reebok would order 200 pairs *per day*! When Paul found out, he went ballistic. The only thing that stopped him firing Steve on the spot was that he had nobody else to replace him in South Korea, plus he was about to order 32,000 pairs and needed his experience.

As I'd predicted, the factory in South Korea struggled to work with our kid leather. It was so thin that you could tear it with your hands like paper. The material wasn't strong enough to withstand the rigours of the manufacturing process. While an additional nylon lining helped, the weakness of the shoe was still a worry and one that had to be remedied if the shoe was to be marketed nationwide. Aerobics was still a small niche, but the size of our orders was enough to get the leather suppliers involved in looking for a solution. The result produced arguably the biggest-ever change in sports footwear manufacturing.

Most leather was firm to ensure street shoes retained their shape. Now the demand was large enough for the tanners to develop a relaxed, soft hide which, unlike glove leather, had substance and strength. The nylon lining could be removed and the shoe could breathe again. This new leather would eventually become mainstream for both sport and street shoes.

But now there was a new problem. Taking away the nylon lining left the shoes with wrinkles in the toes, like they were seconds. The line managers halted production again and asked Angel and Steve Liggett what to do. Angel loved the wrinkles. He knew that the women he'd spoken to in the west coast aerobics studios would find them cute, part of the appeal. He ordered production to recommence and to make sure that the wrinkles stayed in as part of the design.

When the shoe was launched as the 'Freestyle' in 1982, I was worried. In my eyes, it was still too weak to with-stand extreme workouts. But my education in the difference between UK and US consumer habits was furthered when the shoe's longevity, or lack of it, proved inconsequential. Women in America loved them so much that they weren't bothered when they fell apart – they simply bought another pair. If the same thing happened in the UK, the public outcry would have damaged our reputation. We would never have gotten away with such a fragile product, further proof that breaking into America had been essential for our expansion.

CHAPTER 28

Keeping Up

Within two weeks of the Freestyle hitting the shelves in California, they'd sold out. Paul and Angel had hoped for a good uptake but even they were flabbergasted by the demand. Angel was right, Reebok had not just tapped into a retail trend, it had captured a cultural shift towards female empowerment through group fitness, with aerobics and the Freestyle shoe its representation. However, it would still take almost two years for aerobics to become mainstream in the US, longer for global uptake. For that to happen, a major marketing push was authorised.

First, Angel and Paul approached Denise Austin, sister of tennis star Tracy Austin. Denise was California's most celebrated fitness guru and, before she went on stage at a major fitness exposition in Los Angeles, they asked her to wear the Freestyle while she was demonstrating aerobics. Denise fell in love with the shoes and probably would have worn them anyway, but Reebok paid her to appear in them whenever she was in front of the TV cameras or was running exercise classes. And, as Angel had observed at his wife's sessions, what Denise wore, her followers wanted.

After the initial launch in white only, the Freestyle was quickly released in pastel pink and blue, then in bolder hues like red, yellow and orange – colours that both complemented bright aerobics clothing and had never been seen on sports shoes before. Every new release created a clamour that spread from the west coast to the east. Women wanted every new colour that came out.

Nineteen eighty-three saw a high-top version featuring Velcro straps and three padded ankle supports, as well as a version for men's exercise called the 'Ex-O-Fit', which was advertised in typical manly fashion as 'For men who know how to sweat'.

But it was women who were taking sales into the stratosphere as the Freestyle became their choice of footwear not just for the gym, but also for work, leisure and play, and even at A-list events.

Hollywood legend Jane Fonda, who had first launched a series of home exercise videos in 1979, needed no persuasion, paid or otherwise, to join the Reebok tribe. From going barefoot in front of the camera in her first few videos, subsequent instructional tapes in later years showed her wearing Freestyles simply through choice.

Reebok had also unwittingly cross-pollinated sports footwear with urban streetwear, and what an explosive mixture it turned out to be. In New York, the Freestyle shoe was priced at $54.11 including tax and gained notoriety in hip-hop culture as the '5411'. The Reebok Freestyle was now not just the softest and most comfortable shoe on the market, it was also the coolest.

The popularity of aerobics continued to grow exponentially,

giving birth to a whole range of Reebok fashion and accessories. While sales of our fitness gear soared, Nike, Adidas and the others continued to sit back and watch, content in their belief that aerobics and the women's fitness market was just a blip, a mere fad that was here today and would be gone in a flash tomorrow.

By the time they realised it was here to stay, it was too late. Reebok was so entrenched as *the* aerobics company, others had little hope of gaining much market share. For years, we would have the fitness niche all to ourselves.

In the mid-1980s, while Nike sat on the sidelines still focused on men's running shoes, the market for running first began to plateau, then to decline. Again, another company's misfortune provided a much-needed opportunity for Reebok, just at the right time.

Because of the huge clamour for the Freestyle from many different sectors of society, we desperately needed to find more production capacity. Steve already had our factory in South Korea manufacturing shoes for us at full speed, but it wasn't nearly enough. We needed more shoes now. If we delayed, this would open the door for a competitor to feed the frenzy. Thankfully, at that precise time, Nike's apathy meant that sales of their running shoes had slowed to the point where they had to cut back production in the Far East.

Paul immediately instructed Steve to take up all the slack he could find in South Korea. Where Nike had cut back, we placed new orders to keep up with the demand. It was a lifesaver – for us *and* for the factories. Without their reduced Nike output, we wouldn't have been able to supply all the retailers demanding more and more aerobics stock and the whole bubble could have burst.

Naturally, this helped business in the USA, but, because of the incredible demand, our international distributors were now being starved. Paul couldn't keep up with the demand for Reebok aerobics shoes in the US, and, no matter how many orders they put in with the factories, the demand came in higher. Consequently, shoes ordered by distributors in the rest of the world were diverted to feed the USA. Naturally, this caused a lot of complaints, but there was nothing else Paul could do. He held the most important market, and, whatever happened, it was this monster that had to be fed first.

Our other territories were reliant on the USA driving the brand. Without that reinforcement, they would never develop beyond small-time enterprises. That was the power of the USA. As a trend or brand driver, it was second to none when it came to global influence, which is still the case today. Anything that happens in the USA has a huge bearing on what happens in the rest of the world. Japan also has massive leverage when it comes to spreading success, but it's still in a different league to America. I'd finally managed to light the fuse stateside, now all I could do was wait, or rather hope that, with the help of aerobics, the brand would explode on the other side of the Atlantic. If it did, it would take Reebok International with it. If it didn't, well . . . there was actually no other option – it had to.

Back in the UK, the extra royalties we were receiving on Reebok's aerobics range in the US enabled me to employ more people to help manage the distribution network throughout the rest of the world. It was hugely advantageous to take on people who had language skills and could listen to the distributors' moans and complaints in their native language. It made troubleshooting those problems so much easier.

I also began a search for a new base, as I needed to bring Reebok Sports (production) and Reebok International (marketing) together for practical reasons. There wasn't enough room for an office for me at our Bright Street factory, so I was making use of two empty rooms above our accountant's office in Tottington, on the outskirts of Bury. This worked for a while, but it was always intended to be a temporary measure and now I needed to be closer to production. With Jeff no longer there, whenever there were problems at the factory, or somebody had an issue that needed the input or signature of the owner, I would have to drive down to the factory in Bury, and this was becoming a regular occurrence, which disrupted my own plans and schedule.

At the time, we still couldn't be considered a particularly large business in the UK, but we were a success story and something of a celebrity company locally. We had raised the business profile of the town by hosting visits from foreign delegations, dignitaries and politicians. The council were proud to have us in the borough and equally keen to keep us, so I decided to use our popularity points to see if they had any properties for rent that would suit Reebok. They suggested a huge building in Bradley Fold, Radcliffe, on the border between Bury and Bolton.

This former Mather & Platt engineering factory had subsequently been taken over by an equally famous local name, Dobson & Barlow, manufacturers of machinery for the northwest's once-thriving cotton industry. At the start of the twentieth century, there were over 200 cotton mills in the town of Bolton alone. Of the 9,000 townsfolk employed in the industry, over half of them had worked for Dobson & Barlow, cementing their name in Lancashire history. Now, eighty years later, we would occupy their premises, and I envisioned Reebok also enshrined in the annals of the county's development. There was no harm in dreaming.

The sprawling factory was way beyond what we needed, but we embedded ourselves in what was once the old social club. Where once snooker balls clacked on green baize tables in the old billiards room, we now listened to the hum of computers and the purring of fax machines, while the metallic symphony from production lines started to emanate from what was the factory's entertainment hall.

All the structural reforms and administrative reorganisation were merely superficial. The lifeblood of any business comes from the staff, and I was determined to retain as many of my loyal Bright Street employees as I could. However, the new premises were approximately 8 miles from our old factory and most of our current workers had no easy way of making the commute.

I remembered the loyalty and mutual respect between staff and management at John Willie Johnson's factory in Bacup when we first launched Mercury. I'd thought about it many times, how he knew the names of every single employee, treated them all as equal, from managers to cleaners. I'd tried to recreate that environment, to model our factory on a similar friendly footing, and it seemed to have worked. Many of my staff had been with me for years, through thick and thin, organising the lunchtime cricket matches that all the staff and management played in the old factory yard when the weather permitted. It was only right that I repaid their loyalty, so I bought a minibus and arranged for Norman, our stalwart factory manager, to pick them all up in the morning and drop them off at the end of the day.

The expansion of our bases in both Boston and Bury helped in some way to increase production and subsequent storage needs, but there were still other challenges to overcome in the UK. The main one was not to try to do things faster than the progress we were making in America. Expansion in the US had to come first.

It had been my dream and absolute driving motivation to get into the American market. Like Nike, we had a product that needed volume, numbers which could only be attained in a culture where people had money to spend, like America. Nike had 240 million potential customers with lots of disposable income. In the UK, we had a population of under 60 million, the vast majority with no spare cash. There were only pockets of the UK, like Cheshire, Surrey and central London, where women had the money to spend on such luxuries as aerobics shoes. If the housewives in industrial towns like Bury needed footwear, it would be spent on new plimsolls, Wellington boots or other practical items.

For now, I wasn't as interested in building on our expansion in other parts of the world, including the UK; I was just keeping things going with the factory and travelling to Carter Pocock for regular meetings. I was more interested in America becoming what I wanted, which was to be the major player. If I could achieve that, the rest would follow. Paul was doing all the right things and we now had the incredibly popular Freestyle shoes. All the signs were pointing to further growth in the US, which I hoped would eventually open the floodgates to the rest of the world.

By 1984 Paul was doing $13 million in sales. Big numbers, but still representative of what would be termed a small company in the US. In the UK, we had a nice business. We were receiving royalties from Reebok USA, we were manufacturing and selling our own product, we were doing whatever was needed for Carter Pocock, and, because we were working with America, we could obtain products from South Korea, thus lowering our costs, but we were still only turning over less than a million pounds.

It was now a waiting game to see if the rising tide of success in America would ripple across the Atlantic and wash over the UK and the rest of the world.

CHAPTER 29

Changes Afoot

As with J. W. Foster & Sons during their golden days in the early 1900s, it seemed that in the early and mid-1980s Reebok could do no wrong. The 1982 Freestyle, the 1983 Classic Leather and the Reebok Ex-O-Fit all became instant hits. So too did the Victory G, made with an innovative Gore-Tex upper, and the Reebok London and Paris road-racing shoes. We also created a popular shoe made specially for, and named after, a South African runner.

Sydney Maree was a middle-distance runner who had been banned from many international competitions and venues because of sanctions against his country of birth for its apartheid system, even though he was black. It severely limited his race opportunities, but in 1981, having just become a US citizen, he was signed up by Reebok via his agent and invited to compete in the first Fifth Avenue Mile in New York. This twenty-block, straight-line run skirting Central Park pitted Maree against athletes such as Steve Cram, Ray Flynn and Eamonn Coghlan. I stood with Paul and watched as Maree burst through the tape at the Grand Army Plaza in a time of 3 minutes 47.52 seconds, a record that still stands today.

In 1983 he broke Steve Ovett's 1,500-metre world record wearing a Reebok vest and Sydney Maree running shoes. During this era, Reebok consolidated its success in track and field, and raced to the fore in women's fitness. It would soon become a leading force in another sport.

The 'new' soft leather that we had originally developed for the Freestyle was to change the sports-shoe industry for ever. Moving on from shoes with a firm upper that needed to be 'worn in', other companies would follow our path in producing soft, comfortable performance footwear.

Tennis presented an opportunity for this new type of shoe. White tennis shoes in hard leather were the norm at the time, with the Adidas Stan Smith probably the most popular. But by the time they'd been fully worn-in, they looked worn-out. We created the 'Phase 1', a shoe made from our new, soft garment leather and with the same towel lining as the Freestyle. It was promoted as a revolution in men's and women's tennis, and the first shoe that needed no wearing-in. A cheeky advertising campaign helped gain attention during the launch.

REEBOK PUT THEIR BALLS ON THE LINE
If Phase 1 isn't the best tennis shoe you've ever worn, we'll refund your money and send you a free can of tennis balls.

Paul was nervous the advert would backfire and bought two cases of tennis balls, ready for the product returns. Like other shoes before it, the Phase 1 was a massive hit and he only had to give away a few cans. In just our second year after launching a tennis line, we had captured over a fifth of the American tennis footwear market with shoes that looked good both on and off the court.

From being considered as a specialist running-shoe manufacturer, we had now become synonymous with tennis and fitness, famed for shoes that were known just as much for being comfortable and fashionable as they were for being performance-enhancing. Paul knew that, to achieve expansion, he needed to maximise the forward drive of all this positive publicity, and, to him, there was only one way he could do that.

He'd been dropping hints about me selling the brand to him and Stephen Rubin almost every time we spoke recently. Despite our success and growing global awareness, the company was still relatively small and he was worried that there was an underlying lack of commitment to the brand from Stephen, its financier.

Stephen's investment in Reebok had now become significant, and Paul was almost completely reliant on it. He was worried that by not having control of the brand, Stephen might decide to limit his credit line, and that could spell disaster. Without the clout of Stephen's financial backing, Paul would be stranded, unable to fulfil the vast amount of orders he was now receiving, especially for the Freestyle aerobics shoe.

He needed everything tying together, striking while the Reebok iron was hot after our aerobics success. Our 5-star running shoes were also still selling well, but running was now a crowded market, so having a unique product on the 'shoe wall' of sports stores was something we needed to retain at all costs, if only to maximise the brand's visibility on the high street.

The rise of Reebok was gaining speed, and if we were to progress further, we had to do everything possible to keep the momentum going, even if that meant me sacrificing my stake in the brand.

If I sold to Paul and Pentland, Stephen's holding company, Paul knew there was more chance that Stephen would have the necessary commitment to keep providing the finance Reebok needed to expand. There really wasn't much choice.

It was obvious that America was where the vast majority of growth would come, and the company needed to have every opportunity to exploit this success. For *that*, it needed a guaranteed flow of money – and lots of it. It needed Stephen Rubin and, as Paul put it, why would he continue to plough millions into the company if at any time someone (me) could suddenly turn it off?

Until now, I'd casually brushed off Paul's request each time – 'Yeah, yeah, Paul, we'll see'; 'We'll talk about it soon'; 'When the time's right, Paul'. But the time felt right now to seriously think about it.

I thought back to all the key moments in my journey and everything they stood for. Every obstacle, every problem, every challenge had provided a lesson, something that I could take away and use to my advantage in the future: having the courage to walk away from J. W. Foster & Sons; learning to live with the worry while waiting to find out if we were going to be closed down over the unpaid name registration bill; taking advantage of that first opportunity to visit America and the NSGA; being forced to find a way forward after the collapse of Lawrence Sports; learning patience through Shu Lang and his incessant letters; learning to trust my gut instinct after that first meeting with Paul Fireman; and now, knowing that Reebok was not about me, or Jeff – it was about the success of the company.

Rather than fail at this point because I wasn't willing to act, I had to let Reebok go. It was about what was best for the brand.

It was a question of what was more important – me making money or the bigger picture, success in the game? It was about growing Reebok into number one. At that time, the company wasn't run by accountants and suits, it was run by people with a passion for the brand. (Stephen excepted. He had no interest in the brand, but he did provide the money it needed, so we gave him a free pass on his motives.) Like me, those people wanted to see how far this company could go, *that* was the incentive. It was about realising its true potential, something that would only be revealed if it was allowed to grow, with or without me.

What I had learned over and over was that this business required finance and availability of the product. Thanks to Stephen, we now had the finance, so we were at least in the game. In the end, getting the product had proved to be harder. We had been blessed with timely good fortune, and not for the first time in Reebok's history. If Nike hadn't taken their eye off the ball at that precise moment, they would have kept all their production lines running at full capacity in South Korea and we wouldn't have been able to get enough product.

There was nothing left for me to do. Until Reebok USA expanded, there wasn't much more I could achieve either domestically or internationally. Since Jeff's death, the energy had already moved from Bury to the US. It was obvious now that, whatever the next phase was going to be, it was going to have to happen in America first. I had to relieve them of the need to ring me all the time, saying, 'I've got this idea' and 'I was thinking about trying this'. It was just more friction, another thing that would slow them down. They just needed to be allowed to get on with it, unhindered by me as a remote guardian of the final say.

My role had finished. I had supplied Paul with designs, a brand, a five-star opportunity, and a golden history dating back to 1895. What I couldn't do was provide enough money. He had put all his enthusiasm, energy and money behind the brand, and he now had the finance of Stephen Rubin in place. I couldn't stand in the way of Reebok's progress. I'd proved myself as a successful entrepreneur, but you can hold onto things too long. I decided to let go.

In 1984 I agreed to sell the intellectual property (brand) of Reebok International Limited, plus all the shares of Reebok Sports Limited, to a new company set up by Stephen's Pentland Group. This new company now became Reebok International Ltd, licenced for the USA, Canada and Mexico, with me employed as president of the International Division, looking after the rest of the world.

I sold the brand for what at the time was a reasonable figure, with a promise from Paul that if Reebok was successful there would be more money for me. Of course, nobody knew just how big aerobics was going to be. None of us in our wildest dreams thought Reebok would go on to become a multi-billion-dollar company. If I'd had an inkling that it would, then, yes, maybe I would have retained some kind of share. But there's no point in looking back at unknowables. Those kinds of memories change nothing, and only end up leaving your mind in a jumble of knots.

Having signed the papers, I was in effect handing the brand over to the new Reebok International Ltd, with Stephen holding 55 per cent and Paul 45 per cent. I had no regrets at all, just a sense of pressure being lifted. The satisfying addition of money in my bank account helped too, of course. I could step back a little, take a breather and enjoy the rest of the ride, which involved developing the rest of the world while our growth in America blossomed. I was forty-nine. I would relish the next step, travelling the globe without worrying who paid for it.

As it was, the rest of the world couldn't fail to notice Reebok – on TV, on the printed page, on the podium, at major events, at the gym, at work and in shops – and everybody wanted a piece of it. We were receiving enquiries from people all over the planet asking where they could buy Reeboks – from Spain, Portugal, Italy, Greece, Germany, Switzerland, Poland, Czechoslovakia, Sweden, Israel, South Africa, Malaysia, Hong Kong, Singapore, Japan, Australia . . . the list went on. And, unlike before when we had to juggle our cash limitations with the up-and-down demand, we finally had funding in place to finance all the supply we needed. All I had to do was make sure we had distributors in every territory. But first I had a gap to fill closer to home.

Carter Pocock had sold their business, and thus ended our agreement. I never did find out the true reason, but it was probably because they realised their property on Southwark Bridge Road was worth more than the profit they were making from their operation. With Carter Pocock no longer in the role, I needed someone else to take over our UK distribution, but who? Stephen had initially wanted me to handle it, but I made it clear that it was impossible for me to head up the UK *and* to develop other international territories.

At this time, I was still very friendly with Chris Brasher, one of England's finest athletes and a man who would forever be remembered for his pacemaker role in Roger Bannister's sub-four-minute mile. Also, having been inspired by the success of the New York Marathon, he organised the London Marathon, attracting 20,000 runners for its inaugural circuit on 29 March 1981.

Our friendship had endured from the days I was supplying Chris's Sweatshop store and we had shared a few good-natured phone calls over the years, usually with Chris complaining about the price of Reeboks. Since then, Chris and his business partner, John Disley, had set up a distribution company called Fleetfoot, which held the licence to distribute New Balance.

Several years ago, Chris had been shocked when I'd phoned to congratulate him on the success of the London event. I was Reebok, and he was New Balance, competitors in the running-shoe world. But at the time I was sincerely happy for him, and for what he had achieved. A London Marathon would be good for us all, I'd predicted. It would help speed up the import of road running from the USA into the UK. I had been proved right. Both brands had benefited immensely from the event and its subsequent effect of increasing demand for our products.

Now that I was thinking about the best distributor for Reebok in the UK, Chris Brasher again sprang to mind. He was the obvious choice; vastly experienced, and a nice guy to boot. The question was, could we persuade him away from his own distribution company?

I figured there was no harm in trying, so asked him if he'd meet me in the Lake District close to where Fleetfoot was based. After a good dinner, a choice red wine and a fine single malt or two, we had the beginnings of an agreement, a slurred one, but a start nonetheless. I'd like to think it was my charm (and copious alcohol) that persuaded Chris and John to come to Reebok, but, in truth, it was more because of the financial input and connections of Stephen Rubin. With his funding and our popularity, Chris was convinced there was only one direction Reebok could go.

That upward momentum was being made easier not just by the brand awareness Reebok had gained in the aerobics market, but also through continued exposure in major international running events. Steve Jones had won the Chicago Marathon in 1984, smashing the world record in two hours, eight minutes and five seconds wearing our Reebok London shoes. He followed it up by winning the London Marathon in 1985 in a record time of two hours, eight minutes and sixteen seconds wearing what would become the legendary Reebok Paris runners.

History was repeating itself. As in the early days of

Foster & Sons, each high-profile win was propelling our name across the running world, while, additionally, aerobics was simultaneously popularising our brand to women everywhere. We were spinning deliriously in a whirlwind of success, and, since we'd only just touched on the rest of the world, it was clear there was much more to come.

CHAPTER 30

Dealing With the Rest

With Paul Fireman leading the charge in the USA, Chris and John changing their company name from Fleetfoot to Reebok UK, and Stephen Rubin financing both, my focus turned to that little bit of territory remaining called 'the rest of the world'.

Thankfully, I had registered the name Reebok in as many global markets as I could back in 1960 through the patent office of Wilson Gunn & Ellis. It had been a bold decision to spend so much money on this when Jeff and I were just starting out, and it had nearly bankrupted us when the debt remained unpaid. That was the first time I'd met Derek Waller, who subsequently had the winding-up order thrown out of court, enabling us to survive that particular disaster, and Derek was now an integral part of my team, responsible for the legal foundations on which our success had been built.

I'd assumed that our brand was now protected in all the relevant territories, but there were exceptions. Japan was one. A large department store in Tokyo had a name that sounded phonetically similar to Reebok and Derek had been involved in negotiating an agreement.

Spain was another anomaly, and it was here, where our name had been 'pirated', that I would witness his tactical mastery in person. In Spain, anyone was allowed to register a name, irrespective of who owned it. It seemed bizarre, but my previous travels around the world, particularly in Tehran and South Korea, had instilled in me a sense of *anything is possible at any time*.

I arranged a meeting in Alicante for me, Derek and the two Spanish partners who had registered the Reebok brand. I later found out they had actually bought it from a professional service that specialised in registering names of brands that were showing global promise, and that Puma had also fallen foul of this bizarre legal loophole.

We sat down at a table in a private room in a restaurant to discuss ownership of the Reebok brand in Spain. It seemed logical that we, with our twenty-five-year history of first registering then trading under the name, were the rightful and exclusive proprietors, and these two were opportunistic chancers, but in Spain, it seemed, logic played no part in the legal process.

After the appropriate nods and handshakes, Derek began explaining the situation from Reebok's side. He must have talked uninterrupted for about five minutes before he paused, looked at the two blank faces opposite, and whispered to me, 'Joe, they've not understood a word. They don't speak English.'

The meeting was futile. With all the travelling for meetings in America and the UK – naturally conducted in English – it hadn't dawned on either of us that here in Spain we would need to employ the services of a translator. Obviously, it hadn't dawned on the other party either. The only thing we managed to get across was that we would return a few weeks later with someone who could do the translating.

Derek had some Polish friends whose daughter had just returned from working in Spain, and it was with her that we sat back down at the same table two weeks later, holiday rep Yvonna at the head. Perhaps it was her experience of having to deal with complaining holidaymakers every day, but Yvonna had a relaxed and easy manner that immediately placated any ill-feeling between the two parties.

The stand of the two Spaniards was that they'd agree to relinquish their claim on the name only if we agreed to give them distribution rights. The negotiations continued for hours until we reached an agreement whereby we would retain the brand and they would be appointed a ten-year distributorship with the option to extend. We arranged to meet the next morning to finalise the details.

Derek had employed his usual strategy of including at least two clauses in the agreement that he was willing to remove, and at least two others he was willing to amend. As soon as we all sat down again, he dropped his bombshell. He told them that we couldn't agree to the option to extend without Reebok having an option to buy the Spanish distribution company after ten years. Yvonna was still smiling as she relayed the information, but the Spanish contingent looked shocked. 'We need to put a purchase price for the company in the contract,' Derek announced.

There was a chorus of complaint. 'How can we put a forward value on a company we've not even started?' they asked.

'The figure is unimportant,' said Derek nonchalantly. 'We just need it to legally allow the contract to end.'

Smiles return to the Spanish faces. 'Any figure?'

'Yes.'

Yvonna, Derek and I left the room while they discussed how much they thought they could get away with asking for their yet-to-be-launched enterprise. It didn't take long for them to call us back in. They wanted to insert a figure of 20 million pesetas, the equivalent of around £10 million at the time. All eyes were on Derek. He put his fingertips together and stared straight ahead. I could see he'd gone into one of his 'Derek' moments, but the others looked at each other, uncomfortable in the silence. A smile appeared on Yvonna's face. She'd seen it before too. She and I glanced calmly around the room while the Spanish pair looked sheepishly at each other, at us, shuffled papers and waited for Derek to say something, anything.

'Okay,' he said after a minute or two. 'We can do that.' I caught a wink from him as he leaned in to sign the papers. In a few years, the Spanish were to return to us to complain that the figure was way too low, but, by then, Derek had it locked into the contract.

Yvonna did such a good job for us that we asked if she'd be our contact at Reebok Spain for twelve months. Reebok International Limited would pay her salary, while Reebok Spain would provide accommodation. Eventually, they liked Yvonna so much that they employed her permanently.

France was the only other country in the world apart from the UK and USA where we already had what could loosely be called 'distribution'. I had previously set up a deal with a young French runner called Jean-Marc Gaucher, who had called into our factory to buy a few pairs of shoes to take back to Paris to sell to his fellow athletes. We'd regularly sent Jean-Marc small shipments of Reeboks, but now he had decided he wanted to open a shop in Paris and become our distributor. I liked Jean-Marc, he reminded me of myself, eager to get on in life, with good ideas and a good heart. I agreed to set up Reebok France as 50:50 partners, using money from the sale of my mobile home – the 'European office' that Jeff and I had frivolously bought back in the 1960s.

I was to visit Jean-Marc many times as he and Reebok progressed. Each time I went to see him he had a better car, his level of success represented firstly by a small, old Peugeot, whose driver's seat fell out whenever the door was opened, and finally by a shiny Jaguar. With a little financial boost from myself, this penniless athlete had become co-owner of Reebok France and would go on to own his own brand, Repetto, with shoe shops in Paris and beyond. I was pleased to have contributed to his success.

My time on the road was paying off. Spain and France were on board, followed by Reebok Southeast Asia, which was based in Hong Kong but covered Indonesia, the Philippines and Singapore. My most used office became a laptop table pulled from the armrest of a business-class airline seat as I zigzagged constantly across the globe.

For a long time now, I'd enjoyed travelling up and down the UK or around the world on my own, or with a member of my international team. Although Jean was always invited, she preferred to stay home and be close to our now grown-up kids, Kay and David. For the past ten years I'd been away from home for at least half the time. I guess some might say I was neglecting my fatherly duties, and, in hindsight, I was merely repeating the same parental pattern that I had experienced. I was providing financially and materially, but admittedly not emotionally.

Not only had I envisioned, built and created this Reebok merry-go-round, but I had set it spinning so fast that I couldn't get off – but nor did I want to. It was an all-consuming passion that left little time for anything else, family life included. The buzz of seeing Reebok grow was the same as the adrenaline rush I'd felt as a child when winning a race. It made me feel significant, like I was achieving, succeeding, growing. If Reebok hadn't been going in the right direction, I would have felt nothing, invisible, like that boy on the running track so many years ago whose dad only acknowledged him if he won. I still needed to keep moving forward to have that sense of being alive.

CHAPTER 31

Reebok Goes Celebrity

On 18 May 1985, I reached what I'd like to think is just the halfway milestone of my life when I turned fifty. Fifty! Where. The. Hell. Did. That. Go? Life had been full and exciting, that's for sure, but having reached the midpoint I wasn't yet ready to down tools and kick back in a rocking chair, even though I'd sold the brand. I saw it as just the start of the next phase of my life.

Stephen Rubin held a 55 per cent stake and was named chairman of Reebok International Ltd. Paul Fireman retained a 45 per cent share with the titles of president and CEO of Reebok International Ltd, and I, as president of their International Division, needed to finish the job I had started all those years ago and make sure Reebok truly was a global brand.

It did us no harm that Paul in America had begun using the services of Wendell Niles Jr, an influential film producer, and radio and TV announcer. His family had been ensconced in the Hollywood celebrity clique for as long as the Foster family had been involved in making sports footwear. Wendell's dad was a legendary radio announcer and his son had inherited all of his pizazz, along with his contacts – a veritable golden Rolodex of sports and entertainment stars.

As the promotional maestro set to work, our shoes began to pop up everywhere, even on the feet of global legends. In 1985 Cybill Shepherd caused a media frenzy when she showed up on the red carpet to collect her Emmy award in bright-orange, high-top Freestyles. That same year, Mick Jagger donned Reebok trainers to leap around with David Bowie in the music video *Dancing in the Street*. The following year I was in a cinema in Manchester, jumping out of my skin along with the rest of the audience as Sigourney Weaver hunted down extra-terrestrial killers in a spaceship while wearing a pair of futuristic Reebok 'Alien Stompers' in the movie *Aliens*. Reeboks were becoming the rock stars of footwear, and sales exploded.

Our next wave of attack was to increase our standing in tennis, a market in which we already had a 20 per cent share. Through Wendell, Reebok became a major sponsor of international competitions, the most glittering of which were the World Pro-Celebrity Tennis Tournaments. These took place over three days at the beginning of July in Monte Carlo. They were incredibly glamorous events inspired by Prince Rainier in support of his late wife's charity, the Princess Grace Foundation.

With such iconic support and such a fabulous Mediterranean background, celebrities flocked to take on the pros, while CEOs from major retailers were invited to attend and take part in a secondary tournament. The tennis events were always entertaining, but also extremely competitive, with most of the celebrities playing to win, especially Roger Moore and John Forsythe. Lunch was a good time to mix and meet the tennis professionals, who included Roy Emerson, the Australian tennis legend who had won twenty-eight major titles in his illustrious career, and Indian brothers Ashok and Vijay Amritraj.

Reebok always had a VIP box overlooking the four show courts of the Monte Carlo Country Club. The adjacent box had been reserved for Frank Sinatra and, although I never saw him at one of the pro-celebrity matches, I remember one surreal moment when Robert De Niro popped his head into our box to ask if we knew where Frank was. I told him that Frank had a whole floor reserved at the Hôtel de Paris and maybe he would find him there. Everyone was staying at the Hôtel de Paris, which Wendell had reserved exclusively for all the pro, celebrity and corporate guests he had invited.

James Bond has been part of movie culture since the early 1960s and two of the great actors who made the films and its character legendary, Sean Connery and Roger Moore, appeared at one of the tennis events, providing an iconic photo opportunity for Jean as she sat between them. Sean was panicking, patting all the pockets of his 007-style tuxedo.

'I've lost my lunch tickets,' he whispered in his soft Scottish brogue as speeches were made from the garden podium in front.

'I don't think you'll have a problem getting in,' I reassured him before walking to the podium to introduce the present-ers of the tournament trophies. On stage I paused before I spoke, glancing at Joan Collins and Prince Rainier who stood either side of me, and a sea of celebrity faces looked up from the audience. I could make out Chuck Norris, Linda Evans,

Michael Caine and Stephanie Powers, but there were many, many more. *Wow!* I thought. *Just, wow!*

That evening we held a dinner at the Salle des Etoiles, a magnificent venue with a roof that could be opened on warm, dry nights. The dinner was attended by all the players and stars, including, on this occasion, Frank Sinatra. John Forsythe (who played Blake Carrington in the American TV series *Dynasty*) approached my table, hand outstretched, and said, 'Hello, Joe, nice to see you again.'

I was stunned. 'We've only met once, John,' I said. 'How did you remember my name?'

'That's my job,' he replied.

Apart from the glamorous brand association with the Monte Carlo pro-celebrity events, tennis would also provide success with numerous high-profile wins by Reebok-sponsored players, including Michael Chang and Arantxa Sánchez Vicario, who both went on to become French Open champions. Michael was only seventeen years and three months at the time. Not forgetting the long, arduous hours of practice he must have put in, he was a sporting genius, born with an incredible, innate set of skills that every international tennis champion must possess – exceptional hand–eye co-ordination, extreme athleticism and an unswerving will to win. I was thankful that at least I had one out of the three.

Flushed with our success in tennis, we were then introduced to the exclusive world of polo in the UK. Through Major Ronald Ferguson we sponsored events at the Royal Berkshire Polo Club and a special event at Windsor Great Park, when I was presented with a crystal bowl by Prince Charles.

Was this all real? Was I really hobnobbing with royalty in the polo clique, my company providing shoes for Princess

Diana, the Duchess of York, and their children? Shaking my head in disbelief became a regular habit, until eventually rubbing shoulders with the rich and famous became almost the norm.

Reebok was now a brand that was recognised around the world, but it saddened me that not many people in Bolton were aware of its local origins. Very few made the connection between Reebok, J. W. Foster & Sons and my Grandad Joe, creator of both the spiked running shoe and the trainer. I felt it was my duty to do something about that, to honour the previous generations of my family who had laid the foundation stones from which we had now soared.

Fortunately, an opportunity came up to help make that connection. The office was still part of the factory, but the International Division (marketing) now needed to be separate from production. We had appointed a new manager at the Bury mill and consequently I had become less involved with the manufacturing side of things. I now had over twenty overseas distributors to manage and needed to find a separate office for this monumental task. I was adamant that it would be in my hometown of Bolton. Initially we'd located ourselves in Bury so as not to compete locally with Dad and Foster's, but now, with both of them long gone, it was time to come home. It felt the right thing to do and would help local people realise the link with Foster's.

Bolton council made numerous old buildings available, but I was reluctant to take on a refurbishment. I wanted Reebok to be in premises that we could be proud of, not shared, not refurbed, not hidden away. This was my chance to cement Reebok in Bolton's industrial history. Eventually, they offered me a site on Institute Street, close to the town centre. After agreeing on plans, construction began on the Reebok International Division's new headquarters.

Some twenty-nine years after starting the journey with Jeff in a disused brewery in Bury, I stood on the pavement and watched the cranes swing over our new International Division office in my hometown. I wondered what Jeff would have thought of our achievement. He probably would have patted me on my back and said something like, 'I always knew we'd do it, Joe,' even though many times he'd voiced his doubts and worries. I also tried to imagine the faces of Dad, Grandad Joe and Grandma Maria. I'm sure they would have been proud. Grandad Joe would have been honoured that all his initial work had come to this, and Grandma Maria would have made sure I was warm enough. And Dad? I'm going to say he would have been proud, even though he probably wouldn't have voiced it.

CHAPTER 32

A Clash of Cultures

While I'd had my focus firmly fixed on the upbringing of my oldest child, Reebok, I had also become a grandad to my daughter's two children. Kay had married, divorced and married again, having one child with each husband. Paul was born in 1981, followed by Mark in 1986. Life was blissful, on all fronts – family, business and social. How could you not be happy when you had a successful business, a growing family, and your social circle included some of the biggest stars on the planet? Not bad for a boy from the back streets of Bolton!

While business and my direct family had been kept fully apart for the past twenty-five years, mostly through my own choice, Jean had now asked if she could come with me on an overseas trip, largely because some close friends had moved to New Zealand and she would have a chance to catch up with them.

Alec was a printer who had produced all of Mercury's first stationery, but after his business failed he accepted a printing job in Gisborne, New Zealand. While I stopped off in

Australia to finalise a distribution deal, Jean travelled on to New Zealand to spend a few days with Alec and his wife before I joined them.

From New Zealand, Jean and I headed to the launch of Reebok Japan. I'd been to Tokyo several times since my first round-the-world trip and I'd met with many large Japanese companies while trying to choose a distributor, but it wasn't that easy. There was a process to follow, a way of importing goods that was unique to the country.

A trading house had to be used to buy and finance products, handle all the paperwork, customs obligations and foreign exchange rates. They would then sell on to a distributor, who in turn would market and sell to the retail shops.

For us, it added an extra layer of costs that would make our shoes more expensive in Japan than Tiger, now called Asics. We argued that, after appointing a distributor, orders should be placed directly with us. As in most countries, a clearing agent would then be contracted to clear the goods through customs. But our battle to negotiate a way around the trading house process came to nothing, and eventually we appointed a combination of Marubeni as the trading house and Sumitomo as the distributor, both to operate together as Reebok Japan.

In Tokyo, the executives at Reebok Japan wined and dined Jean, treating her like royalty and showing her the sights of the city, while I spent four hours in a tedious meeting. By the time we were seated as special guests at dinner that night, my wife was more than impressed with the hospitality. And then it all went south.

Jean and I sat as guests of honour at a table right next to a low stage. As the main course was served, the house lights dimmed and the headline show began. I watched Jean's eyes open wider and wider, her cheeks glowing a darker shade of scarlet with every second. Reebok Japan had booked four English strippers, and they were currently flaunting their flesh directly at the guests of honour as though it was a private floor show.

I caught sight of our hosts, who'd failed to spot the horror on Jean's face. Instead, they were beaming as they sought my approval of the 'English' entertainment. When the show finished, Jean glowered in my direction, her high spirits sunk without trace. To make matters worse, the four smiling strippers then joined us at our table, 'dressed' but only slightly less naked. They had obviously been told to give me, as the guest of honour, the most attention, and Jean's disgust grew in direct proportion to their professional flirtatiousness.

The girls eventually left. Jean turned to me and hissed, 'I want to leave, NOW!'

I made the excuse that my wife was feeling tired, thanked our guests for an enjoyable evening, and we took a limousine back to our hotel in silence. Once in our suite, Jean exploded.

'This is obviously what you do all the time when you're supposedly *working* away.'

What could I say? It was a different country, a different culture. They didn't understand us as much as we didn't understand them. It was one of many cultural clashes that I had come across on my travels, but it was unfortunate that this one involved Jean. Our hosts thought it would be a special treat for me because they were English girls. It would have been if Jean hadn't been there. But we were in their domain and therefore Jean should have respected their hospitality and been more open-minded about it, even if it didn't fit in with her way of thinking. On my next trips, I travelled without her – a mutual choice.

It wasn't just socially that the Japanese and British cultures were disparate. As well as the trading house system, there was a difference in the actual way of running a business, as we would later find out when Reebok Japan bought shares in a golf course. This made Reebok International Ltd, as 25 per cent shareholders, part-owners of the same. It seemed bizarre, but our Japanese distributors saw this as a perfectly logical way to expand our brand in the country. Because of this, we also quickly found out that there was more profit in owning a golf course than there was in selling shoes!

The European way was easier to understand, and Italy was my next destination. I flew to Milan to meet with Umberto Columbo, CEO of the Italian shoe brand Divarese, part of the Benetton Group and located in the town of Varese some 35 miles north. Umberto obviously knew the shoe industry and Benetton knew all there is to know about distribution, which is why they were top of our list of potential distributors.

That evening, Umberto drove me through stunning countryside to the top of the Sacred Mountain in the hamlet of Santa Maria del Monte. We sat on the terrace of a small restaurant, drinking Italian wine and soaking up the gorgeous views over the red rooftops of the village as the sun sank beyond the fields and meadows of Lombardy and Piedmont, and the last sparkles of Lake Varese fizzled out. It was a perfect setting to count my blessings. All through my travels, I'd tried to remember to make time to pause and appreciate, to live in the moment. It was definitely one of those times, and there were more to come just around the corner.

Having been through Umberto's business proposal with

Derek Waller, we signed the paperwork that permitted him to set up Reebok Italy, the latest addition to the international group. Initially, it would operate out of the Divarese factory before moving to its own office and warehouse.

I had a travelling companion on this visit, Angel Martinez, the star man behind our aerobics coup, since promoted to vice-president of marketing for Reebok International Ltd. Gianfranco Terrutzi, head of sales for the newly created Reebok Italy, had invited us to the Italian Formula One Grand Prix as guests of the Benetton racing team. It was an opportunity we weren't going to miss. Neither of us was what you would call a 'petrolhead', but what male in his right mind would turn down an invitation like that?

Gianfranco had joined Reebok from Adidas. His overexuberant manner ensured he was remembered by everyone he met and talked about by those he didn't. Consequently, he knew everyone. He arranged a tour of the pits for me and Angel, had us driven around the track in the steward's car and made sure I got to wave the chequered flag to signal that the Friday practice session had ended. It was another boyhood dream come true.

The international group was expanding rapidly. At that time, we were taking on at least one new distributor every quarter and Germany was next on my hit list. I wanted to launch Reebok Germany in the lion's den. We knew there was no space for Reebok running shoes in the sports stores throughout Germany, as Adidas and Puma were so strong, but aerobics was different.

The CEO of Intersport Germany had been well aware of this new fitness craze in America. He was desperate for a piece of the action and wanted us involved in his stores.

Keen for me to see his operation, he picked me up from the airport in his powerful Mercedes and we drove to Heidelberg, home of the Student Prince. We made the trip in good time on the autobahn. You tend to when you're travelling at 200 kilometres per hour. It was a quick visit in several ways, but enough to secure an exceptionally good order for our Freestyle shoes.

But now we needed to go bigger. I made several visits, interviewing prospective candidates for the position of CEO of what would become Reebok Germany. We'd already planned a big launch at the 1986 September ISPO sports goods exhibition in Munich, complete with Broadway-style music and dance, so the pressure was on to find someone to fill the position. I decided that man would be Richard Litzel, who, despite his stiff, formal manner on first impressions, turned out to be a very warm and kind character. With the appointment ticked off my list, there were now only ninety-nine other things I needed to do before the launch.

Just days before the ISPO, while Derek Waller was crossing the t's and dotting the i's of all the paperwork needed for setting up a German company, I heard that Richard would not be taking up the role of *Geschäftsführer* after all.

'What are we going to do?' I asked Derek.

'There's only one thing for it,' he replied. 'You're going to have to be the CEO.'

And that's how I came to be bestowed with the grand title of *Geschäftsführer* of Reebok Deutschland GmbH along with all the accompanying responsibilities. Great! Just what I needed: more work.

The ISPO was a big success, or at least I was told it was. I was in hiding, keeping a low profile after Derek warned me that Puma's lawyers were looking for me. They saw Reebok's use of lateral striping as an infringement of their own 'Formstripe'. Trying to stay low-key wasn't easy seeing as I was now the CEO and we wanted as much publicity and exposure as possible. However, I kept away from the Broadway show, limited my time on the Reebok stand, and managed to avoid being hunted down by Puma's legal team for the time being.

There was no way I could carry on as *Geschäftsführer* of Reebok Deutschland while also being president of the International Division, so, on my return to the UK, Derek and I met up to figure out how I could free myself from the role. As we batted ideas back and forth, the phone rang. It was Richard Litzel. We hadn't heard a thing from him since he backed out. He wanted to explain why he'd not taken up the position. When we'd approached him he was the *Geschäftsführer* of Wilson, the tennis racket company. He hadn't expected the Reebok appointment to take so long, which meant that he would be leaving Wilson just before the ISPO exhibition. His conscience hadn't allowed him to do that, and he'd been willing to pass on the opportunity rather than let Wilson down. I told him I admired his ethics but asked if he would be willing to come on board now. Thankfully, he said he would, thus lifting one responsibility from my shoulders.

At the 1987 ISPO, with Richard as Reebok Germany's CEO, the US marketing team organised a special-invitation show at a private venue. Wendell had arranged for Hollywood film star Jane Seymour to be flown in to address the German sports retailers. Jane had started as a dancer, moved into acting (perhaps most memorably as a Bond girl in *Live and Let Die*), and was now one of the many A-list actresses who wore Reeboks. Again, it was a massive success. We were now fully fit and ready to go head-to-head with Adidas and Puma on their own turf, but in aerobics, not in running.

In many of the smaller countries, the arrangements weren't quite as clear-cut as in Germany. Some of the distributors carried other lines as well as Reebok. Switzerland was one such territory, and it was here I was to meet our new man, Ruedi Sigg. Ruedi had fingers in a wide variety of pies. He held Swiss distribution rights for Nintendo games and Matchbox model cars, as well as owning a chain of toy shops and a publishing business.

Ruedi had a remarkably colourful history, having spent some time in the USA where he learned to fly. His other accomplishments included becoming a downhill ski champion, a rally driver and a 100-metre sprinter. He was a prime example of someone squeezing 100 per cent out of his allotted time on the planet.

When I visited him in Basel, he decided to drive me to the top of a steep hill to show me the point where Switzerland, Germany and France meet. It was a dark winter evening and there was a foot of snow on the ground, but that didn't stop Ruedi racing off rally-style, wheels spinning and snow spraying behind us. I could only see a thick blanket of white in front but Ruedi assured me we were still on the road, more or less. I clung to my seat in terror as we sped through a forest, narrowly missing trees, then came to a skidding halt in a clearing at the top of the hill. Here lay the next challenge. With my legs already wobbling, I clambered behind Ruedi up an icy wooden tower. It felt more like an endurance course than a sightseeing trip, but it was certainly memorable and forged a bond of friendship that remains today.

In the summer of 1987, I travelled to Poland, a country still trying to assert itself in the face of Soviet influence in communist Eastern Europe. Derek Waller had instigated the journey. He had Polish friends, including Yvonna, our translator in Spain, and, through him, a businessman had asked if we would consider manufacturing in Poland, which at that time would have been the only way to sell Reeboks in the country.

I took a flight to Warsaw with a colleague, checked into the Hilton hotel and met with Derek's contact. We discussed the possibility of production, but, apart from football, there seemed to be very little appetite for sports footwear in Poland. The total lack of any arrangements for me to meet with sportswear manufacturers made this glaringly apparent. It was a disappointing conclusion, but a memorable trip for several other reasons, one of which was the sight of cars queuing, up to twenty-deep, to get petrol in the centre of the city. Another was the amazement of being charged just a couple of US dollars for lunch-for-two in the Hilton.

However, the most unforgettable, and also haziest, memory I had of that Poland trip was of the afternoon on the day of my departure. We had been invited to meet the sports minister, who presented us with some commemorative coins and keyrings before inviting us to join him for a drink.

We moved into a small room that had lounge chairs around a table. On the table was a huge bowl of fresh strawberries, plus four vodka glasses. After inviting his female assistant to join us, I lost count of the number of toasts we made, clinking glasses of 70 per-cent-proof slivovic, our cheeks bulging with strawberries. I just about retained enough sense to check my watch and remind our jolly host that we had a flight to Manchester to catch, which was due to leave shortly. He swatted away my concern and filled the glasses one more time. 'To good friends and safe travels,' he slurred, before asking his assistant to call for a limousine.

By this time it was getting seriously close to our take-off time. Despite the alcohol taking the edge off my anxiety, I knew there was no way we would navigate check-in and passport control in time. I needn't have worried. Instead of dropping us at the airport terminal, the limousine drove straight to the steps of the waiting BA flight, no check-in, no immigration control. A stewardess at the top of the stairs hid her frustration behind a well-practised smile and poured us into two seats on the first row, where my colleague and I slept like babies until the plane touched down in Manchester. I've managed to avoid slivovic ever since.

CHAPTER 33

A Rollercoaster Ride

Reebok International Division was now a significant group and I had moved on from adding more countries to managing them and their individual needs. There was a growing demand from them for apparel. Branded clothes provided public exposure, much more so than shoes. As we didn't have an apparel division at the time, each country was allowed to produce a small amount of their own, as long as it was approved by the international HQ in the UK, as per my previous arrangement with Carter Pocock.

We encouraged the distributors to work together on apparel, in many cases using the same manufacturer. Mostly, the apparel was kept simple, just tracksuits, athletic vests and shorts and t-shirts. The odd one out again was Spain. In the early days, their business came mainly from tourists in the coastal regions, so they'd decided to produce a line of swimwear. Not exactly what we had in mind, or what was 'officially' allowed, but they argued their case well and we were receiving a nice royalty from it, so we let them continue.

Paul, however, wanted global uniformity in the Reebok apparel range. His vision was that wherever you went in the world you should see the same product. There was one line across the whole of America, so there should be just one line throughout the world, he reasoned. Perhaps this blinkered thinking was down to his fear of flying – he hadn't travelled much so hadn't experienced many different cultures beyond the US. I argued that it was a counterproductive stance. If you were in Norway, for example, you'd want warm clothes. If you were in southern Europe, you'd want lightweight, cotton garments. In America, an XL-size t-shirt would be like a dress if worn by someone in Japan. It was about understanding different markets, something that had become a specialist subject of mine. But Paul's intransigence ruled and he set up an apparel division that offered a generic global range without consulting my International Division and overseas network.

The day came when all distributors were invited to view the new clothes at the Boston headquarters. Our international group were excited to see what clothes they could order for their territories as the Apparel USA team introduced the range. A respectful silence descended on the room as Paul Fireman stepped onto the stage. He thanked everybody for their attendance and invited them to place their orders.

A short while later, Paul's apparel team had surrounded him, concerned about the lack of interest expressed. Paul climbed onto the stage again and called for attention. 'You have to place your stock orders now. This is the global product range for next season. You'll not be allowed to buy apparel from any other source from now on, and we have to place your orders with the factories this week.'

There was a mass shaking of heads from the international distributors. They were confused and came to me for clarification. I told them not to panic, to place their orders now for some of the global products on display if they wanted some, but added that if they weren't sure, not to buy anything for now.

Paul was concerned by the scant orders that had been placed. I reminded him of my warning that without bringing the international network into the early stages of design, the whole system wouldn't work. Reluctantly, he agreed to let me handle the situation. I told the distributors not to worry, to just concentrate on footwear for now, and to trust in me to find a solution.

The first thing I did was to appoint an international apparel manager who would be based in Boston and work alongside Apparel USA to establish some global co-operation. We set up a small team in Boston to co-ordinate footwear, apparel and marketing within the USA, while I also created a team in Bolton to manage other overseas regions, allowing me to work on strategy and promotions.

While in America, my life was turned upside down in one phone call. I was in Paul's office with Derek Waller. Paul was showing us the new Pac-Man arcade game he'd installed in his office 'to help him relax'. Derek and I raised our eyebrows and exchanged glances. The phone rang, sparing us from making comment. Paul picked it up. His demeanour suddenly changed from playful to deadly serious. 'It's Jean,' he mouthed as he passed the phone to me.

Jean was sobbing down the line, barely able to talk. I managed to pick out the two words that said it all: 'Kay . . . leukaemia . . .'

I lowered the handset to the cradle, replacing it carefully as if not wanting to break the calm. Derek and Paul stared.

'It's Kay. My daughter. She's got leukaemia.'

Kay was a bright, bubbly girl with an unrivalled joie de vivre. She loved her hairdressing job, adored her two boys, and her zest for life was infectious. How could it be that she was now staring death in the face at the age of twenty-seven?

Paul immediately picked up the phone and instructed his secretary to book me on the next return flight to the UK.

It was the first time I'd flown on Concorde, the world's fastest jet aeroplane at the time, but the three-and-a-half-hour flight still seemed endless. My stomach was knotted, my head all over the place. Why Kay? What about her boys, Paul and Mark? They were still so young, just six and one.

Over the next twelve months, Kay had to undergo an agonising series of chemotherapy treatments followed by a bone-marrow transplant. Most of that time was spent in hospital, often weeks on end in an isolation ward. I'd delegated to other colleagues as many of my trips overseas as I could, but there remained some prearranged business meetings abroad that only I could attend to, despite my reluctance to leave Kay.

During the time I was in the country, I would finish work and drive straight to the Christie Hospital in Manchester every day to spend time with her in the evening.

Her boys moved in with me and Jean, and while we were both able to see Kay many times, children under ten were prohibited from visiting. Trying to explain to two tear-stained faces why they couldn't see their mum was heartbreaking. All we could do was try to keep them as happy and reassured as we could.

Kay was able to leave hospital only on a handful of

occasions, when her blood cell count was stable enough and she wasn't sick from the numerous rounds of chemotherapy. One of those times was to attend the opening of our new International Division office in Bolton on a frosty morning in December 1987.

I stood on the stone steps of the entrance where six months previously, with the help of Paul Fireman, I had buried a stainless steel, hermetically sealed time capsule (filled with a pair of Reebok shoes, plus paperwork relative to the time) and addressed a huge crowd consisting of our factory workers, my family, several journalists, members of the public and a handful of local dignitaries.

Now, we had added a touch of Hollywood to the proceedings. Charlton Heston was working in the UK at Pinewood Studios at the time and was top of the list to appear at the opening ceremony. Other celebrities included Veronica Hamel, star of the hit TV series *Hill Street Blues*, our actor/ producer friend John Forsythe, Ashok Amritraj from the pro tennis circuit, and Major Ronald Ferguson (father of the Duchess of York) from the polo world.

To the delight of Kay, Wendell had also persuaded 'He-Man' Dolph Lundgren to attend our celebrations, and my biggest thrill was watching him and Kay laughing and chatting together.

I talked about the rise of Reebok to number one in the world, and about how proud I was, not just for me, but for the town of Bolton too. At this point, Charlton Heston was due to unveil a wall plaque, but he was late. I didn't want to lose the media, so asked Mum to step up and pull the curtain drawstring instead. She was thrilled to oblige, then even more so when Charlton arrived and gave her a big hug before we ran through the procedure once again for the photographers, this time with him doing the unveiling in his typically smooth fashion.

To follow the opening ceremony, we had arranged for Manchester's Hallé Orchestra to perform at Bolton Town Hall. Apart from all our workers, we had also invited all the international distributors and over 200 schoolchildren. It was a phenomenal event, straight from the showbiz playbook thanks to Wendell.

As I stood in the wings taking in the spectacle, I wondered what my dad would have made of it all. Not one for making a scene, he probably would have thought there was no need for all that fuss, that it was a waste of money. He liked to keep things plain and simple, but Reebok had gone way past that point a long, long time ago.

CHAPTER 34

Death, and a Rebirth

As Kay continued her battle against leukaemia, I visited Monte Carlo with Wendell Niles to discuss that year's pro-celeb tennis tournament with Prince Rainier at his palace. We were met at a guarded side door and led through a warren of carpeted corridors to a grand reception area where the prince arrived escorted by a footman. I couldn't help but be a little impressed as Wendell greeted him like an old friend. He later told me that he was, having known Princess Grace thanks to his Hollywood connections.

As we sipped on flutes of champagne, the prince asked a lot of questions about Reebok, then Wendell mentioned Kay and her struggle with leukaemia. Prince Rainier was visibly saddened. He left the room, returned with a signed book about Monte Carlo which he insisted I gave to my daughter and said he hoped to see her at the next tennis tournament. Hope was all I had too.

Although I didn't want to accept it, in my heart there was a realisation that Kay wasn't going to make it. Her condition hadn't improved. If anything, she was getting worse, the treatments seemingly having little effect other than to wipe her out for the subsequent weeks.

She did have spells of reasonable health, however, and, in the summer of 1988, Kay was able to leave the hospital on two more occasions. The first was to attend a charity event in June that Reebok had organised (again with the help of Wendell). 'Bolton's Night of Stars' raised a staggering £11,500 towards funding to build a hospice in the town, and my Hollywood acquaintances John Forsythe and Dolph Lundgren both made an appearance.

The following month, Kay was strong enough to come with me and Jean to Monte Carlo for the pro-celebrity tennis tournaments we were sponsoring. We booked a suite in the Hotel de Paris and took her youngest son, Mark, along with a babysitter, while Mark's brother, Paul, stayed with his father.

As ever, it was a glittering affair, icons of Hollywood mingling with all-time tennis greats and corporate sponsors such as us. At a special dinner one night, Roger Moore came up to our table and presented Kay with a gold necklace that Wendell had bought her. Jean, Kay and I were all speechless, Kay because 'James Bond' had just approached them, and Jean and I because it was an incredibly thoughtful and generous gesture from Wendell.

By the time we returned to the UK in early summer, Kay was exhausted and admitted back into hospital. I knew that time was running out, but whenever it seemed her time had come, she would bounce back to relatively good health.

The twentieth of October 1988 was the last day that my heart would ever be whole. I was at a Reebok event in the

USA when the news came through. Kay had died suddenly. There was no gradual or even rapid decline. Had I known she was at death's door, obviously I wouldn't have travelled. She had just slipped away.

My memories of who told me, where I was, how I reacted, are still hazy. I only remember concerned eyes, the bareness of the walls, sudden claustrophobia. I needed to get out of the office, to do something, as if, in being active, I would find a solution and the harsh reality of what I'd just heard would no longer be true.

Although I had been in this building, this office, on this side of the pine-wood desk looking at the back of framed family photos so many times, it suddenly felt unrecognisable. I felt tiny, cold, vulnerable, like a child lost in a sea of strangers, desperately trying to find familiarity, both aesthetic and emotional. I needed warmth, comfort. I needed to be a million miles from the sterility of the corporate world. I needed to be back in my bedroom, pressed against my mum, her arms around me and my brother, listening to Dad's calm voice as we watched the world burn together.

I will never forget the journey home. Fate had provided much good fortune and many opportunities throughout my life, just at the right time. But that day I learned that fate could be cruel too. Buckled into my seat on that journey to my dead daughter, the cycle of shock-denial-yearning had plenty of chance to replay over and over during the 3,000-mile flight, my mind refusing to settle, to believe. It was a violation of the natural order, parents weren't supposed to outlive their children, it wasn't right.

Everything that I recognised felt like a lie. The plastic overhead panels above the seats, the smiles of the cabin crew, the floor of clouds through the plane's window. I'd seen them all before, accepted them as part of my journey, expected them next time, remembered them from last time. But now they felt different, as though they were just props on a movie set, all part of this great conspiracy to trick me into thinking that my daughter had died. They were all culpable. If they all went away, maybe so would the lie.

I closed my eyes. I trusted nothing, no one, pushing back in my seat when drinks and meals were offered. I thought maybe alcohol would cushion my brittle state of mind, but Johnnie Walker, my comforting companion who had smoothed the way in so many stressful social encounters, had deserted me too. Just another fake friend in my world of disbelief.

'Devastated' is an often overused word. Its arbitrary employment in trite situations has rendered it ineffectual as a way of describing the pain of paternal bereavement. The complete and abject desolation of a father losing his daughter comes not just from the torment of powerlessness, but also from the knowledge that you would never again see your child's infectious smile across the room, nor be the recipient of her admonishing expressions during your moments of teasing and mischief. And no more would you feel that swell of emotion from sensing her maternal pride as she watched her boys play football or sit on their grandad's knee as he made them smile with his silly stories.

But most of all it's the feeling of parental bankruptcy. No matter from which school of parenting you come, or how old your children are, a father's principal duty to his daughter is to protect. I was supposed to be the guardian of her path to the future, the sentinel who would help keep harm at arm's length, enable opportunity to shine through, and strike down despair so that happiness could prosper. And in this, I had failed.

Jean and I dealt with Kay's death in different ways, as is often the case with a bereaved couple. While her emotions were outward, for all to see, mine were kept tightly bound inside, pressurised to the point of exploding. Like my dad, and his before, I mirrored their belief that, when the going gets tough, the tough bottle it up; that emotions are to be dealt with privately, not shared.

Jean grew angry at my apparent apathy. She wanted equality in the hurt. She couldn't understand why I wasn't *feeling* the same frustration, rage, guilt, blame. Insults were thrown, anger released. Words became weapons, brandished to wound. Accusations flew about my life's priorities – and some of the mud stuck. Why did I put Reebok before family? *Had I*? I began to question my choices.

My whole life had been about momentum, progress, growth and success. Yes, maybe I can say it was more about my own sense of achievement, and, initially, that was my driving force. But, once that vacuum of significance in my life had been filled, accomplishment was more the means by which I could provide for my family. It was the only way I knew.

Perhaps the hairline cracks in our relationship had already formed, but Kay's death widened the fissures. In years to come, the chinks would join together and form an irreparable chasm.

I had lost a daughter, but Jean had lost her best friend. She was also to lose the closeness of her grandchildren. Paul and Mark were separated and went to live with their respective fathers.

I had endured the ultimate tragedy and, because of it, my

very being had been stripped to the core, raw, exposed. I'd worked hard building Reebok, but now I was going to have to work even harder to rebuild myself.

CHAPTER 35

A Founder's Role

The changes were bound to come as Reebok grew and new people were brought into the US operation. Paul had stepped back and the new board wanted more control of the international business. Consequently, my role in acquiring new distributors across the globe was becoming less significant by the day. At the start of 1989 it was suggested by the board that I departed as president to take on a 'founder's' role, as a kind of Reebok ambassador. 'Joe, you're getting on a bit now, we want to ease your lifestyle.'

The 'suggestion' was inevitable. Reebok was turning over $3 billion a year. It was a big company and they didn't want to just look after America and leave me to manage the rest of the world. They were wanting to control everything by putting their own man in position, someone who they could tell what to do instead of letting me do what I wanted without consulting them. The board saw me, as the founder, as being too independent and free to make decisions that hadn't come from inside their executive boardroom.

From my side, the loss of Kay had altered my perspective on life. When Kay was taken, so too was part of my passion, my spirit, my drive. I was ready for a change, and, as with so many things in the telling of my story, the timing of their 'suggestion' was perfect.

I didn't want to fight any more; I didn't need to. Rather than deal with the pressures of business, of doing deals, managing offices and people, my new role as an ambassador would enable me to enjoy the fruits of previous labour without needing to sell myself and/or the business to others. I didn't need to be thinking ahead, drawing battle plans, striving and reaching. After a lifetime of aspiration, I'd already achieved my dream, and now it was time to live in the present, to appreciate what I had.

That didn't mean there would be no travelling. I'd lost count of the number of times I'd flown at 35,000 feet on the way to business appointments in exotic and not-so-exotic destinations. I'd met so many new people, made dozens of new friends. In my new founder and ambassador role, I would still go to the European ISPO trade shows, and I was still invited to the international meetings and new product launches, but my involvement in decision-making at Reebok was finally at an end.

Over the next year as an ambassador, there were major transformations within the business. Reebok had launched an innovative basketball shoe that allowed adjustable, custom cushioning thanks to individual chambers that inflated with a button pump. Like so many of our shoes, the 'Pump' was almost inevitably a sell-out hit, both on the court and the street.

Later, following Dee Brown's infamous 'blind' basketball

dunk in the 1991 NBA Slam Dunk Contest, when he stopped mid-court to pump up his high-tops, the shoes would become one of those rare footwear icons, like Doc Martens or Jordans. Reebok would enter the hall of fame with Pumps ninety-one years after my grandad had instilled near-legendary status in his spiked pumps.

Another event that was perhaps more pleasing to me as it helped marry the company with its birthplace was the buzz that Reebok would soon become the official shirt sponsors of Bolton Wanderers Football Club, eighty-five years after Grandad had initiated sports sponsorship by paying elite athletes to wear Foster's shoes. It would be the ultimate honour for what had started as a local sports company.

It seemed that many of the seeds that Grandad Joe had planted at the turn of the century were now coming to fruition and I was even more intent on promoting the company's heritage. I still wanted to continue my mission to let the world know how and where this sportswear Goliath had built its foundations.

On 31 December 1989, a year into my role as ambassador, I decided to completely step back from Reebok for good. As throughout my life, it was all about the timing. If Kay's death had taught me anything, it was that spending time with people you cared for – and who cared for you – was truly the most important thing. If we hadn't lost Kay, maybe I would have stayed involved a little longer, but I was ready to step away. More than being ready, I needed to. In the current circumstances, there was no more contribution I could make to the company's progress.

I had given it my all for the past thirty-five years – eating, sleeping and breathing Foster, Mercury and Reebok – and I couldn't help but wonder what life would be like now that I was leaving it all behind.

I'd convinced myself that it would be a pleasure not having to pack a bag every month, not having to step off a plane in a new destination and find my way around as a stranger, however much I'd enjoyed that journeying in the past. But the reality of it all was different. My high-flying lifestyle, even as an ambassador, was like a drug, difficult to come off.

For the first few months, I was at a bit of a loss as to what to do. From the moment I awoke I was constantly anxious, thinking I was supposed to be doing something, going some-where, speaking on the phone to someone. It took a long while to adapt to the change, to know that when I woke up, I had no commitments and that doing *nothing* but mowing the lawn that day was okay.

But it had definitely been the right time to pull away. Reebok had changed. In my eyes, since going public in 1985, it had become a numbers company, and I was not a numbers man. Decisions were now based on reports from accountants and lawyers, the bottom line paramount, the personality absent. It *had* to be, now that shareholders needed to be appeased. But inevitably this had hammered a nail in the coffin of entrepreneurship, which was the lifeblood of business passion.

During my time, marketing had always been the most important part of the business, making sure that the company was delivering the product that the athlete wanted, and then making sure others wanted it too. This was only possible if you had your eye on the ball by being out there, talking to the sportsmen and women. If you could convince the players that you had exactly the right product, the rest would follow. You just had to ensure you were paying the right people to be part of your team.

I was fifty-five years old, healthy, fit but unfulfilled. I was still feeling the pain of losing my daughter and I needed to move on for my sanity. I'd only ever been good at two things in life – badminton and business – and I was far too old for the former. It was a new business challenge I needed to rediscover my entrepreneurial spark – 'use it or lose it', my Grandma Maria always used to say about the brain.

The early 1990s was a period of historic change. The Berlin Wall had come down, the Hubble Space Telescope had gone up, and Nelson Mandela had regained his freedom, to an extent.

Of all the places where I had established a Reebok network, South Africa was by far the most sensitive, and it was here that I was asked to go for one last business trip before I left.

Since the early 1970s, I had been supplying small volume to Stephen Stone of Jokari in Cape Town. Paul Fireman had found out, and he wasn't happy.

'Joe, what the hell are we doing in South Africa?'

'We've had a small distributor there for years,' I explained.

'Well, it's a problem. The USA has a boycott on South Africa. We can't be seen to be ignoring it!'

'It might go under the radar,' I offered.

'We're called Reebok, for God's sake!' He was shouting down the phone now. 'Our company has a South African name. That's bad enough without doing business with the goddamn country!'

'But . . .'

'We need to stop supplying.'

I argued that if Reebok stopped the supply, the demand would still be satisfied through trans-shipment and we would lose control. I was keenly aware that 'underground' illegal shipping was already going on in countries where Reebok hadn't yet appointed a distributor. Opportunists who saw a major brand in a region without official representation had popped up like Whac-A-Mole. In previous years I'd tried to knock them back down, but it had been futile.

I suggested to Paul several action points. Firstly, that he needed to better publicise the company's association with black activists who were wearing Reeboks at the time; secondly, to make it known he supplied South Africa simply to control the brand; and, thirdly, to emphasise the fact that Reebok had arranged to pay all royalties from sales to the Save the Children charity. The company had already presented the charity with a cheque for £20,000 to help with their provision of legal aid to alleged 'young offenders' who had been prosecuted by John Vorster's governing National Party.

But it wasn't to be. Paul conferred with his legal advisers who told him that it was too difficult to get the message across, and it was much easier and safer to simply say that Reebok didn't supply South Africa.

I told Stephen Stone that Paul would no longer be able to supply him with Reebok products. He was stunned and pointed out that we had a distribution agreement. He stood to lose a lot of money if we cut off his supply.

He demanded a meeting with Paul, but all that was subsequently offered was that he would be Reebok's 'distributor of choice' when the apartheid problem had been resolved. A month after that meeting I was subpoenaed by the South

African High Court to appear as a witness in a case brought by Stephen Stone against Reebok.

The day before the court case, I wandered into a local mall and spotted a photograph of Nelson Mandela pointing to Vorster on the cover of a book. It was captioned: *I want your job*. Mandela had been freed from prison but was under house arrest and resistance to a change in the apartheid system was still strong, so I was surprised to see a book for sale that so blatantly challenged the existing political situation. It made me think that change was perhaps near, and would not be as violent as we were led to believe in the UK.

In court, the Reebok legal team was on one side of the room and Stephen Stone's was on the other. I was on Stephen's side, but only to give my version of events. The case was over quickly and I'm sad to say that Stephen lost. He was a good man and, fortunately for him, financial ruin was avoided when he managed eventually to pick up the distributorship of Nike.

It felt like a defeat for one of my territories, and an undeserved one at that, but just like Reebok had let go of me, I had to let go of South Africa. I no longer had the authority to influence Stephen's case that I would have had were I still part of the inner circle.

Even though I am, and always will be, the founder of Reebok, there were moments after I left when I experienced the pain of feeling like an outsider. It was only my new business aspirations in property management and development that kept my spirits lifted during those occasions.

Although I no longer had an active role, as the founder, I still retained an office in the International Division headquarters in Bolton. One day after I'd stepped away, I returned to the office and sat at my desk. I still hadn't got round to clearing out my personal possessions. I didn't see the need as no one else was using my particular space. Or at least that was the reason I liked to think. In reality, it was possibly a fear that, if I packed it all away, the memories would fade.

On my desk a headline – 'Reebok brings Hollywood to Bolton' – blared from an edition of the *Bolton Evening News* printed after the star-studded opening of the headquarters. *If that hadn't sealed our history with the town, nothing would*, I thought.

I looked up at the family photos still lining the wall then gazed out of the office window at Bolton Parish Church, the playground of my youth. I pictured myself standing in my Scout uniform laughing with Brian and other members of my troop until Skip, our leader, called us to attention. I replayed the dance-hall days when nothing was anywhere near as important as chasing girls. I recalled the days of flying around the badminton courts with teenage speed and agility. They were great days, but I was lucky – so were many others.

Now here I was, sat in a multi-million-pound headquarters in Bolton having founded a global empire that quoted its revenue in the billions. It was a long way from the difficulties Jeff and I faced when we first began the Reebok journey. Back then, we'd struggled to raise just a few hundred pounds for new machinery that we had to carefully position at the edges of the workshop for fear of the floorboards giving way. We'd had to borrow equipment from the ever-generous John Willie Johnson, and obtain loans from Mr Stop Heart and Jean's uncle just to stop us going under.

The international business had now topped $1 billion.

The USA outshone even that as it continued to grow to over $2 billion and Reebok International Ltd was being hailed as the fastest-growing company in America ever, largely thanks to an agent in California watching barefoot, Lycra-clad ladies in his wife's fitness class and thinking, *They need shoes.*

I still had a copy of a monthly newsletter titled *Sports Goods Intelligence* in which Reebok had been nicknamed 'Numero Uno' and Nike the 'Eager Beavertons', because we were the leaders and they were now the chasing pack. When I'd first read this in the late 1980s I'd expected to feel more euphoric. I'd had to read it over and over to try to get it to sink in, to experience the elation that I thought I'd feel when I first started chasing that dream. But I realised that, by that stage, after such a meteoric climb, overtaking Nike and Adidas had become matter-of-fact. The real buzz was not from Reebok reaching the top; it came from simply being considered to be in the race. I became aware that I was no longer bothered about crossing the finishing line first; just like on the jogging track at that hotel in Tokyo, I was too busy enjoying the run. Unlike my boyhood days when extreme physical exertion still wasn't enough to beat those boys who were born runners, I was the founder of something that had the DNA of a winner, a natural-born winner.

I realised that this was the thing I'd been trying to attain all my life – not to come first just once by sheer, extraordinary physical and mental effort, but to know that at any time I wanted I could win; to have that inner spirit and utmost belief that you're one of life's winners. No longer did I need to push, push, push for the praise of someone else; this was all about me, about knowing I had become a major player because a long time ago I had wanted to be.

These days, now in my eighties, you might see me in the morning walking Pepe, my dog, on the streets of Bolton. My head will probably be down, but not because I yearn for those heady Hollywood days of the Reebok rollercoaster – I'm keeping an eye out for Reebok trainers. Even now I still seek out that buzz of seeing *my* shoes on the feet of people in *my* hometown. And, who knows, perhaps one of those young people with whom I cross paths will read this book and be inspired to dream big too. They might be currently unemployed, they may be stuck in a job they despise, but with dedication, and the right amount of luck, there's no reason why they can't begin their journey now and become world-beaters. If a simple shoemaker can, then anything is possible.

Who and what made a difference

As I look back over the years and try to pinpoint the key to Reebok's success, my mind always conjures up the faces of those who played a vital part.

It goes without saying that, for any company, its staff are the key, the main asset. I was fortunate to have a loyal and hardworking staff who were prepared to ride with us through the ups and downs, never doubting or complaining, even when we had to temporarily lay them off on several occasions.

Among the staff, we had particular heroes like Norman Barnes, who joined us in the days when we were still Mercury and stayed with us until the closure of the UK factory. Norman had many qualities and set the bar high when it came to reliability; he was always the first to arrive in the morning, never slacked on the job, and was completely trustworthy, especially when I needed someone to keep production running smoothly after Jeff died.

Peter Halligan was another stellar worker. He joined us to operate a clicking press when we moved to Bright Street, then took on various roles as the factory grew and moved to Bradley Fold, where he was eventually appointed as manager. After the factory closure, Peter came to me to help collect old Reebok and Foster's shoes; he even found one pair of Mercurys. All are now safely stored and catalogued in the Reebok Archive in Boston, USA. Peter also undertook a great deal of historical research into the innovative advertising means and methods of my grandad back in the 1900s, some of which is included in this book.

Then there was my family. Jeff was the most important of all the people who were part of the Reebok story and, although we were very rarely together socially, we were the best of friends and never had a serious disagreement in or about the business. I don't know if he was content just to look after the production or he simply wanted a quiet life, but he never interfered with decisions I made regarding marketing or sales, even the near-disaster caused by my allowing Lawrence Sports to be our exclusive global distributor.

Jeff was a keen cyclist and on most weekends he would enter in 25k, 50k or even 100k races. In the early days, Jeff would drive himself to these events, but on some occasions he'd lend his car to me and Jean on the proviso that we pick him up at the end of the race. We got to spend the day at the coast or in the Lake District, and he'd get a lift back, albeit being physically sick sometimes. The same happened when he entered running events and I often wondered why he put himself through such ordeals. I think it may have contributed to the stomach cancer that eventually led to his early death.

Grandad Joe was the first person who influenced both Jeff

and me to risk everything and eventually give birth to the Reebok brand. Apart from starting the family business and laying the foundations for future generations of shoemakers in the family, it was Grandad who inspired me and Jeff to take a leap of faith and leave the sinking ship that was Foster's, to set out on our own. Subconsciously, he had instilled the belief in both of us that if he could do it, so could we. He was a business pioneer, a born leader with the vision to see what the market needed before the market itself knew.

This brings me to Grandma Maria, who took it upon herself to look after my wellbeing in the factory when I first started by delivering mugs of warm milk and keeping the fire burning in my workroom at the famous 'Olympic Works'. They may have been small acts of kindness, but without my grandma's coddling, who knows if I would have endured one cold winter after another. Maybe I would have sought a more comfortable way to earn a living and then this story would not have been written.

Neither Jeff nor I really bonded with Dad. He was never there, which led to an air of indifference between us. It wasn't that he travelled, but after work he would go to the local pub, or once a week he would be on home guard duty. As for Mum, mothering was her nature. She dutifully accepted both sides of the argument when Jeff and I left Foster's and Dad stopped talking to me. I'm sure she also attempted to get him to reconcile, in her own soft, subtle way. Mum died just short of her ninety-first birthday, but dementia had taken her away from us some five years earlier.

On an entrepreneurial journey such as Reebok's, however, it's not just your own family and staff who play a vital role; it's also the individuals beyond the inner circle. As I've mentioned in the book, some of them were the elusive gate-keepers who provided access to the next stage, and without meeting, befriending and truly listening to them I could have found myself in a perpetual loop of inertia, similar to what happened at J. W. Foster & Sons when my dad and uncle were in control. Having built a cosy nest of financial comfort, they didn't want to look beyond their immediate vicinity. It was either too much effort or too much of a distraction from the day-to-day demands of running a business. But, by being so insular, they missed out on so many opportunities that would have propelled the company to much greater heights.

I guess some people set a cap on their goals, while others seek the moon and beyond. I think you have to know from the outset exactly what you're striving for depending on your mindset. For me, it was taking the company as far as it could go, and, for that, it had to enter the big arena to take on the A-list sports shoemakers.

The 1960s was a difficult time for shoe manufacturers in the UK. At least once a month I would receive notice of an auction to be held on the premises of the latest company to go out of business. I had attended a few auctions previously, but it was my incredibly good fortune to have sat next to John Willie Johnson on one occasion. Little did I know that I had just met another man who would leave an indelible impression on me with his generosity and friendship. I enjoyed the time I spent with him as he told me of his experiences while we travelled together to various auctions. I did meet him again later in life, as an old man of ninety, but while the memories were there, age and dementia had taken their toll. He died while I was away from the UK and regrettably I was unable to attend his funeral.

There are lots of other people who have been important to the survival of Reebok, especially in its early days. Bob Brigham was one, who, along with his brother Ellis, inherited the F. E. Brigham outdoor activities shop, which at the time was in Collyhurst, Manchester. Bob was to move the shop to the centre of Manchester and extend his business to many outdoor sports venues throughout the UK, renaming it Ellis Brigham. Certainly, the FEB rock-climbing boot helped Reebok survive during the time of the Lawrence Sports disaster. On more than one occasion, it was necessary for me to drive to Manchester to collect a cheque from Bob, race back to the bank – sometimes having to knock on the door – to get the cash to pay our staff their weekly wages.

Bob was also my first companion at my initial NSGA show in Chicago back in 1968. It took a while for me to build up the courage to attend as Reebok were tiny at the time, and were it not for the company of Bob I might not have had the guts to go at all. We stayed friends for a long time, but the last time we met was in 1995 to celebrate my sixtieth birthday.

I was to learn a lot from the numerous attempts and failures to find a way into the US market, but nothing can compare with the Shu Lang experience. We both tried extremely hard for over four years to make our distribution agreement a success before we finally called it a day. The time with Shu was a testing ground. It taught me a lot about what we really needed to succeed in the States, unfortunately things that neither Shu nor I had at the time.

I made a point of visiting Shu in Philadelphia on my return from an NSGA show. Shu put on a party and brought in some of his customers and family members to meet me. Quite recently his daughter Jodi made contact, which prompted a second visit to Philadelphia to look through the exchange of letters that Shu had kept on file from back in the 1970s. Jodi told me that sadly Shu had died just a couple of years earlier, aged eighty-six.

Derek Waller you will remember was the lawyer I was introduced to when Reebok was faced with a winding-up petition in the early days. Derek was to become a good friend and a regular travel companion as I met with potential global distributors. He oversaw the initial agreement with Paul Fireman and represented me at the time I decided to sell the intellectual property to Reebok USA, which was then in the control of Stephen Rubin's Pentland Industries. His manner may have been odd, but his intellect was phenomenal, and on many occasions I thanked my lucky stars that he was fighting for me and not against.

Another Derek, Derek Shackleton, known to all as 'Shack', helped rescue Reebok when Lawrence Sports went out of business. He was the very epitome of professionalism. Shack may have been a born salesman with all the patter and charm needed to earn a lot of money, but he was undoubtedly a people person, always interested in their personal lives. He knew all the sports shop owners and kept a book with their family details, birthdays, kids and whether they smoked etc. I learned a lot from Shack, in many ways, not just his attention to detail, but also through his emphatic willingness to help whoever he could. Shack eventually moved on from Bata to become the distributor for the Italian Diadora brand. He was taken ill in the 1990s and died suddenly.

Harold Lawrence, the owner and managing director (CEO) of Lawrence Sports, was another man whom I admired a great deal and, like Shack, he was also always quick to offer help when needed. When I first met him, he was in his seventies and was slowly handing the business over to his son-in-law. Unfortunately, he didn't realise how important Shack was to the business, so when Shack left, taking most of the sales team with him, this, along with the manufacturing problems caused by his son-in-law's inexperience, caused irreparable damage to Lawrence Sports.

In the early days of Reebok USA, I would spend a lot of time with Paul Fireman as we clawed our way out of his start-up problems. His decision to go 'full-time' and shut down his existing business had surprised me, but it showed just how committed he was to the cause – he was Reebok through and through. What made him different, and ultimately successful, compared to other distributors we tried in America was that we weren't a 'bolt-on' to an existing set-up, whereby the aim was to simply raise a little extra money in addition to their existing revenue. There were other factors too, including his financial connections within the Jewish community and the timing. When we achieved our five-star ratings in *Runner's World*, the road-running market was beginning to boom in the States. It was this combination of elements that ultimately led to the next stage in our progression.

Of course, the catalyst for the monumental shift in Reebok's success was Stephen Rubin. Not only did he come up with the finance Paul needed, but he also seemed to provide a challenge that irritated Paul on many occasions. It was a relationship that led to Stephen being referred to as 'the grit that gets into the oyster and forms a pearl'; or, to put it another way, Stephen provided elements of friction that Paul needed to overcome to progress.

My relationship with Stephen was invariably good and I

always found him to be a gentleman. Stephen recently sent me an email in answer to a question I had posed to his office. They passed it straight to Stephen and he sent a very sincere response and best wishes.

Without the vision of Angel Martinez, the company would not have seen the phenomenal sales uplift that led to Reebok being named the fastest-growing business in the history of America. It was Angel who had the foresight to spot a new trend, and then to help to design and produce such a revolutionary shoe – the first fitness footwear to be made and marketed exclusively for women. Our early dominance of the aerobics craze was responsible for Reebok's annual revenue rising from $3 million to $13 million, then $300 million to a staggering $1 billion in consecutive years. Naturally, this incredible growth isn't all down to Angel, but just like me and Grandad Joe, he planted the seed that would flourish and mature into a sports brand known all over the world.

I can't end this chapter about 'people who made a difference' without mentioning Wendell Niles. Wendell took everything Jeff, Paul Fireman and I had created and showcased it to maximum effect, bringing A-list stars and celebrities to the Reebok family. This consequently bridged the gap between sports footwear and casual shoes, enabling us to go mainstream not just on the track, field, pitch and court, but also on the street.

It's worth saying that Wendell wasn't exclusive to Reebok, however. He came to us already loaded with a contacts book of the glam and glitzy, partly due to his dad's influence but also through his representation of Wilson tennis rackets and Louis Roederer champagne. Wendell became a good friend, introducing me to a lot of Hollywood stars and, of course,

Prince Rainier of Monaco. But, more than that, his concern for my daughter Kay when she was ill with leukaemia was genuine and gave Kay some blissfully happy moments. As we did some research for this book, I discovered that Wendell had died. Thankfully I'm now in regular contact with his lovely wife, Nelle.

There were many, many more people I haven't mentioned who contributed to Reebok becoming the number one sports goods company in the world, ahead of Nike and Adidas. Unfortunately, at my age, most of the people who made a difference have passed away, but I do remain in contact with some of the Reebok International team. And, since retiring at the beginning of 1990, I've enjoyed travelling through Europe to meet up with Jean-Marc in Paris, Richard in Munich, Umberto in Varese and Ruedi in Basel. I enjoy these get-togethers and the chance to recall those exciting days of Reebok's incredible rise to the top, and the spirit it generated.

Developing Reebok was never just a job. It wasn't something you did day-to-day to make a living. Everybody I worked with was excited to be part of the success, to be able to contribute in some way to it, and, to a certain extent, everybody had the freedom and opportunity to do that. For the most part, everybody at the top was approachable, keen to hear ideas for progression, whether those ideas came from the factory floor or the boardroom. That is what instils a good 'spirit' in a company. We worked *with* people; we didn't tell them what to do. When people have to keep their heads down, watch the clock, and they don't feel part of the success, that's when their role becomes a job and the spirit of the company suffers.

Naturally, the larger a company becomes, the harder it is to maintain that inclusive spirit. Having said that, Phil Knight managed it at Nike even when it grew to be a multi-million-dollar organisation. He took steps to keep the right people around him, but also made sure he didn't put people between him and those who helped him grow. I can happily say that we managed to retain the spirit at Reebok, all the way from the days of Norman and David, our apprentice, right through until I sold the company in 1984. And for that, I look back in pride at the success we achieved, which wouldn't have been possible without the hundreds of Reebok-passionate colleagues who contributed along the way.

Some of the earliest influences on me as a person weren't people, they were institutions. Most of my social and recreation activities revolved around St Margaret's, the local church, half a mile from where we lived, and where Mum would send us to Sunday school. The church would hold events and Christmas parties for the children, with a film show where we'd laugh at Charlie Chaplin, Laurel and Hardy, or Abbot and Costello. St Margaret's had a bowling green and four tennis courts, but while the bowling green was still in use, the tennis courts and the pavilion had become disused and derelict. Friday night was Cubs, where Jeff and I joined the rest of the troop gathered in one of the two halls adjacent to and part of St Margaret's Church, while the 28th Bolton Scout Troop occupied a cellar in the same building. Over the past ten years, I've reacquainted myself with some of my fellow troop members, including Brian Wilby, who we 'lost' on the snowy march to Patterdale.

After the Second World War, my extracurricular activities continued to be centred in and around St Margaret's, where I joined the badminton club, which was to be my passport to travel while doing national service in the RAF. Apart from badminton, social life at St Margaret's revolved around the Saturday night dances, until our group of friends spread its wings and discovered the bigger dance venues in Bolton, where I first met Jean.

National service was to change everything as, at varying times, the boys in our friendship group were called away for two years, destroying the social dynamic. We would return two years later to find the group no longer existed, so, for the most part, as the boys returned they would reunite with the girl they left behind and settle down to married life, just like me and Jean.

Jean and I married twelve months to the day after I returned to Bolton. At first, she was the most supportive wife any man could hope for, more or less singlehandedly raising our two children without complaint at my mental, and often physical, absence. At the time Kay died, my son, David, was working in design at Reebok. After that, he moved on to set up his own company.

Jean's family had little money, but they supported and encouraged the venture Jeff and I had embarked on. They were instrumental in persuading Jean's uncle to lend us £500 when things got tough. I also have very fond memories of Steve, Jean's dad, who, after retiring, would get on his bike to help with dispatching orders and always refused to accept any money for his time. Steve gave us the support Jeff and I had sought from our own dad. Unfortunately, and somewhat understandably, Jean's tolerance for my single-minded focus on business waned in the later years and our marriage reached the end of the road in 1993.

Finally, at the risk of sounding like an Oscar winner, I'd

like to thank Lady Luck. Without her on my side, none of this would have been possible. Every entrepreneur, without exception, needs a little good fortune their way. I had plenty, and from the bottom of my heart, I hope you do too.

ACKNOWLEDGEMENTS

I have been writing and rewriting my memoir for a number of years and feel compelled to thank a lot of people, mostly friends and family for pushing me to get it written and for helping me when my memory failed.

Firstly, I must thank all those who worked for Mercury and Reebok in the early days at our Bolton Street and Bright Street factories in Bury, as well as all those who, during the later years, helped drive Reebok to become the No. 1 sports company in the world – especially Paul Fireman and Stephen Rubin for turning the dream Jeff and I had back in 1958 into a reality.

With regards to the researching of this memoir, I am most in debt to Peter Halligan, a loyal and trusted employee who spent endless hours scouring old newspapers for those incredible J. W. Foster ads. Peter also traced many old Reebok, Mercury and Foster's shoes that are now in the Reebok Archive in Boston.

This brings me to Erin Narloch, the curator of the Reebok Archive, who applied her wonderful skills to safeguarding

Peter's precious finds within a special climate-controlled protective area. Erin also scanned hundreds of items to add to the treasure chest of photographs, some dating back to the early 1900s, which she has made available online and for use in this memoir.

When I struggled with the structure of my memoir, a friend, Roy Cavanagh MBE, who himself has written numerous sports books, especially about him being a lifelong fan of Manchester United, helped me move my story on.

Joe Cawley, a storyteller and award-winning writer of incredible talent, was a driving force in bringing my book to life. His knowledge of the industry led to the introduction of a literary agent and the path towards a publisher.

This literary agent is Euan Thorneycroft of A. M. Heath, whose enthusiasm and passion for the project sprinkled a little more magic dust as it drew closer to being published by the team he entrusted with my memoir.

Under the skillful control of Ian Marshall, that publishing team at Simon & Schuster has helped turn over one hundred years of my family's achievements and my experiences into a book that I am very proud of, and one that I hope you enjoy reading.

My grandson, Mark Hardman, is a graphic designer who has not only kept my hard-worked computer in good order but has also developed and managed the website https://reebokthefounder.com/ where you can trace the history covered by this memoir. Mark was also instrumental in introducing me to Joe Cawley.

Lastly, most thanks go to Julie, my wife, my true friend and my travelling companion. While not part of my life during my Reebok working days, Julie has relived my experiences over the years and accompanied me on many Reebok revisits. She has become my invaluable 'external hard drive' when, as mentioned above, my own rusty internal memory fails.

I thank you all.

INDEX

Abbot and Costello 292
Abrahams, Harold 17
Adidas 38, 39, 53, 89, 90, 112, 132, 135,
    148, 151, 153, 200, 207, 218, 223,
    230, 255, 258, 281, 291
  market domination of 105, 107
  trademark infringement claimed by
    104
advertising 13, 58, 118, 134–6, 141, 147,
    148–54, 166, 170, 230–1, 284
aerobics 216–20, 221–4, 227, 232, 235,
    237–8, 255, 258, 290
Aggressor cycling shoes 61
air pads 60
Alec (printer) 251–2
Alien Stomper shoes 246
Aliens 246
Amateur Athletic Association 94
Ambleside Youth Hostel 26
Amritraj, Ashok 247, 265
Amritraj, Vijay 247
Amsterdam Olympics (1928) 17
Anderson, Bob 166, 167
Antwerp Olympics (1920) 17
apartheid 229, 277–9
Apparel 262
Applegarth, Willie 14
Argentina football boot 89
Arkwright's 47
Arsenal FC 16

ASCO 210–13, 211, 212, 231
Asics 101, 252
Associated Shoe Company 210–13,
    231
Astaire, Fred 189
Aston Martin 119
Athens Olympics (1896) 9
Athletics Weekly 50, 102, 147
Austin, Denise 221–2
Austin, Tracy 221
Australia 121, 236, 247, 252
Aztec trainer 172–3, 185, 196
  midsole problem with 204–7, 209,
    210
  Reebok USA survival aided by
    discounted sales of 210

badminton 29, 30, 37, 46, 158, 208,
    277, 280, 292–3
bank loans 62–3, 80, 122, 128, 184,
    208
bankruptcy 124, 210, 239, 270
Bannister, Roger 37, 91, 236
Barnes, Norman 102–3, 226, 292
  as foreman production manager
    203, 283
  joins Mercury 68–9, 203, 283
  retirement of 283
baseball 214
basketball 274–5

Bata 122, 127–8, 174, 177, 184, 199, 203, 204, 205
  Aztec trainer manufactured by 204–7, 209, 210
Bawdsey Manor 36–7
Bawdsey, RAF 34, 35
Beatles, The 73
Belgium 105
Benetton 254, 255
Berlin Olympics (1936) 14, 21
Berlin Wall 277
Big Freeze 95
bingo 58, 59
Black, Doug 86–7
Blake sole-sewing machine 32–3, 50, 60
Blunier, André 180, 186
Board of Trade (UK) 108, 114, 198, 199
Bolton, Zeppelin bombing of 15
Bolton Crematorium 143, 200
Bolton Evening News (BEN) 17–18, 45, 53, 280
Bolton Harriers 13
Bolton Parish Church 280
Bolton Primrose Harriers 6, 9, 13
Bolton Royal Hospital 100
Bolton Street factory 56–8, 67, 96, 203, 250
Bolton Town Hall 266
Bolton United Harriers 17–18, 21, 118
  founding of 13–14
Bolton Wanderers FC 16–17, 25, 38, 58, 89, 275
Bolton's Night of Stars 268
bonding exercise 184
boot camp 34
boot technology 122–3
Boston Camping 165–6, 191–3
Boston Marathon 101
Bowerman, Bill 171
Bowie, David 246
Boy Scouts 26–9, 34, 280
Bradley Fold factory 225–6, 284
brand association 248
brand awareness 237
brand loyalty 207
brand registration 80
branding 2–3, 17, 39, 43, 49, 67, 74–7, 80–1, 84, 86, 90, 94, 103, 117,

127–31, 135–8, 140–7, 148–9, 164–7, 177, 185, 188, 190, 193–5, 202, 209, 211–12, 214, 218–19, 224, 231–8, 239–43, 245, 254, 261, 278, 285, 288, 290
Brasher, Chris 91, 102, 103, 236–7, 239
Brian (Scout friend) 27–8
Brigham, Bob 86–7, 108–9, 111, 112, 114, 123, 127, 287
Brigham, Ellis 86, 287
Bright Street factory 168, 169, 201, 203, 209, 225, 226–7, 234, 284
Brill Bend technique 115
Brill, Debbie 115
British Airways (BA) 104, 162, 260
British Shoe Corporation 75, 76
Broadway 256, 257
Brooks 148, 170
Brown, Dee 274–5
Brown, Paul 203
budget-price trainers 128–9
Bukta 90
Burghley, Lord 17
Burnden Park stadium 58
  fans crushed at 25
Bury FC 58
Bury Felt Ltd 98
Bury General Hospital 73
Bury Times 61, 68
Butlin, Billy 62

Caine, Michael 248
calfskin 31
California Runner (company) 158
California Runner shoe 158
Camborian side-lasting machine 60
Canada 114–15, 121, 174, 185, 234
Cardington Reception Unit (RAF) 34
Carter Pocock 140, 141, 144–5, 227, 236, 261
Carter, President Jimmy 133
cash flow 62, 122, 122–4, 127–8, 129, 130, 147, 152, 203
Castle Irwell course 18
celebrity culture 188–90, 222, 245–50, 257–8, 265, 267–8, 280, 290–1, 292

Challenger cycling shoes 61
Chang, Michael 248
channel machines 60
Chaplin, Charlie 292
Chariots of Fire 17
charity events 268, 278
Charles, Prince 248
chart ratings 167, 170, 172, 174, 175,
      190, 196, 204, 212, 234, 289
Chicago Marathon 237
China Runner 180, 186
Christie Hospital 264
chrome-tanned leathers 65
Chrysler Building 109
Classic Leather shoe 229
clicking 80
climbing boots 86–7
Coe, Sebastian ('Seb') 193
Coghlan, Eamonn 229
Collins, Joan 247
Columbo, Umberto 254–5, 291
comfort zone 190
commercial design 172
commission-only sales 88, 94
competition 38–40, 41, 101–2
complaints 82, 138, 224, 241
Connery, Sean 247
conscription 33–8, 41–2, 73, 106,
      293
Cortez shoes 171
cost-effectiveness 138
cotton industry 6
cotton mills 225
Cram, Steve 229
Crewe course 18
cricket shoes 47
Crompton, Samuel 6
cross-border shipping 174
cross-country 116, 119, 132
Cuba 214
cultural identity 95
culture clash 55, 213, 251–60, 262
cushioning 7, 110, 119, 170, 216, 274
Cycling 61, 62
cycling shoes 60–1, 81
Czechoslovakia 235

Dancing in the Street 246
Dassler, Adi 14, 39, 105

Dassler, Rudolf 39, 105
De Niro, Robert 247
Deane Road factory 9, 13, 15, 17, 20,
      23–4, 31
decency, paramount need for 2
DeLuxe shoes 39, 66, 96
design and development 203
design motifs 104, 193–4, 212, 218
Diadora 288
Diana, Princess 249
discounts 31, 64, 126, 134, 206–7, 210
Disley, John 236–7, 239
disposable commerce 107–8
Distance Running News 166
distribution 39, 45, 48, 75–6, 97, 112,
      114–17, 121, 128, 130, 132–9,
      136, 140–7, 148–54, 158–9,
      161–3, 172, 175, 177, 185–6,
      192–3, 199–203, 208–12, 224,
      236–7, 241–3, 249, 252, 254–5,
      258, 261–6, 273, 277–9, 284,
      287–9
distribution rights 241, 258
Divarese 254
diversification 22, 117–18, 125, 129
Dobson & Barlow 225
Doc Marten 275
double revolving scourers 60
Dunlop 90, 140
durability 65, 170, 171, 172
Dynasty 248

E. Suttons 71
eBay 33
edge trimmers 60
Eldon, Stan 102, 103
Electrolux 76
Ellis, Mr (clerk) 75–6, 78–9
Emerson, Roy 247
Emmy Awards 246
Empire State Building 109, 209
espionage 35
ethylene-vinyl acetate (EVA) 171, 205,
      206
Etonic 170
Eurosport 108
EVA (ethylene-vinyl acetate) 171, 205,
      206
Evans, Linda 247

Ex-O-Fit shoe 222, 229
exponential growth 222–3

F. E. Brigham 287
FA Cup:
　1946 stadium disaster 25
　Final, 1923 17
　Final, 1958 58
Fab-Road trainers 102–3
Fab-XC shoes 103
Fairbrother 88, 90
Far East 69, 129, 165, 209, 212, 223
fashion and accessories 223, 261–3
FEB rock-climbing boots 87, 111, 287
feedback 82, 135
Felixstowe, RAF 35
fell-running 93–4
Ferdinand, Archduke Franz 15
Ferguson, Maj. Ronald 248, 265
Fernee, Brian 158, 159
Fifth Avenue Mile race 229–30
Finland 132
Finn Aamodt 129, 130
Fireman, Paul 72, 162, 165–8,
　　169–70, 172–4, 177, 184–5, 190,
　　191–7, 198–9, 200, 202, 203,
　　204, 206–13, 214, 215, 216–19,
　　221, 223–4, 227, 229–35, 239,
　　262–4, 265, 273, 277–8, 288,
　　290
　as Reebok International Ltd CEO
　　245
　time capsule buried by 265
First World War 15–16
fitness gear 216–20, 221–3
fitness running 132, 221, 230
fitness training 221–2, 281
'5411' shoe, see Freestyle shoe
5K road events 132
Fleetfoot 236, 237
　renaming of 239
Flynn, Ray 229
foam rubber 171
Fonda, Jane 222
football 58–9, 275
　1946 stadium disaster 25
　boot technology 122–3
　footwear 16–17
　sports shops 87

wage capping 87
　World Cup (1954) 89
　World Cup (1966) 100
Formula One (F1) 255
Forsythe, John 247, 248, 265, 268
Fosbury Flop technique 115
Foster, Bessie (mother) 2, 19, 25, 34, 61,
　　142, 265–6, 292
　death of 285
　husband's death affects 143–4
　during WWII 22–4
Foster, David (son) 142, 143, 145, 201,
　　243
　at Reebok 293
　birth of 100–1
　second birthday of 109, 113
Foster, Diane (niece):
　birth of 101
　father's death affects 200
Foster, Ian (nephew):
　birth of 95–6
　death of 99–100, 101
　ill health of 95, 99
Foster, James William ('Jim') (father)
　　3–4, 25, 31, 32–3, 34, 81, 88,
　　146–7, 249, 250, 285
　BEN interviews 45
　Bill's feud with 19–20, 40, 41, 43–5,
　　46, 66–7, 202
　birth of 15, 51
　complacency and indifference
　　exhibited by 39–40, 41
　death of 51, 143–4
　ill health of 42–3, 143
　indifferent nature of 44–5, 47–8
　Joe's showdown with 50–3, 54–5
　reactive nature of 42
　sports shop owned by 67, 142
　during WWII 22–4
Foster, Jean (sister-in-law) 81, 92, 198
　first child born to 95
　inheritance of 201–2
　Jeff marries 75
　Jeff's death affects 200
　Joe buys her out 202
　second and third children born to
　　101
　son's death affects 99–100, 101
　supportive nature of 190

Foster, Jean (wife) 46, 54, 62–3, 81–3, 88, 91–2, 113, 118, 126, 142–3, 199, 201, 243, 263
  daughter's death affects 271
  first child born to 73–4
  Joe meets 31
  Joe's relationship ends with 33–4
  Joe resumes relationship with 41
  Joe weds 43, 186, 293
  marital problems of 195–6, 253–4, 271, 293
  overseas trips of 251–4, 268
  second child born to 100–1
  supportive nature of 30, 54, 145, 190
Foster, Jeff (brother) 67–8, 69, 74, 80, 86, 91, 98, 105, 117–18, 122, 134, 149, 152, 153–4, 158, 190, 194, 196, 203, 225, 233, 239, 243, 250, 280, 290, 293
  athletic prowess of 46, 60, 92, 198, 284
  becomes a father 95, 101
  birth of 19
  brother's mutual respect for 46
  cancer diagnosis of 199, 284
  childhood of 22–4
  death of 200, 204, 234, 283, 284
  factory acquired by 56–9
  family feud affects 42, 44–5
  father resists modernisation ideas of 44–8, 50–3
  and father's death 143
  ill health of 198, 199–200
  Jean marries 75
  National Service of 41–2, 106
  reactive nature of 42
  in Scouts 26, 292
  shoemaking course attended by 48–9, 55, 60, 201
  son's death affects 99–100, 101
  works for Fosters 31, 32
  during WWII 22–4
Foster, John (brother) 143
Foster, Joseph William ('Joe'):
  Achilles tendon rupture of 158, 159
  ambassador role undertaken by 273
  ambitious nature of 3, 44–8, 50–3, 79–80, 81

  badminton prowess of 29–30, 37, 46, 158
  becomes a father 74, 100–1
  becomes commission-only sales agent 88
  birth of 19
  childhood of 3–5, 22–9, 292
  daughter's death affects 268–72, 274, 275, 277
  18th birthday of 34
  entrepreneurialism of 55, 277, 285
  factory acquired by 56–9
  family duties neglected by 243–4, 271
  family feud affects 40, 41–2, 43–5
  fashion business founded by 117–18
  father resists modernisation ideas of 44–8, 50–3
  and father's death 143–4
  first Concorde flight of 264
  first NSGA event attended by 108, 110–13, 114, 232, 287
  'founder's' role of 273
  as *Geschäftsführer*, Reebok Germany 256–7
  grandmother names 19
  grandmother spoils 32
  as International Division president, Reebok International Ltd 235, 245, 257, 261, 273
  Jean meets 30, 31
  Jean's relationship ends with 33–4
  Jean resumes relationship with 41
  Jean weds 43, 186, 293
  Jeff's death affects 200–1, 204–5, 225
  joins Fosters 31
  joint venture proposed by 148–52
  Lake District visits of 142–3, 237, 284
  loans secured by 62–3
  marital problems of 195–6, 253–4, 271, 293
  National Service of 33–8, 43, 293
  nephew's death affects 100, 101
  optimistic nature of 54, 131, 141, 174
  outsourcing lesson learned by 130
  passing-out parade of 34
  proactive nature of 42
  in RAF 293

Foster, Joseph William – *Continued*
  Reebok founded by 33
  Reebok sold by 234
  rejoins Fosters 38–9
  in Scouts 26–9, 34, 280, 292
  shoemaking course attended by
    48–9, 55, 60, 201
  steps away from Reebok 275–6,
    279–80
  teenage years of 29–30
  thinking time valued by 145
  32nd birthday of 109
  time capsule buried by 265
  weighing scales incident involving
    197, 200
  during WWII 22–5
Foster, Joseph William ('Joe') (paternal
    grandfather) 16, 32, 50, 53, 57, 67,
    81, 94, 116, 144, 249, 250, 275,
    284–5, 290
  Bolton United Harriers founded by
    13–14
  death of 18
  Joe born on birthday of 19
  marketing prowess of 13, 14–15,
    16–18
  Midas touch of 17–18
  spiked running shoe invented by, *see*
    main entry
  WWI affects business of 16
Foster, Kay (daughter) 88, 91, 100, 113,
    142, 145, 201, 243
  birth of 74–5
  death of 268–72, 274, 275, 277,
    293
  grandfather's boat named after 143
  ill health of 263–5, 267–8, 291
  leukaemia diagnosis of 263–4,
    267–8, 291
  marriages and divorce of 251
  Monte Carlo trip enjoyed by 268
Foster, Maria (paternal grandmother)
    18–19, 21, 47, 57, 250, 285
  death of 43–4
  Joe spoilt by 32
  sons' feud affects 40, 43
  during WWII 23–4
Foster, Mark (grandson) 264, 268, 271
  birth of 251

Foster, Paul (grandson) 264, 268, 271
  birth of 251
Foster, Robert (nephew):
  birth of 101
  father's death affects 200
Foster, Sam (paternal great-grandfather)
    6
  death of 18–19
Foster & Sons, *see* J. W. Foster & Sons
Foster, William ('Bill') (uncle) 15, 21,
    31, 32, 42, 49, 53, 55, 81, 82, 96,
    146
  athletic prowess of 17
  BEN columns written by 17–18
  complacency and indifference
    exhibited by 39–40, 41
  death of 66
  hand-sewn footwear by 19–20, 39
  Jim's feud with 19–20, 40, 41, 43–5,
    46, 66–7, 202
Fosters, *see* J. W. Foster & Sons
four-minute mile 91, 236
France 87, 92, 105, 107, 242–3, 258
Fred Martin Agencies 114–15
Fred Perry 188
free shoes 14
Freestyle shoe 220, 221–4, 227, 229,
    230, 246, 256
French Open 248
Fukuoka Marathon 101

G. T. Law & Son 37
Gaitskell, Hugh 95
Ganley, Len 141
Gaucher, Jean-Marc 242–3, 291
Geinjack, Bob 39, 96
General Motors (GM) 133
genius, defined 12–13
Germany 15, 21–4, 100, 105, 106, 123,
    128, 132, 178, 235, 255–8
gharry 34, 35
Gigg Lane stadium 58
global conquest 72
global reach 79, 91, 101, 105–13,
    114–20, 121, 146, 190, 200, 240,
    245, 284
goat-kid skin 216–17
golf 161, 254
Gore-Tex 229

Grace, Princess 246, 267
Grand Army Plaza 230
Great War, *see* First World War
Greece 235
Green Flash trainers 140
Greengate & Irwell Rubber Company 57
guillotines 60
gym shoes 216–20, 221–2

Hallé Orchestra 266
Halligan, Peter 284
Halstead, Nellie 18
Hamel, Veronica 265
hand clicking 68
hand-lasting jacks 60
Hawaii 186–8
Hawkins 87
Henderson, Joe 153
Heston, Charlton 265–6
high-top shoes 222, 246, 275
Hill, Albert 17
Hill, Ron 118–20
Hill Street Blues 265
Hitler, Adolf 21
hole-punching machines 113
Hollywood 188–90, 222, 245–50, 257–8, 265, 267–8, 280, 290, 292, 293
Holmes, C. B. 21
home exercise videos 222
Hong Kong 177, 179, 180–90, 235, 243
Hoover 76
Horse and Vulcan pub 9, 15
Hôtel de Paris 247, 268
HS Corporation 176, 183, 184–5
Hubble Space Telescope 277
Hull RLFC 16
Hummel 128

Ibrox Park stadium, Glasgow 11
illegal shipping 278
image 104, 193–4, 212, 218
importation 102, 112, 132, 216, 237
India 179, 247
Indonesia 243
inflation 174
Ingles of Leeds 59
inheritance 18, 47–8, 66, 201, 246, 287
injection moulding 122–3

innovation 6, 12, 42, 107, 115, 170–2, 177, 229, 274, 284
Institute Street factory 249–50
International Sports Goods, Camping Equipment and Garden Furniture trade show 105–9
Intersport Germany 255
Iran 178–9, 181, 240
ISPO 256–7, 274
Israel 235
Italian Grand Prix 255
Italy 235, 254–5

J. W. Foster & Sons 88, 89, 112, 116, 138, 142, 146–7, 184, 202, 210, 229, 238, 249, 276
  army boots repaired by 16, 22
  competition affects 38–40, 41
  cross-country shoes manufactured by 16
  demise of 66–8
  expanded footwear range of 16
  family feud affects viability of 19–20, 40, 41, 43–5, 46, 286
  fifties downturn 38–40, 41, 45–9, 50
  football/rugby football clubs supplied by 16–17, 67
  founding of 53, 57
  hurdling shoes manufactured by 16
  Jim becomes sole owner of 66
  Joe and Jeff leave 50–3, 131, 200, 214, 232, 284–5
  limited company status of 20
  Maria takes over at 18–20
  marketing 45
  'Mercury rising from the ashes of' 62
  new designs developed by 42
  sales and distribution 45
  sandals manufactured by 22
  spiked running shoes manufactured by 5, 6–10, 12–15, 16, 17, 37, 64–5, 94
  trainers manufactured by 89–90, 249
  US distribution deal 39
J. W. Foster (Athletic Shoes) 12
  founding of 9
  renaming of 15
Jack (best friend) 24–5
Jagger, Mick 246

Jaguar 96, 98, 193, 243
James Bond (007) franchise 247, 257, 268
Japan 77, 79, 101–2, 132, 156, 167, 176, 185–6, 187, 214, 224, 235, 239, 252–4, 262
Jim (sales manager) 199
Johnson, Ethel 18
Johnson, John Willie 71–2, 98, 99, 226
    death of 286
Jones, Steve 237–8
Jordan 275
Joyce (Bessie's friend) 61, 62, 80

kangaroo skin 31–2, 216
Kay 143
Kay, Norman 61
Kelly, Grace 246, 267
Kershaw, David 61, 68, 69, 74, 81, 292
Kiddell, Canon 30
Kmart 162, 163–5, 166, 189
Knight, Phil 102, 166, 176, 214–15, 292
Kodak 76
Korean Central Intelligence Agency (KCIA) 182
Kosice Marathon 101

Lang, Jodi 287–8
Lang, Shu 132–9, 145, 146–7, 148, 154, 202, 287–8
    joint venture proposed by Joe with 148–52
launch promotion 102–3
Laurel and Hardy 292
Lawrence, Harold 116, 121, 288–9
Lawrence Sports 116–17, 121–6, 128–30, 140–1, 146, 192, 233, 284, 287, 288–9
Leatherflair 203
    founding of 117–18
    Lawrence Sports collapse impacts 125
    Miss Blackburn models for 118
Lesser, Dick 208–9, 211
Liberal Party (UK) 210
Liddell, Eric 17
Liggett, Steve 207, 216, 217, 219, 220
liquidation auctions 69–70
Litzel, Richard 256, 257

Live and Let Die 257
Liverpool FC 16
Liverpool Shoe Company 210
Lofthouse, Nat 58
London Marathon 236, 237–8
London Olympics (1908) 14
long-distance running 11, 33, 102, 118, 214
Lord Nelson pub 58, 74
Lotus and Delta 75, 76
Louis Hoffman 88, 90
Lovelock, Jack 21
Lundgren, Dolph 265, 268
Lycra 281

McCormick Place 108, 111
McGoldrick, John 206
Macmillan, Harold 73
mail order 136, 149, 215
Malaysia 235
Manchester City FC 17
Manchester United FC 16, 58
Mandela, Nelson 277, 279
marathon running 101, 236, 237
Maree, Sydney 229–30
marketing 13, 14–15, 16–18, 45, 61–2, 76, 91, 93, 193–4, 196
Martin, Peter 114–15
Martin, Rolf 114–15
Martinez, Angel 214–20, 221, 290
    as VP, Reebok International Ltd 255
Martinez, Frankie 216
Marubeni 252
Matchbox 258
Mather & Platt 225
mega-brands 135
Melbourne track shoes 53
Mercedes 256
Mercury Sports Footwear 251, 276, 283
    budget shoe created by 64–5
    cycling shoes manufactured by 60–1
    first apprentice taken on by 61–2
    founding of 59, 86, 226
    freelance agents taken on by 61, 62, 87
    Jean's family lend money to 63, 280, 293
    Jean's uncle's belief in 63, 280
    limited company status of 75–7

loans secured by 62–3, 280
pounding-up machine loaned to 72
renaming of 75–9 (*see also* Reebok
    Sports Limited)
second-hand machinery acquired by
    60–1, 72
sole presses installed at 67–8, 72
stability of 74–5
Mexico 174, 185, 234
Mitre 90
Monaco 291
monopoly 67, 86, 88, 90, 128, 167
Monte Carlo 246–8, 267–8
Monte Carlo Country Club 247
Moore, Roger 247, 268
Motter Tektura font 104
Mountaineering Activities (MOAC) 108
Mustang shoes 136

Nathan, Malcolm 176, 177, 184
National Party (SA) 278
National Service 33–8, 41–2, 73, 106,
    293
National Sporting Goods Association
    (NSGA) 133, 155–9, 204, 233
  1968 event 108, 110–13, 114, 287
  1979 event 161–2
  1980 event 196, 198, 204–5
  Aztec displayed at 196, 205
  Joe determines annual visit to 114
  Joe's first-ever visit to 108, 110–13,
    114, 232, 287
NBA Slam Dunk 275
networking 133, 160–1
New Balance 102, 166, 170, 218, 236–7
New York Marathon 236
New Zealand 21, 121, 251–2
Nichols, Alan 177, 181, 184
Nike 135, 150, 166, 167, 171, 193, 200,
    207, 209, 214, 218, 279, 291, 292
  apathy of 223, 234
  charts topped by 170, 173
  'Eager Beavertons' sobriquet of 281
  founding of 102, 171
  waffle soles pioneered by 171–2
Niles, Nelle 291
Niles, Wendell, Jr 245–7, 257, 265, 267,
    268, 290
  death of 291

Nintendo 258
Nokia 103, 132
Norris, Chuck 247
Norwegian Army 129
nostalgia 53
NSGA (National Sporting Goods
    Association) 108, 110–13, 114, 133,
    155–9, 161–2, 196, 198, 204–5,
    205, 232, 233, 287
  Aztec displayed at 204
nylon half-soles 53

Old Horse Show 14
Olympic Games 67, 118, 214
  1896 9
  1908 14–15
  1920 17
  1928 17
  1936 14, 21
  1964 185
Olympic Works 9, 15, 18, 20, 21, 23,
    44, 53, 285
  compulsory purchase order issued
    on 67
Onitsuka 101
Opal 107
orienteering footwear 102
outsourcing 69, 130, 144
Ovett, Steve 230
Owens, Jesse 14, 21
Pac-Man 263
Painting the Town Red 189
Palais dance hall 30
Pan Am 177, 181
parachute shoes 129
Parker Shoe Company 129–30
Parker's 98–9
patching machines 60
patent law 75–6, 239
pattern-cutters 60
Pentland Group 210, 232, 288
  Reebok bought by 234
Pepe (dog) 282
Perry, David 188–9
Peter (accountant) 83–4
Peters, Martin 100
Phase 1 shoe 230–1
Philippines 243
Pinewood Studios 265

Pittards of Yeovil 119
Pocock, Christine 144
Poland 235, 259–60
polishing machines 60
polo 248–9, 265
Portsmouth FC 17
Portugal 235
pounding-up machines 71–2
Powers, Stephanie 248
Prefect spiked shoe 114–15
Princess Ballroom 57
Princess Grace Foundation 246
promotion 18, 102–3, 132, 147, 151,
    246, 263
prototypes 171, 217, 219
Puma 38, 53, 90, 114, 115, 132, 135,
    153, 200, 255, 257, 258
  market domination of 105

Raelbrook 78
RAF Bawdsey 34, 35
RAF Cardington Reception Unit 34
RAF Felixstowe 35
RAF Yatesbury 34–5
Rainier, Prince 246, 247, 267, 291
rating numbers 167, 170
rear-foot control 173
Rebow 78
Reebok Archive 284
Reebok Deutschland GmbH 255–8
Reebok France 229, 242–3
Reebok International Limited
    (distribution and marketing arm),
    see Reebok UK
Reebok International Limited, Inc., see
    Reebok USA
Reebok International Ltd:
  Bolton HQ 249–50, 261, 265–6,
    279
  creation of 234–5
  distribution and marketing arm
    236–7, 239, 249
  Fireman CEO and president of
    245
  Fireman steps back from 273
  golf course acquired by 254
  Joe International Division president
    of 235, 245, 249–50, 257, 261,
    273

Joe steps away from 275–8, 279–80
Joe takes on 'founder's' role 273
Martinez VP of 255
Rubin chairman of 245
time capsule 265
trademark infringements 257
turnover 273, 280–1, 290
TV exposure of 235–6, 246
Yvonna taken on by 242
Reebok Italy 255–6
Reebok Japan 252–4
Reebok London road-racing shoe 229
Reebok Paris road-racing shoe 229,
    238
Reebok Southeast Asia 243
Reebok Spain 241–2
Reebok Sports Limited (manufacturing
    arm), see Reebok UK
Reebok UK 104, 193–4, 212, 276
  Adidas claims trademark
    infringement by 104
  athletic shoes manufactured by 90
  Aztec trainer manufactured by
    172–3, 185, 196, 204
  Bata terms eases cash flow of 127–8
  Board of Trade sponsorship taken up
    by 108, 110–11, 114
  Boston Camping deal with 165–6,
    191–2
  Bright Street factory 98–9, 132, 136,
    225–6, 284
  budget-price trainers manufactured
    by 128–9
  California Runner manufactured by
    158–9
  Canadian contract 114–15
  Carter Pocock agreement with
    140–1, 144–5
  chart ratings sought by 167, 170, 172,
    173, 174, 175, 190, 196, 204,
    212, 234, 289
  Classic Leather shoe manufactured
    by 229
  competition affects 101–2
  cross-country shoes manufactured by
    99, 103, 116, 119
  cycling shoes manufactured by 90
  DeLuxe shoes recreated by 96–7
  design motifs 104, 193–4, 218

distribution and marketing arm 146, 174, 203, 225, 234, 236–7, 239, 242

distribution gamble 114–17

Eire government approaches 97–8

European market expansion of 105–9, 229, 240–3

Fab-Road trainers manufactured by 102–3

Fab-XC shoes manufactured by 103

FEB boots manufactured by 87, 111, 287

5-star rating awarded to 167, 170, 172, 173, 174, 175, 190, 196, 204, 212, 234, 289

Fleetfoot becomes 239

football boots manufactured by 89–90

founding of 1–3, 33, 146, 200–1

Fred Martin Agencies approaches 114–15

image 104, 193–4, 212, 218

Jagger wears trainers by 246

Joe buys sister-in-law's share of 202–3

Joe sells 234–5, 288, 292

Joe's thinking time benefits 145

Lawrence Sports collapse impacts 124–6, 140, 146, 284

literature 146, 149, 151

London road-racing shoe manufactured by 229

manufacturing arm 82, 203, 225, 234

midsole problem encountered by 204–7, 209, 210

MOAC joint venture with 108

modest rise of 99

Motter Tektura font adopted by 104

MPs refer to Trading Standards 195

Mustang shoes manufactured by 136

naming of 77–9

Norwegian Army commission 129–30

'Numero Uno' sobriquet of 281

original name of, see Mercury Sports Footwear

parachute shoes manufactured by 129

Paris road-racing shoe manufactured by 229, 238

pioneering nature of 150

Prefect spiked shoe manufactured by 114–15

Puma claims trademark infringement by 153

Reebok USA royalties paid to 227–8

relocation of 95–104

reorganisation of 203, 204

Ripple trainer manufactured by 127–9

road-running shoes manufactured by 101–2, 116, 119, 130, 141, 169–70, 218, 237, 289

rowing shoes manufactured by 129

rugby boots manufactured by 72, 89, 90, 116

running pumps manufactured by 90

running shoes manufactured by 94, 99, 104, 118–19, 132, 255

schools supplied by 64, 114, 126, 132, 135–6, 147, 149, 266

seventies turmoil affects 174–5

sister-in-law inherits Jeff's share of 201–2

sixties growth of 95–104, 286

skateboard shoes manufactured by 129

Spanish investment in 240–3

Starcrest identity adopted by 104, 194

subcontract work put out by 129–30

track and field shoes manufactured by 99, 107, 116, 119, 230

trademark infringements 104, 153, 195, 201, 240

trainers manufactured by 102–3, 116, 123, 126, 127–9, 153, 172–3, 246, 249, 282

Union Jack branding of 194–5

US expansion of 105, 107–13, 114–20, 121–4, 130–1, 132–9, 148–9, 148–54, 169–77, 174, 186–90, 191–7, 227–8, 234–5 (see also Reebok International Ltd; Reebok USA)

Victory G shoe manufactured by 229

Reebok UK – *Continued*
   'Welcome Reebok' banner 183
   widespread brand awareness achieved
      by 141
   winding-up petition issued to 82–5,
      91–3, 173, 201, 239
   World 10 running shoe
      manufactured by 118–20, 217
Reebok USA 148–9, 174, 199, 202,
   203, 242
   aerobics shoes manufactured by
      216–20, 221–4, 227, 229
   discounted faulty Aztecs aid survival
      of 210
   Ex-O-Fit shoe manufactured by 222,
      229
   fitness gear line of 216–20, 221–3
   Freestyle shoe ('5411') manufactured
      by 220, 221–4, 227, 229, 230,
      246, 256
   gym shoes manufactured by 216–20,
      221–4
   high-top shoes manufactured by 222,
      246, 275
   intellectual property acquired by
      234–5, 288
   Nike's apathy benefits 223, 234
   Phase 1 shoe manufactured by 230–1
   refunding of 208–12
   royalties from 228
   tennis shoes manufactured by 230–1
Repetto 243
retail market 74, 86, 111, 123, 130, 138,
   155, 162, 166–7, 170, 208, 211–13,
   223, 246, 257
ripple soles 127–9
Ripple trainer 127–9
road running 101–2, 119, 141, 169–70,
   218, 237, 289
   explosion in 101
   mainstream growth in 130
road-running shoes, *see* running shoes;
   training shoes
Rogers, Ginger 189
Rossendale College 61
Rossendale Valley 56
Rothwell, Linda 203
roughing machines 60
rowing shoes 129

Royal Air Force (RAF) 24, 293
   Cardington Reception Unit 34
Royal Berkshire Polo Club 248
Rubin, Stephen 210–13, 231–2, 233,
   234, 235, 237, 245, 288, 289–90
rugby football 72, 89, 90, 116
Runner's World 132, 147, 152, 153, 154,
   166, 173, 180, 188, 196, 212, 215,
   289
   chart ratings 167, 170, 172, 174, 175,
      190, 196, 204, 212, 234, 289
   Nike gets star billing in 171, 173
running shoes 5, 6–10, 13, 20, 31,
   33, 42, 53, 64–5, 81, 89, 94, 99,
   101–2, 104, 118–19, 130, 132,
   167, 176, 186, 198–9, 216–18,
   223, 230–1, 237, 249, 255 (*see also*
   training shoes)
Russell, Arthur 14–15
Ryan, Frank 39, 66, 96–8

Saab 193, 194
Sacred Mountain 254
Saint Helens RLFC 16
St Margaret's Church 26, 30, 292–3
sales and distribution 45
Salford Red Devils RLFC 16
Salle des Etoiles 248
Sarah, Duchess of York 249, 265
Saucony 170
Save the Children 278
screw-in studs 53
sealed product samples, defined 207
Second World War 21–5, 35, 106, 292
Seymour, Jane 257–8
Shackleton, Derek ('Shack') 72, 116,
   117, 121–2, 125, 127, 128, 177,
   196, 199, 204, 206, 289
   death of 288
Shepherd, Cybill 246
shock-absorbency 171, 205
Shoe & Leather News 59
Shrubb, Alfred 11–12
side-lasting machines 60
Sigg, Ruedi 258–9, 291
Sinatra, Frank 247, 248
Singapore 235, 243
skateboard shoes 129
skateboarding 129

Skip (Scout master) 26–9, 27, 280
Smith, Stan 230
Snazzy Fox 119
soccer, *see* football
sole presses 67–8, 69, 70, 72
sole-sewing machines 32–3, 50, 60
sole traction 7, 171, 173
sourcing agents 212
South Africa 121, 229, 235, 277–9
South Korea 176–7, 180–5, 184, 185,
    195, 204, 207–10, 219, 223, 228,
    234, 240
Southeast Asia 165, 175–6, 243
Soviet Union 259
Spain 235, 240–3, 259, 261
spiked running shoes 5, 6–10, 12–15,
    16, 17, 37, 64–5, 94, 216, 249
spinning mule 6
SPOGA 105–9
sponsorship 93, 108
sport psychology 172
sporting goods exhibitions 105–11, 114,
    155–9, 161, 198, 256–7, 274
sports agencies 114
Sports Goods Intelligence 281
Sports International 133
sports magazines 50, 61, 62, 102, 108,
    132, 135, 147, 152, 153, 154, 166,
    167, 170, 171, 173, 180, 186, 188,
    196, 212, 215, 289
sports retailers, *see* retail market
Sprintmaster 42
squash 208
Stan Smith shoe 230
Starcrest identity 104, 194
Steve (wife's father) 293
Stone, Stephen 277, 278–9
Stoppard, Mr ('Mr Stop Heart') (bank
    manager) 62, 80, 280
street shoes 130, 165, 219–20
Student Prince 256
Stylo 128
subcontracting 129–30
Sumitomo 252
Supreme cycling shoes 61
Sweatshop 90–1, 102, 236
'sweaty' brands 218, 222
Sweden 235
Swinging Sixties 73

Switzer, Kathrine 101
Switzerland 235, 258

Taiwan 176, 181
tanning 65, 219–20
Taylor, Elizabeth 30
Taylor, Mr (sales agent) 62, 63–4
television exposure 235–6, 246
10K road events 132
tennis 88, 188, 208, 221, 230–1, 246–8,
    257, 265, 267–8, 290, 292
tennis shoes 230–1
Terrutzi, Gianfranco 255–6
Thatcher, Margaret 174, 175
thinking big 138
Three Towers 93
Tiger 101–2, 132, 135, 148, 166, 176,
    214, 252
time and motion 206
time capsule 265
Times Square 109
Tokyo Olympics (1964) 185
Tootils 78
Total Environment Sports 133–4
Tour de France 91
track and field 99, 107, 116, 119, 132,
    136, 230, 290
Trackmaster 42
traction, *see* sole traction
trade journals 59, 135, 147, 152, 153,
    154, 166, 167, 170, 171, 173, 180,
    186, 188, 196, 212, 215, 281, 289
trade shows 105–14
trademark infringements 104, 153, 195,
    201, 240, 257
trademarks 78–9, 104, 153, 232
trading house system 252, 254
Trading Standards (UK) 195
training shoes (trainers) 89–90, 102–3,
    116, 123, 126, 127–9, 153, 172–3,
    216, 246, 249, 282
Trans World Sports 133
Trimley Heath 35
turnover 273, 280–1, 290
TWA 197
28th Bolton Scout Troop 26, 292

Umbro 90
Union Jack branding 194–5

Unitarian Chapel, Ainsworth 43
United States:
  consumer culture 207
  Iranian Embassy siege 179
  Joe held up by Immigration in 186–7
  Reebok expansion into 105, 107–13,
    114–20, 121–4, 130–1, 132–9,
    148–54, 158–9, 160–8, 169–77,
    186–90, 191–7, 201 (*see also*
    Reebok USA)
urban streetwear 222
USSR 259

vegetable-tanned leathers 65
Velcro 192, 222
Vicario, Arantxa Sánchez 248
Victory G shoe 229
Vorster, John 278, 279

WAAA Championships, 1932 18
Waffle-sole trainer 171
waffle soles 171–2
wage capping 87
Walker, Johnnie 270
Waller, Derek 84–5, 91–3, 142, 146,
    173, 184, 196, 212, 239–42, 255,
    256–7, 259, 263, 288
wearing-in 230
Weaver, Sigourney 246
*Webster's New School and Office
    Dictionary* 77

Weltmeister football boots 53
Wembley Stadium 17, 58
West Germany 100
West Ham United FC 17
Whac-A-Mole 278
The Wheatsheaf pub 19
wholesale 13, 140–1
Wilby, Brian 292
Wilson 257, 290
Wilson Gunn & Ellis 75, 80, 82, 92,
    173, 239
Windsor Great Park 248
Women's Amateur Athletic Association
    (WAAA) 18
Women's Royal Air Force (WRAF)
    34, 36–7, 38
World Cup:
  1954 89
  1966 100
World Pro-Celebrity Tennis 246–8
World 10 shoe 118–20, 217
World War I, *see* First World War
World War II, *see* Second World War
WRAF (Women's Royal Air Force) 34,
    36–7, 38

Yale University 39, 82, 96, 112
Yatesbury, RAF 34–5
Yvonna (holiday rep/translator) 241–2,
    259